Amateur Craft

Amateur Craft

History and Theory

Stephen Knott

Bloomsbury Academic
An imprint of Bloomsbury Publishing Plc

B L O O M S B U R Y
LONDON · NEW DELHI · NEW YORK · SYDNEY

Bloomsbury Academic

An imprint of Bloomsbury Publishing Plc

50 Bedford Square
London
WC1B 3DP
UK

1385 Broadway
New York
NY 10018
USA

www.bloomsbury.com

BLOOMSBURY and the Diana logo are trademarks of Bloomsbury Publishing Plc

First published 2015

British Library Cataloguing-in-Publication Data
A catalogue record for this book is available from the British Library.

ISBN: HB: 978-1-4725-7735-1
       PB: 978-1-4725-7734-4
       ePDF: 978-1-4725-7736-8
       ePub: 978-1-4725-7737-5

Library of Congress Cataloging-in-Publication Data
Knott, Stephen (Stephen D.)
Amateur craft: history and theory / by Stephen Knott.
pages cm
Includes bibliographical references and index.
ISBN 978-1-4725-7735-1 (hardback)
1. Handicraft—Social aspects. 2. Hobbies—Social aspects. 3. Amateurism. I. Title.
TT149.K59 2015
745.5—dc23
2014045833

Typeset by RefineCatch Limited, Bungay, Suffolk
Printed and bound in India

CONTENTS

ILLUSTRATIONS

Figures

Plates

ACKNOWLEDGEMENTS

This book derives from PhD research undertaken at The Royal College of Art and the Victoria and Albert Museum between 2008 and 2012 that was funded by the Arts and Humanities Research Council through its Collaborative Doctoral Award scheme. The thesis allowed a degree of freedom and experimentation that I did not think possible in doctoral level research, and I would like to acknowledge the dynamism, enthusiasm and encouragement of my supervisory team – Glenn Adamson, the then Head of Research at the Victoria and Albert Museum (now director of the Museum of Art and Design, New York), and Hans Stofer, head of the Jewellery and Metal department of the Royal College of Art. I would like to also thank the staff and students at these two institutions.

I would like to thank the Trustees of the Crafts Study Centre, Farnham, Surrey, for their generous support in providing funds for sourcing the images and copyright licences. In sourcing the images I would like to thank Neil Parkinson and Cathy Johns of the Royal College of Art Library, the Yale Centre of British Art, the Haas Family Art Library at Yale, the Bodleian Library, the Hartley Library at the University of Southampton, and Kay Peterson and Wendy Shay at the Archives Center of the Smithsonian National Museum of American History. Thanks to Winsor & Newton for providing permission to reproduce nineteenth-century advertisements of their products. The artists mentioned in the thesis have also been generous in their provision of images: Jeff McMillan, James Rigler, Trey Speegle, Simon Starling, Chris Eckersley, Rory Dodd and Linus Ersson. I would like to thank the railway modellers and model engineers Mike Chrisp, David Crossley, Peter Bossom, Grahame Hedges, and particularly Leslie Bevis-Smith, Clive White and Tim Watson of the Model Railway Club. Their openness and willingness to support my research has been invaluable.

I want to acknowledge the kindness of my parents and family, in particular for their patience, warmth and generosity throughout the research. Writing up the research within the environs of my parents' chicken farm and the frequent discussions helped me through tough moments. Finally, I would like to thank my partner Kimberley, for the many conversations about the ideas raised in the book, suggested avenues of research, copy-editing, image editing and putting up with my inability to unglue myself from the computer screen during the manuscript preparation. Her enthusiasm and support have proved vital, as have our countless busman's holidays.

INTRODUCTION

*There is a charm about the fact that one has succeeded in accomplishing some object,
or overturning some obstacles by oneself, alone and unaided. . . .*

*In mechanics for example, an amateur likes to show, as a rule, that he can chuck a
rough piece of stuff in the lathe and shape it off into a rod, an oval, or a ball, as the
case may be; and when the job is done he loves to turn around and let you see the
results, and tell you at the same time that he learnt the art himself – from a book
perhaps. He may tell you, too, that he is on an office stool all day, and has never been
in a shop all his life, and as far as he can see at present is never likely to be so. . . .*

*He has picked up fragments from papers and books, or scraps from other sources,
and these he has put together arranged them in his mind, tested some with his hands
and considering the difficulties he has had to surmount by his own resources, has no
doubt succeeded with tolerable success.*

'AMATEURS', *DESIGN AND WORK* (19 FEBRUARY 1881), P. 141

This characterization of amateur craft, written in an editorial of the Victorian handyman journal *Design and Work* (1876–81), bears all the hallmarks associated with voluntarily chosen work. There is no compulsion to undertake the activity, no financial remuneration, and the object made – 'a rough piece of stuff' shaped into a more pleasing form – seems distinctly superfluous. Deploying skill to such a trivial end would doubtless be questioned as art by scholars, artists and theoreticians; the maker failing to adopt critical distance from his work through his desire to show off. This exertion of labour-power would not interest many economists, Marxist scholars or sociologists either as the output lacks value, whether in terms of exchange value, function or political statement. Many would consider practices like this amateur mechanic's work unimportant, not worthy of critical attention and certainly not significant enough to merit an entire book.

I aim to contest this dismissive set of assumptions, and demonstrate how amateur craft has made a vital and important contribution to the material culture of the modern world, and remains the freest, most autonomous form of making, within structures of Western capitalism at least. Under no financial obligation, amateur craft allows an individual to make something for the love of it alone, without the pressure of deadlines or the need to please a patron. Indeed, the space and time afforded by amateur craft is integral to the survival of a whole range of craft practices, from greenwood carpentry to bookbinding. As craft theorist and cabinet-maker David Pye stated in *The Nature and Art of Workmanship* (1968), 'the very best quality' production will depend on makers doing it 'for love and not for money', those who are able to pour excessive resources of time and money into activities that are economically unviable in other everyday spaces of modern capitalism.[1]

These unique conditions of amateur craft practice have thrust the phenomenon into the limelight in recent years. Kirstie Allsopp's advocacy of handmade additions to the home on British television, the journalists of *Wired* magazine who urge us to tinker with and adapt technologies like 3D printers to our own will, steampunk embroiderers and IKEA-hackers: all vouch for the importance, both personal, financial and psychological, of making. We can conceive of the amateur craftsperson as the capitalist *bricoleur*, a re-working of the anthropologist Claude Lévi-Strauss's term to describe making from that which is to hand, updated to the conditions of mass production and consumption.[2] But being an amateur, or a capitalist *bricoleur*, is not a simple path to the unfurling of subjective desire. Like the mechanic described above, amateurs are beset by limitations, whether to do with inadequate materials or tools, or a lack of space and time, and often rely on the fragments and scraps of modern culture – the commercially available tools, materials, external advice and readymades that have already passed through various networks of exchange. Attention to the history of amateur craft shows how it is linked to these structures of everyday life, and does not represent simple, individual opposition against 'the machine', as so often presumed.

In this book I challenge the overly individualist reading of amateur craft and instead propose that its practice is differential within modern capitalism, following French theorist and sociologist Henri Lefebvre's conceptualization of difference.[3] Amateur craft is inherently dependent on the routines of everyday life, the structures symbolized by the 'office stool' in the quote above – the division of labour, entrepreneurship, the adulation of productivity, and the accumulation of capital. Yet it simultaneously constitutes a spatial-temporal zone in which these structures can be stretched, quietly subverted, and exaggerated. Limitations to amateur craft practice demand our attention, as it is the constrained freedom of amateur craft that produces distinctive configurations of work. For example, creating a home workshop tailored to individual need is a model of hyper-efficiency, a system of management that would make any company boss envious, and concentration on processes of making rather than the final output leads to experiences of joy and play that are close to resembling the utopian dream of unalienated labour. So often overlooked, amateur craft is more complex, innovative, unexpected, roguish, humorous and elusive than its use as a cover-all term for inadequacy and shoddy work (amateurishness).[4]

This book treats amateur craft to much-needed philosophical and historical investigation and is envisaged as a primer to a much more detailed consideration of the subject within art history, material culture studies, modern history and cultural theory. I do not present a comprehensive account of amateur practice within any particular craft medium or focus on a specific period or geography. Nevertheless there is a narrative arch, with later case studies from 1950s' USA, the period of the famous DIY boom, representing an intensification of characteristics of amateur craft practice evident in the earlier British contexts of Victorian self-help.[5] The aim is to develop theories of modern amateur craft practice, substantiated by historical case studies that challenge our stereotypical presumptions. Each chapter will look backwards to the emergence of the modern amateur but, echoing the 'elastic chronological structure' of Glenn Adamson's *The Invention of Craft*, will also refer to examples within art and design practice of the last twenty years that reference, deploy or exploit amateur conditions of making.[6] I adopt a sceptical approach to recent projects that try to mobilize amateurism as a 'movement' (the craftivism movement, for example),[7] and instead attempt to describe the importance of amateur craft while avoiding framing it as a new 'ism'. A critical assessment of such projects will show how recent practitioners, and society more generally, continue to grapple with amateur craft's mercurial qualities.

When Andy Warhol went to the theatre, he stated that he was not interested in watching professional actors who do the same thing every day. He preferred the amateurs: 'whatever they do never really comes off, so therefore it can't be phoney . . . you can never tell what they will do next'.[8] Throughout the book amateur craftspeople are centre stage and, like their thespian counterparts, their honesty, mistakes and unpredictability make for a captivating show.

History of a definition

Amateur practice has not always required scholarly defence. From the Renaissance to well into the eighteenth century, European definitions of the word were consistent with its Latin root – 'amare' (to love) – and it was associated with virtuous activities undertaken for their own sake. The disassociation from need was particularly important as it rendered amateur practice a symbolic expression of a gentleman's ability to spare resources of time and money, as well as those of his female spouse and dependents.[9] Cultural cachet was assigned to excellence within various activities, from husbandry, travel writing and scientific discovery for men, to the female 'accomplishments' of piano playing, foreign languages, embroidery, and even dairy management and other rural pastimes that became popular in the latter half of the eighteenth century.[10]

The Industrial Revolution, often dated in Britain between 1750 and 1850 and later in Europe and America, disrupted these conventions. Commercial production of artistic supplies and tools, as well as guidance in how to use them through manuals and advice literature, meant greater access to the things needed for amateur craft. The culture of work shifted, reflecting the rise of what could be described as middle-class values: aristocratic idleness and autonomous pursuit of knowledge was viewed with greater suspicion in comparison with self-help and productivity. Nineteenth-century philosopher Arthur Schopenhauer represented the old order and privileged the autonomy of 'dilettanti' – those who 'pursue a branch of knowledge or art for the love and enjoyment thereof'. In his 1851 work *Parerga and Paralipomena* he stated that it was from dilettanti, and not from the professional ('paid servant'), 'that the greatest work has always come', lamenting the 'want, hunger or some other keen desire' of engaging in a task out of necessity.[11] Schopenhauer's 'dilettanti' was a configuration of amateur practice that chimed with the values of gentlemanly society of the pre-industrial age where it was only the elites who could afford to pursue a task out of love alone. A more heterogeneous understanding of amateur practice emerged with economic growth and industrial progress, and from the late eighteenth century was defined, like the burgeoning middle classes, by diversity. The unpaid aristocratic virtuoso was joined by a vast array of amateur makers – women engaging in home arts, beginners learning a craft, tourists capturing a scene through watercolour, and throughout the nineteenth century an increasing number of middle-class workers wanting to fill spare time with useful and enjoyable practices. As a result, amateur practice increasingly became associated with conditions of making (labour), rather than mere curiosity or a love of acquiring knowledge.[12]

Equipped with newly available tools and materials, middle-class individuals could excel in voluntarily undertaken labour and were less concerned with being compared to artisans (even though many of them might have been artisans). Amateur activity offered the middle classes a chance to gain social and economic advantage from working in their free time in quasi-imitation of their aristocratic counterparts, yet with productivity as the cornerstone of what constituted moral virtue. This celebration of productivity was critical to the development of a middle-class mentality, which Karl Marx argued was a consequence of a totalizing understanding of work characterized by alienation, where both an individual's means of life, desires and activity were ruled over by an 'inhuman power'.[13] Marx perceptively recognized the shift in the culture of work that accompanied the Industrial Revolution and his thought influenced subsequent generations of scholars, including German sociologist Max Weber, who claimed that capitalism and its ideological bedfellow, economic rationalism, had pervaded all spheres of culture in the nineteenth and twentieth centuries and curtailed the possibility of genuine freedom.[14] Industrialization and the alienation that it fostered challenged Schopenhauer's idealistic assessment that the amateur could achieve some kind of distinctive autonomy outside the grip of capital.

Another consequence of this expansion of amateur craft practice in the nineteenth century was the notional competition between the newly equipped amateur and the professional. Amateurs threatened to match the skills of professionals who were already struggling to defend the technical worth of their labour against the mechanical power of steam and the accelerating division of labour. The presumed threat of higher levels of skill among amateur craftspeople sowed the seeds for the dichotomization of amateur practice from professional practice as artisans, craftsmen and artists used the word amateur pejoratively to denote lack of commitment, poor skill and ineptitude rather than doing something for its own sake. Throughout the nineteenth century, expertise, skill and excellence were tied to monetary remuneration within a 'profession', with the amateur reduced to a dabbler, or feminized through an association with domestic handicraft that has proved pervasive. This division continues to live with us today.

A comprehensive treatment of amateur craft is impossible unless this oppositional split between professional and amateur is questioned. If Marx famously summed up the character of modernity whereby 'all that is solid melts into air',[15] my attempt is to show how the amateur craft practitioner attempted to make experience 'solid' once more through making, within this disruptive temporal environment.

Method and structure

Amateur craft has a peculiar historiography. Although there are countless medium-specific publications intended for amateur audiences – just think of the constantly full and replenished shelves at bookstores labelled 'Craft/DIY' – there are very few works that provide a model for studying amateur craft in any detail.[16] Most existing academic work sits within the discipline of sociology. Robert Stebbins's *Amateurs, Professionals and Serious Leisure*, a book derived from a series of interviews with amateur and professional practitioners across different vocations undertaken during the 1970s and 1980s, is one work that attempts to provide a model for understanding amateur practice. Stebbins challenged the marginality of amateur practice by suggesting a new category of 'serious' amateurs who demonstrated high levels of perseverance, skill and training, and who generated profit from their activities, setting them apart from the occasional dabbler.[17] While this treatment challenges the idea that all amateurs can be lumped into one category (defined by poor skill) Stebbins's concern is to map a series of amateur stereotypes based on an ascending scale of seriousness. Like the recent article on do-it-yourself practice by design historian Paul Atkinson in *The Journal of Design History*,[18] Stebbins seeks to categorize the characteristics of amateur labour that are inherently elusive and complex, an approach that fails to recognize the oscillation between 'amateur' and 'professional' at any given time. A report published by the Policy Study Institute in 1991 adopts a similar sociological method, using a range of questionnaires sent out to amateur societies and organizations in five areas in the UK to try to understand the social, cultural and economic value of amateur arts. Their conclusion that 'statistics and tables alone can appear cold', caution in regards to 'ring fencing' amateur activity, and their recognition of the inter-dependence of amateur and professional modes of practice at least point to the limitations of the sociological method in grasping the full importance of what amateur craft offers its practitioners beyond issues of demography and public funding.[19]

A methodology appropriate to the study of amateur craft practice must be more sensitive to its fluid and flexible status, and aware of how it has been continually marginalized as a subject of study. The work of cultural theorists who engage with the philosophy of the supplemental proves particularly useful: from Jacques Derrida and the inter-war scholars associated with the Frankfurt School, such as Siegfried Kracauer and Walter Benjamin, with their predilection towards 'inconspicuous surface-level expressions', to craft theorist Glenn Adamson, whose book *Thinking Through Craft* seeks to redress craft's presumed supplementary and inferior position compared with modern art.[20] The work of theorists of everyday life, such as Gaston Bachelard, Michel de Certeau, Sigmund Freud, Ben Highmore and Joe Moran is also helpful because they focus, in their different ways, on how the minutiae of human experience reflect a haphazard, irrational and sometimes unquantifiable mediation of broad supra-individual structures. In addition, their work helps provide solutions to the problems of lack of evidence, demonstrating ways in which novels and literature, oral history, psychology and aesthetic theory can be used to highlight supplemental arenas of culture.

However, as mentioned above, it is Lefebvre's critique of the everyday that proves the most useful theoretical mechanism for understanding amateur craft. Unlike most Marxist scholars who marginalized the significance of any expressions that derived from leisure (see Chapter 2), Lefebvre devoted his career to the understanding of such practices. He coined the phrase 'differential space' to refer to cultural expressions that depart from the conventions of everyday life while simultaneously relying on them.[21] While Theodor Adorno and Hannah Arendt, and many other scholars besides, merely saw the expression of the amateur as akin to a permitted freedom within alienating structures, Lefebvre was always alert to the potential 'something else [that] is always possible'[22] that might break free from such structures, even if he did not analyse amateur craft head on.

Something of the contrasting attitudes towards everyday expression in twentieth-century Marxist scholarship can be seen in recent work within consumer culture. The discipline's emphasis on the multivalent experiences of consumption has brought attention to amateur making via the concept of 'craft consumption'.[23] This term builds on a swathe of literature that situates the consumer, not as passive, but as a proactive, productive agent in cycles of capitalist production and consumption.[24] The attributes of the craft consumer, or the producing-consumer (prosumer)[25] have merited particular attention of late in the light of sophisticated technologies – such as the 3D printer, open source technologies, and a culture of online participation and civilian journalism – that promise to bring production to the home and disseminate critical power to the hands of non-experts. Such phenomena, however, have encouraged a fairly simplistic response, even among academics. There are those that are 'for' the idea of democratic access to tools, where an individual can express some form of antagonistic, subjective response to capitalist hegemony, or usher in a 'Third Industrial Revolution' from behind his or her computer screen.[26] Then there are those who are less optimistic about amateur participation and view such decentralized practices as mere illusions of control that merely reify existing capitalist structures in various ways.[27] These are hyperbolic extremes that I aim to navigate by focusing on the specific way in which non-experts engage with the tooling that is available to them.

From the perspective of social history, amateur practice has received some medium-specific attention, particularly within film and photography. Patricia Zimmerman and Bernhard Rieger explain how improved film technologies throughout the twentieth century allowed amateurs to create their own home movie fantasies,[28] and film historian Charles Tepperman has argued how mid-century amateur film in America constituted a 'vernacular pragmatic imagination'.[29] In the realm of photography, Annebella Pollen and Juliette Baillie's co-edited series of short essays 'Reconsidering Amateur Photography' for the National Media Museum's *Either/And* website has probed deeper into the various features of amateur practice within this field, from Karen Cross's account of the technical focus of photography evening classes to British writer Graham Rawle's analysis of the 'salacious titillation' that lay behind 1950s literature for the amateur art photographer.[30]

Steven Gelber's monograph *Hobbies* on the culture of productive leisure in the twentieth-century USA is one of the most substantial histories devoted to the continuation of work in free time that shows an awareness of the relationships between amateur craft and its opposites. He shows how characteristics of professional work structured the productive occupation of leisure time, stating that 'hobbies developed as a way to integrate the isolated home with the ideology of the workplace'.[31] In Chapter 2 I explore this relationship between work and home, mainly through the case study of Victorian self-help, but rather than see the practice of amateur craft as merely a 'disguised affirmation of work' as Gelber does in his study, I outline the various differential configurations of labour that result from the fusing together of the productive work ethic and free time. I show how the dominance of the 'work ideology' is subtly twisted or refracted when it enters into the realm of amateur practice, and I give examples of how work, productivity, aesthetics, play and labour are continually negotiated in this spatial-temporal zone.

Unlike the scholarly literature on amateur craft that is hard to find, direct evidence is everywhere, from knitting circles to Sunday painting groups. Such groups and societies provide an instant point of access for any anthropological investigation or oral history on amateur craft, and many studies on the subject proceed from this basis.[32] In Chapter 3 I use a few interviews and site visits in my analysis of amateur railway modelling, but I do not wholly rely on this method due to the tendency for individual amateur practitioners to give accounts that often re-enforce existing stereotypes of amateur practice, either as unbridled subjective expression or as an escape from the everyday grind. Instead, I primarily look at the structures that surround any given amateur craft, relying heavily on manuals, guidebooks, how-to pamphlets, critical reception of amateur craft and advertisements for supplies targeted at the amateur, giving the analysis a textual and visual focus that reflects its historical and theoretical leaning. I am aware that this literature cannot give an unmediated account of actual making and the criticism of advice literature as a reliable source, an argument well articulated by design historian Grace Lees-Maffei.[33] Yet this focus on the infrastructure surrounding amateur craft highlights the importance of the meeting point between individual autonomous activity and broader structures, in line with my argument that amateur craft cannot be just defined by self-expression through making, but is inherently constrained, mediated and socialized.

The book has three thematic chapters: amateur surface intervention, amateur space, and amateur time. The first chapter accounts for the emergence of the amateur as a surface intervener in the nineteenth century, equipped and able to make marks on two-dimensional surfaces. After explaining how the surface can be freed from its marginal position within art history, I will narrate the history of amateur surface intervention, not through accounts of individual practice but through the things that made amateur craft possible. These include *bases* – the blank canvas upon which amateur dreams unfold; *carriers* – easy-to-use tools understandable to an inexpert public; and *arbiters* – the manuals, guidance and advice that explained how a process was undertaken. I analyse the products produced by commercial art supply firms such as Winsor & Newton, Reeves, and LeFranc et Cie, to see how amateur craft was shaped by the tools and materials, such as paint in collapsible tubes, which democratized certain processes that were previously difficult to access for individuals outside guild association or elites. These new tools and materials did not simply invite the non-expert in to existing practices, but instead opened up new capabilities and modes of practice – in the case of paints in collapsible tubes, the ability to carry paints with you or to tuck them tidily away. In their study on contemporary DIY, Elizabeth Shove, Matthew Watson, Martin Hand and Jack Ingram stress the importance of new tools in shaping practice and how they 'rearrange the distribution of competence', and their attention to the network of relationships that lie behind the use of any tool proves incredibly helpful in framing amateur surface intervention as dependent on infrastructures of supply for their expressive content.[34]

The case studies in this chapter will relate to the most accessible forms of amateur craft: drawing, and painting in watercolour and oils. I argue that amateur access to these tools fundamentally altered conditions of artistic production from the nineteenth century onwards as the audience became increasingly aware of how paintings were made. Such access also played a major, yet often forgotten, role in the formation of *avant garde* ideas as the demystification of how the painted surface was built up compelled artists to distinguish the exclusivity of their skills and prompted departures into theoretical realms of practice. The shifting dynamics of modern artistic production prompted by amateur access and anxiety about what constituted artistic skill *vis-à-vis* the amateur and the readymade will be reflected in the major case study of the chapter: the commercial production of the paint-by-number kit in post-war America, and its subsequent appropriation by trained artists such as Andy Warhol and Jasper Johns.

For the second chapter the focus is the space of amateur craft, both the garages and workstations where work takes place, and the spaces created by amateurs. I will explore in greater depth the central hypothesis of the book: that amateur craft represents what Lefebvre termed 'differential space', a space of production that departs from the normal conditions of everyday life, yet tangentially relates to, and depends upon, its structures. I focus on the question of amateur labour – how it can be defined and how it relates to various philosophies of work. Amateur space is not merely a site where the individual ego is given the opportunity to flourish through manual work, or an antagonistic response to capitalism, and neither is it a space of alienation as some Marxist scholars have argued. Instead amateur space rehearses the ideologies drawn from its presumed opposites while subtly refracting them in the process. This is epitomized by the late-nineteenth-century 'professionalization' of amateur space, where the prevailing ideology of Victorian self-help filtered through to amateur activity and led to unusual forms of production and labour organization.

The connection between amateur space and everyday life will be shown by studying the unusual attributes of amateur spaces of work – the self-built, portable and tailored workstations in garages or sheds. In addition, I will illustrate the complex and ambiguous productivity of the spaces that amateurs produce through an exploration of the late nineteenth- and early twentieth-century movement of suburban chicken keeping. The production of eggs to supplement the household economy was rarely intended to replace large-scale production, yet its appeal – that has proved to be long lasting – is predicated upon its differential productivity that is both functional and ornamental at the same time.[35] Reference to artist Simon Starling's *Burn Time*

(2000), which includes chickens in nebulous matrixes of making, pays homage to this idiosyncratic productivity.

The third chapter provides a number of explanations as to why individuals voluntarily carry on labouring in their free time, despite the fact that there is no clear economic compulsion to do so. Starting with a critique of Adorno's notion that free time is essentially unfree, I argue that amateur craft practice is driven by a will that is unaffected by the end product and its associated economies, and is instead reflective of a desire for a different productive utopia or system where an individual temporarily takes control of the conditions of his or her own alienation. I will look at the human desire for joy, play, autonomy and sociability that is often integral to amateur craft practice, as well as the limitations of 'free time' that derive from its temporary and ephemeral position in Western capitalism.

The constrained freedom of amateur craft practice only facilitates a partial or temporary escape from everyday life, which I explain with reference to Fredric Jameson's conceptualization of utopia, and demonstrate through the example of amateur railway modellers (from the late nineteenth century to the present) who build miniaturized, highly detailed and complex alternative universes. These model railways often depict a bygone era, and there is a perception that the hobby is steeped in nostalgia. Yet the differential experience of time in making these models relates back to everyday life, whilst simultaneously stretching its parameters. For artists and designers working today in a post-disciplinary environment, the prospect of making in conditions that depart from the norm has proved attractive, and I will conclude this chapter by assessing the ways in which artists self-consciously and temporarily inhabit amateur time.

Through analysis of the forgotten, the mundane, the inexpert and obvious, this book explains how and why amateur craft practice has become so essential to the experience of everyday life. The story of modern amateurism is about the continuation of autonomous action within the constraints of capitalism. Amateur craft practitioners negotiate limitations of skill, space and time, motivated by the desire to temporarily control their own labour. Thus, it is no surprise that prospective employers pose the question to their nervous interviewees: 'Do you have a hobby?'

1

Surface

Using enamel paint

George and Weedon Grossmith's comic novel, *The Diary of a Nobody* (1892), explores the daily toil and trivialities of Charles Pooter, a City worker living in a suburban house called *The Laurels* in Holloway Road, North London, who is desperate to attain a position of middle-class respectability. The opening diary entries record Pooter's bumbling encounters with tradesmen who are renovating the house he has just bought, but Pooter does not simply stand by and watch. Aspiring to greater self-sufficiency, Pooter contributes to these efforts of home improvement alongside his wife Carrie who 'is not above putting a button on a shirt [or] mending a pillow'.[1]

In this wave of enthusiasm for home decoration, Pooter, on the recommendation of a neighbour, buys a couple of tins of red 'Pinkford's enamel paint' and proceeds to cover a variety of household objects in a red layer, including flower-pots, the servant's wash-stand, a chest of drawers, the spines of his Shakespeare plays, a coal scuttle and the family bath, much to the annoyance of his wife who laments this 'new fangled craze' (Figure 1.1). This infatuation with red enamel paint comes to a farcical end, however, when Pooter prepares a hot bath to alleviate a 'painter's colic' that had developed while applying the substance. The heat of the water strips off the inexpertly applied layer of red enamel on to his body, giving him the appearance of a 'second Marat'.[2]

As a form of surface intervention – the physical manipulation of the two-dimensional plane through the application of a surface layer – Pooter's effort with Pinkford's enamel seems particularly amateurish; his ill-fated foray epitomizes the dominant stereotype of amateur surface intervention as a misguided, mimetic act of decoration, personalization or ornamentation, reflecting a lack of technical capability and the superficiality of middlebrow taste. However, this tendency to critique, marginalize, ridicule or ignore amateur surface intervention on account of its poor quality or naivety has deflected attention from the significant modern cultural phenomenon that lies behind it: access to affordable, commercially produced tools and materials that allowed individuals, like Pooter, to engage in tasks previously undertaken by tradesmen or specialists.

This chapter accounts for the growth of this infrastructure of tools and materials that allowed individuals to add a layer on to objects after the initial process of commodity exchange, with a particular attention on the simplest forms of surface intervention: drawing and painting. The 'things' that facilitated intervention are the focus[3]: ready-mixed paint, pre-stretched canvases, brushes, paintboxes and manuals, produced commercially from the late eighteenth century onwards. As examples of new technology that invite the non-specialist to practise, these tools

I painted the washstand in the servant's bedroom

FIGURE 1.1 *Pooter applying Pinkford's enamel paint. Illustration by Weedon Grossmith.* The Diary of a Nobody *(Harmondsworth: Penguin, 1965).*

and materials 'reconfigure the distribution of skill', as stated by Elizabeth Shove et al. in *The Design of Everyday Life* – an important work that builds on Bruno Latour's understanding that technologies and artefacts 'script' our engagement with them rather than being subservient to our will.[4] Their twenty-first-century examples include self-levelling house paint that enables the amateur decorator to achieve a smooth, good surface finish. But within the longer history of tool access, the portable *camera obscura* that made it possible for eighteenth-century tourists to capture a scene, paint in tubes and the all-in-one 1950s paint-by-number kit can be added to this list of 'smart' tools. Competence and ability, enmeshed in the pre-modern era within the skilled labourer (and often protected through guild association) was re-distributed across a wider network from the late eighteenth century onwards, with the increasingly sophisticated tools, materials and literature incorporating complex tasks into their domain.

This brings us back to Pooter's inglorious use of red enamel paint, which was not mere literary or comic embellishment but a direct reference to new brands of enamel paint developed from the mid-1880s that allowed non-specialists to cover surfaces – including baths – in self-drying enamel paint. Only a few years before the publication of *Diary of a Nobody*, weekly publications targeted at the diverse array of Victorian handymen, such as the *Illustrated Carpenter and Builder* (1877–1971) and *Amateur Work* (1881–96), ran advertisements for brands of enamel paint, such as Celestial Enamel, Aspinall's Enamel and Prices's Chez Lui Enamel (Figure 1.2).

Before the introduction of these brands, enamelling, and in particular enamelling baths, typically involved a series of complex tasks – it was 'a highly skilled job' according to paint historian Harriet Standeven.[5] For a start, the enamel paint needed to be mixed in the right quantities from a combination of strained white paint, varnish, and enamel varnish; several coats were needed to prepare for the final glossy surface; the material had to be 'flowed on' to the surface quickly in one continuous movement without leaving gaps, as the work could not be touched up; and, if greater durability were required, baths would have to be sent to specialists for stoving, where the surface layer would be fired on in large kilns.[6]

New enamel paints decentralized this process into the home. Chez Lui enamel, as the editor of *Amateur Work* noted, resembled paint in both appearance and its behaviour when being applied, the material changing only during the process of drying: '[Chez Lui] will present a surface almost as smooth and as glossy as porcelain, while that of ordinary paint, even at its best is somewhat rough to touch.'[7] It was these self-levelling qualities of the new technology – that it dried to a smooth finish – that were so valued, particularly in the contexts of increasing concern about sanitation and cleanliness.[8] Readers of *Illustrated Carpenter and Builder* recommended both Chez Lui and Aspinall's enamel as they were easy to use, could resist both hot and cold water when dry, had a wide colour range and could be used on a variety of surfaces – including wood, stone, glass and metal.[9] Moreover, the process was so straightforward that instructions guiding the enameller on the side of the paint-tin sufficed as adequate instruction, anticipating the famous tagline of the British stains and paint manufacturer Ronseal: 'It does exactly what it says on the tin.'[10]

The availability of readymade enamel paints in the late 1880s provoked responses that often accompany the democratization of any skill. Skilled labourers and commentators alike were happy to poke fun and identify the faults and mistakes associated with non-specialist practice.[11] Indeed, the domestic use of Aspinall's Enamel was the subject of an 1896 song written by W. M. Mayne for the well-known and well-travelled caricaturist, entertainer and Yorkshireman, Mel B. Spurr.[12] The first verse reads:

When a woman enlists under Aspinall's banner
She ought to be kept in restraint in some manner.
Just give her unlimited scope, and full powers,
And she'll alter the Town in a very few hours.
St Paul's would be painted Emerald Green:
The Houses of Parliament Ultramarine,

THIS IS THE
"CHEZ-LUI" ENAMEL !

CHEZ-LUI Enamel dries hard without heat.
CHEZ-LUI Enamel dries with glossy surface.
This is the Home, once so dingy and mean,
Which now is the brightest that ever was seen,
  Through the use of CHEZ-LUI Enamel!
This is the Master, so happy and proud,
When his friends, in astonishment, came in a
  crowd
CHEZ-LUI Enamel is not softened by hot water.
CHEZ-LUI Enamel is made in every colour.
To look at the Home, once so dingy and mean,
Which now is the brightest that ever was seen,
  Through the use of CHEZ-LUI Enamel!

FIGURE 1.2 *Chez Lui enamel advert*. Illustrated Carpenter and Builder *22 (17 February 1888), p. 142.*
Courtesy of Bodleian Libraries.

And Westminster Abbey a sealing-wax Red,
With a sweet peacock Blue for the tombs of the dead.
And I don't think a woman is right in her head
Who would put peacock Blue on the tombs of the dead.[13]

Pooter's misapplication of red enamel paint, and the ardour of the housewife armed with Aspinall's enamel are two pejorative characterizations of amateur surface intervention that are often feminized (see Figure 1.2). The amateur is portrayed as lacking knowledge about how tools and materials work, with a will to beautify without skilful execution, and an inability to regulate labour power, as is the case with the obsessive enameller described in Mayne's lyrics.

Throughout the book I want to move beyond this rhetorical marginalization (and feminization) of amateur craft practice, and in this chapter I do so by focusing on the things that decentralized surface intervention (classified below as bases, carriers and arbiters). In the hands of amateurs, new tools and materials enabled individuals to express personal taste and creative autonomy, but they equally set the parameters of what could be achieved and the type of practice that unfolded. The amateur surface intervener was not suddenly able to do anything he or she so desired. Competence was distributed between the maker and the tool, as Shove et al. have stated.[14] Their argument supports the claim that amateur surface intervention is not merely a subjective act of expression but an appropriative and dependent act: the ability of an individual to harness an entire network of production.

To prioritize the importance of the amateur's interaction with tooling is one goal for this chapter. But the second key hypothesis is that the advent of tool and material accessibility thrust the issue of distributed competence and appropriation into the realm of artistic production. As explored below, the late eighteenth and early nineteenth century ushered in a period of chemical and technological progress that fuelled the commercial provision of artistic supplies, which removed the need for artists to engage in the tasks that previously preceded the production of a painting, such as stretching canvases or grinding colours. As the French artist Marcel Duchamp stated in a series of interviews in the 1960s – all art was readymade from this moment on, when equipment and supplies, like paint in tubes, were industrially produced.[15] But rather than seeing this as evidence of de-skilling within art, the end of the craft of painting, and the beginning of the conceptual age, as many do,[16] I build on recent theory to suggest that skill was simply re-configured and did not disappear. Artist and amateur alike were faced with readymade abundance, but this did not lead to a clear meeting point between the amateur on the 'way up' and the professional artist on the 'way down', 'under the auspices of deskilling', as claimed by the theorist John Roberts.[17] Although amateurs and artists might go through similar processes of choosing and applying surfaces, they move in different directions, with different intentions and goals for their work.

Let us return to enamel paints to demonstrate this.

A couple of decades after the popularization of Aspinall's and Chez Lui, Duchamp was also messing about with enamel paint. His 1916–17 assisted readymade *Apolinère Enameled*, uses as its base a tin-plate advertisement that is remarkably similar in composition to the Chez Lui advertisement (Figure 1.3). Duchamp manipulated the readymade into a misspelt, humorous message to his poet friend Guillaume Apollinaire: he carefully erased the 'S' of Sapolin – an enamel paint product – and added 'ère' and 'ed' in white paint.[18]

We could situate Duchamp's playful surface intervention within the art historical narrative of art's increasing distance from representation; art used not to depict something, but to reference

FIGURE 1.3 *Marcel Duchamp,* Apolinère Enameled *(1916–17). Gouache and graphite on painted tin, mounted on cardboard. 9⅝ × 13⅜ (24.4×34cm) Philadelphia Museum of Art: The Louise and Walter Arensberg Collection, 1950 © Succession Marcel Duchamp/ADAGP, Paris and DACS, London 2014.*

the relationships and mechanisms within the artworld: Apollinaire was an influential critic besides being Duchamp's friend. We could frame it as a surface intervention with an 'internalized', philosophical, aesthetic and political language, what Thierry de Duve termed 'a reprieve', 'an avant-garde strategy devised by artists who were aware that they could no longer compete technically or economically with industry'.[19] Surface interventions as diverse as the Impressionist foregrounding of sketch as the final artwork, the celebration of surface flatness in Maurice Denis and Paul Gauguin, or Jackson Pollock's abstract expressionism could be woven into this artistic strategy whereby the craft of painting plays second fiddle to the idea, spirit or aesthetic point being made.

Yet Duchamp's use of an enamel advert as his base cannot be ignored. He places his own act of surface intervention in a similar league to the hordes of amateur surface interveners, who are using Sapolin to coat their bedframes, or other domestic surfaces. For both Duchamp and the amateur enamellers (like the fictional Pooter), artistic labour is reduced to the production of the final layer: marking, signing, decorating, in short adding the final layer to an object produced by the labour of others. In this environment, artistic labour was akin to choosing and appropriating – or as Duchamp stated, selecting whether to use red or blue tubes of paint.[20]

Duchamp provocatively laid bare these new relationships of artistic production with all of his readymades, and he achieved this through skilful manipulation of the surface as shown through the signature of R. Mutt on the surface of *Fountain* (1917) that signalled artistic game-playing.

By contrast, many enamellers shared Pooter's plight and were unable to achieve the surface finish they desired. However foolproof the instructions or sophisticated the technology, individual competence could not be effaced and skill was still required. For example, to use Aspinall's or Chez Lui enamel, users had to ensure surfaces were dust-free and smooth before starting and that the paint was left to dry for 12 hours in between the application of the required three to four layers.[21] Skill and know-how concerning the material applications on to surfaces was still important in the era of the readymade. Surface interveners of different guises were exploring the material potential and limitations of increasingly accessible and sophisticated technology, some to achieve an effect that would have previously been beyond their capability, others to make deliberate points about conditions of artistic production and labour.

This case study on new enamel paint technologies constitutes a microcosm of the chapter's aim: to describe how new technologies made amateur surface intervention possible, and to explain the subsequent impact on artistic production once the alchemy associated with an artistic process has been deconstructed. When art is reduced to an appropriation of the labour of others, how one approaches the materiality of the final surface layer is, I argue, integral. This material understanding of surface intervention presents a lens through which a new reading of modern art history is possible, building on recent work that places skill, labour, the use of tools and material manipulation centre stage.[22]

The effort to etch amateur surface intervention into narratives of modern art history demands three successive conceptual moves. First, the surface has to be foregrounded as a contested zone of material and metaphorical manipulation. Its status as a mere conduit through which meaning and depth is expressed needs to be challenged. Using an interdisciplinary source base – drawing from Jacques Derrida's assault on the expectation of art's autonomy, and recent theories of material culture – the surface is shown to contain multiple depths.

Once the surface has been rescued from its intellectual marginalization, I will then account for the history of the things that facilitate surface intervention: the bases, carriers and arbiters. The ability of the amateur to become surface intervener and unravel the mystery of artistic production is predicated on the accessibility of these tools and materials that were produced in increasing quantities from the late eighteenth century onwards and marketed to a heterogeneous array of artists, middle class hobbyists and anyone else with time and money on their hands by firms such as Winsor & Newton, Reeves or LeFranc et Cie.[23] Far from constituting exhaustive company histories, the attempt is to deconstruct selected commercially supplied artistic tools and materials through object analysis to show how they were made, how they simplified various practices of surface intervention, how they were used and, consequently, how they were implicated in the evolving dialectics of de- and re-skilling in artistic practice. Although I only cover various forms of painting in this analysis, the codification of bases, carriers and arbiters is intended to offer a rubric for the deconstruction of any amateur craft.

As a complete all-in-one invitation to art, the paint-by-number kit produced in large quantities in the USA during the 1950s concludes this history of accessibility to artistic supplies. As a medium that reduced the artistic process to a simple '1–2–3', critical hostility to the kits comes as no surprise despite the best efforts of promoters to accentuate their pedagogic potential. However, by completely fragmenting the processes of making a painting, the paint-by-number kit, whether consciously or not, exposed a repressed truth about all art in the modern era: its reliance on the non-artistic labour of others and the reduction of the artist's role to application of the outermost layer or finishing off. The conceptual depth of this seemingly ephemeral fad underlines the importance of situating amateur surface intervention within broader art historical narratives, as attempted above by relating the history of enamel paints to Duchamp's *Apolinère*

Enameled. Several artists have at least been partially aware of the revelatory power of paint-by-number kits, and the chapter closes with a critical assessment of the various appropriations of this much maligned and misunderstood medium: from Andy Warhol's *Do It Yourself* Series of 1962, to Jeff McMillan's 2009 paint-by-number installation, *The Possibility of an Island*.

The philosophy of the surface

> Even what is called *ornamentation* (parerga), i.e. what is only an adjunct, and not an intrinsic constituent in the complete representation of the object, in augmenting the delight of taste does so only by means of its form. Thus it is with the frames of pictures, or the drapery on statues, or the colonnades of palaces. But if the ornamentation does not itself enter into the composition of the beautiful form – if it is introduced like a gold frame merely to win approval for the picture by means of its charm – it is then called *finery* and takes away from genuine beauty.

EMMANUEL KANT, *Critique of Judgement* (1790), p. 57

Alongside frames, draperies and colonnades, the surface can fall under Kant's definition of parerga. An adjunct to art, *parerga* refer to the intermediate zone between the form of an object and the field of subjective experience, at best extrinsic to the work of art, but with the capability of despoiling 'genuine' beauty. Kant's construction of the autonomous aesthetic judgement that privileges 'design' or 'form' signals the theoretical marginalization of the surface in post-Enlightenment art and material culture, a critical trajectory continued in the twentieth century by Adolf Loos's assault on surface ornamentation and by Clement Greenberg's art criticism.[24]

Greenberg's marginalization of the surface as 'kitsch' – as a simulation, dependent, popular and facile – epitomizes this tendency to marginalize surfaces in aesthetic theory.[25] His classification of what constituted a kitsch surface was particularly pressing because the abstract paintings he encoded with aesthetic depth, such as Jackson Pollock's 'all-over' work, bore a close resemblance to the flat two-dimensionality of wallpaper.[26] This elevation of Pollock's flat surface compared to the flatness of advertisements, wallpaper or, indeed, amateur surface interventions, has much to do with the development of an internalized progressive language of an artistic *avant garde* mentioned above. Greenberg's adherence to Kantian notions of aesthetic autonomy can be taken to represent the persistence of the assumption that compared with form, or depth, surface only serves to augment, distract, placate, conceal or deceive the innocent autonomous subject who is striving to assure his distance from the 'mere' representation of an object.

In an attempt to foreground the potential of the surface as a mobile site of meaning, its relationship to both exterior and interior elements of the artwork must be problematized. Critiquing Kant's assumptions of what is 'intrinsic' to art, and therefore what also is extrinsic, Derrida situates the parergon (singular of parerga) in a more fluid position as a shifting boundary between interior and exterior. He asks why the garment or colonnade constitutes a parergon: 'It is not because they are detached but on the contrary because they are more difficult to detach and above all because without them, without their quasi-detachment, the lack on the inside of the work would appear; or (which amounts to the same thing for a lack) would not appear.'[27]

The parergon, or the supplementary adjunct, defines the interior meaning of an object through the linguistic construction of a binary opposition. However, this is not just definition by opposition, as Derrida points to the parergon's *quasi* detachment, situating its meaning within both exterior and interior contexts. He describes the parergon as 'standing out',[28] showing how this intermediary space can be conceptualized independently, between exterior and interior but merging with both. Derrida's invitation is to consider the parergon as an abstract entity that is manifest through certain objects, but not tied to them.[29] In the deconstruction of a painting – from its material grounds, painterly marks, varnish, framing, placement in a room, position within networks as commodity of exchange and architectural setting – the parergon negotiates throughout, constructing the interior–exterior binary by virtue of its quasi-detached role.

Derrida's method of analysis is primarily conceptual and linguistic; he is not concerned with the material properties of the parergon (including the surface). This is where the study of material culture must be brought in to help rescue the surface from its marginal position. Attention within this sub-discipline to the material properties of objects demonstrates how the surface is not a quasi-detached entity as Derrida suggested, but materially tied, amalgamated and embroiled. Karl Knappett's argument that 'an object cannot be properly grasped independently of how it relates to the body and indeed to its underlying area', is reflective of a rich stream of writing fuelled by Alfred Gell's and Latour's problematization of the resolute division between subject and object, human and non-human.[30]

While such works have highlighted the networks of social relations and individual agency that determine the production, dissemination and use of objects, few fail to locate the material surface as the site of this dynamic relationship. Notable exceptions include Grant McCracken's essay on pre-eighteenth-century patina, Celeste Olalquiaga's study on nineteenth-century perceptions of dusty surfaces and a chapter in Alfred Gell's *Art and Agency* devoted to the mesmeric potentiality in abstract, patterned surface decoration of Iatmul lime containers.[31] However, these works situate the surface as a site of fixed meaning, rather than as a material entity whose meaning is constantly being negotiated through processes of maintenance and ongoing labour. McCracken cites Pierre Bourdieu and Thorstein Veblen to equate various features of patina with reductive and static concepts of eighteenth-century strategies of distinction and overlooks how fashion continually re-appropriates patina in new social-historic circumstances.[32] Olalquiaga is more poetic in her description of dust as the debris of a previous era's aura, a sheen of historicity that mediates perceptions of the object beneath, describing dust as a 'failed commodity' that continually speaks of all it has ceased to be.[33] But dust, like patina, is not a passive surface effect. It is active; it can be manipulated, maintained or wiped, as shown by Manuel Charpy's study of nineteenth-century French antique dealers who deliberately applied dust and distressed the surfaces of furniture and *objets d'art* to lend them the vaunted badge of historicity.[34]

Victoria Kelley and Glenn Adamson's edited volume, *Surface Tensions*, sets a standard for exploring the materiality of surfaces and how an object's meaning, cultural position and form are mediated by the management and manipulation of surface effect.[35] Exemplary of this approach is Kelley's own work in which she demonstrates how patina and other signs of age and wear are continually maintained and regulated through different strategies of cleaning, dusting and polishing; different approaches to surface intervention that are socially specific. For example the social cachet attributed to objects that showed their age through material effects on the surface would not make sense in poorer communities 'in which objects that showed their age did so in ways that undermined their value'.[36] There is a certain sense of social competition in how best to regulate surfaces as Kelley's case studies demonstrate, and as evident in a scene in J. G. Ballard's novel *Millennium People*, when one character praises the new invention of spray-on-mud in an aerosol can: 'An effective way of impressing people in the office car park on Monday mornings. A quick spray on the wheels and your colleagues will think of rose pergolas and thatched cottages.'[37] Ballard here parodies middle-class sensitivities to surface, in which an added layer can transform an object's meaning and lend it social and cultural cachet.

Surface mediation is both materially and metaphorically loaded: its constant regulation – through cleaning and other forms of maintenance – demonstrates its power as the vehicle through which depth is articulated. In addition, the material activity of the surface determines the entire meaning of the object beneath, all the way down.

The artistic surface

Studies of material culture, mentioned above, demonstrate the importance of paying attention to the material qualities of the surface and help challenge the presumption of the surface's superficiality. The material constitution of the surface is equally important in the study of painting and sculpture. However, with the notable exception of research on surface analysis for the purposes of conservation and preservation,[38] art history has largely forgotten the importance of the material surface, merely situating this zone as a conduit to biographical, formalist, semiotic or socio-historical study. This is particularly surprising given that the surface, and particularly its outermost layer, was at the centre of debates about modern painting from the mid-nineteenth century onwards.

For Eugène Delacroix and Jean-Baptiste-Camille Corot (and subsequently the 'Impressionists') the surface was not merely a layer that assisted the spectator's journey to greater symbolic depth. These artists confronted their audience by presenting the *ébauché* – the preparatory painted sketch – as a finished artwork in its own right, exposing the textured surface in its full matte glory. They defied a significant tenet within the Davidean Academic pedagogy of the time: they refused to flatten a composition through the application of a final layer of varnish, which was seen as a testament of artistic skill.[39] For art historian Albert Boime, this shift represented: '[The] displacement of distinct phases: the germinal experiment and the final execution took place on the canvas simultaneously – no intermediate stage between impulse and act hampered the final expression.'[40] This displacement, positioning the *ébauché* as a completed work, was controversial not because it demonstrated a lack of talent but because it aroused incredulity due to its incompleteness. Many critics equated such paintings to unfinished, facile, feminine daubs, due to the prevailing attitudes about artistic skill, but Baudelaire read the same surface as masculine, full of vigour and raw, equating the academic application of the *fini* with the femininity of domestic polishing.[41]

Regardless of critical preference, treatment of the outermost layer of the surface became essential for designating authorship within the new commercial art market of the nineteenth century and could be used as a weapon to signal rejection of artistic conventions. The type of material surface intervention could form an artist's signature style, described by Ulrich Lehmann (after Charles Baudelaire) as a *poncif*, a 'recognisable formal trait that distinguishes the artist's output from works by other artists competing in the market'.[42] The *poncif*, according to Lehmann, operates between the artist's own clichéd subjectivity – the calling card that indicates authorship – and the demonstration of these features in any given context. Drawing attention to the materiality of the surface – exposing facture – not only signalled a challenge to technical definitions of what a painting should be within the art establishment and its increasing redundancy as an accurate representational practice, but ensured that the artist's skill was distinguishable in a new commercial environment where photography and mechanical printing procedures could replicate the varnished smoothness of academic painting with ease.

The metaphorical depth of material marks in painting was lent particular aesthetic and social cachet in an era that witnessed the rise of photography and the ascendancy of the smooth, flat, photographic finish. The disregard for surface smoothness as contrasted to the authenticity of expression associated with gestural Impressionism is brilliantly evoked in a passage of Marcel Proust's *Remembrance of Things Past* (1913) where the narrator recalls his mother's opinions on the photographs in his room.

> She would have liked me to have in my room photographs of ancient buildings or of beautiful places. But at the moment of buying them . . . she would find that the vulgarity and utility has too prominent a part in them, through the mechanical nature of their reproduction by photography. She attempted by a subterfuge . . . to introduce, as it might be, several 'thicknesses' of art; instead of photographs of Chartres Cathedral, of the Fountains of St-Cloud, or of Vesuvius she would inquire of Swann whether some great painter had not made pictures of them, and preferred to give me photographs of 'Chartres Cathedral' after Corot, of the 'Fountains of St-Cloud' after Hubert Robert, and of 'Vesuvius' after Turner, which were a stage higher in the scale of art.[43]

Although still a photograph, 'Chartres Cathedral after Corot' possesses more aesthetic (and moral) worth according to Swann's mother on account of the 'thicknesses' suggested in the photograph. As photography and its mechanical reproduction begins to monopolize the surface as a representational site, the materiality of the painted surface becomes the site where an artist's individual *poncif* and thus autonomy is located; the recognition of its thicknesses determining its status as a marker of correct, if middlebrow, taste. In French sociologist Pierre Bourdieu's taxonomy of taste,[44] appreciation of a textured surface is reflective of an individual's understanding that art can, and indeed should, point to its own form and historical development in resistance to the representational homogeneity of photographic flatness. However, the appreciation of textured surfaces was not just introduced as part of nineteenth-century art connoisseurship. Amateur surface interveners wanted to produce their own textured surfaces and endow photographs and paintings with their own mark or *poncif*, something reflected by the popularity of 'touching up' photographs with watercolour paint.[45]

Attitudes to academic *fini* and the properties of the photographic surface are two quick examples that rescue the artistic surface from its presumed superfluity and place marginal material phenomenon as the central focus of study. This approach is integral when attempting to insert amateur surface intervention into broader narratives of art history. Both works of art and amateur productions can be subject to a material anthropology of the surface that looks into how the surface layers were put together, the materials and technologies used, how the practitioner achieved such effects through varying levels of skill, and the extent to which such interventions were facilitated by the labour of others (those who made the tools and materials that were relied upon). This craft-centred anthropological approach to amateur surface intervention, however, is historically contingent. It can only be applied in an era of tool accessibility, when it was possible for individuals to have a go at replicating the labour of the artist.

What is needed for amateur surface intervention

All surface intervention requires three different categories of mediating agents – bases, carriers and arbiters:

- 'Bases' are the objects that provide the blank surface on which the amateur operates, such as paper, pre-primed canvases and sketchbooks. They constitute the very foundation of a work, yet themselves are already a result of a series of productive procedures.

- 'Carriers' are the tools and kits that provide the vehicle through which practice takes place. They are the mark-making objects that contain metamorphic qualities – objects whose *raison d'être* is to transform the blank, non-figurative base into objects imbued with creative enterprise, such as pens, paintbrushes, paint in tubes, as well as paint-boxes and kits that represent the collection of these objects, complete *invitations* to art in convenient carry cases.

- 'Arbiters' are objects, external to the materiality of a work, that shape the way in which the surface is manipulated. This is manifest textually in manuals and 'how-to' books, which inform the amateur of techniques, standards of taste and histories of style. Arbiters range from simple didactic pamphlets for the beginner to large tomes on the history of a specific medium. In addition to such literary support, there are also material aids, such as perspective devices, that assist the amateur in bypassing complex procedures of artistic production. (These two means of arbitration exist interdependently: the handbook often provides instruction for use of a device.)

The use of bases, carriers and arbiters is common to all art, regardless of chronology or geography. However, the nineteenth century witnessed both the growth of firms like Winsor & Newton, who ensured amateur access to craft processes, and a culture of knowledge dissemination that Glenn Adamson characterizes as the 'Age of the Reveal': 'No longer would [craft expertise] be exchanged tacitly, bit by bit, behind the closed doors of a workshop but traded exhaustively, in the wide open arena of the marketplace.'[46] Commercially produced bases, carriers and arbiters undermined the alchemy formerly at the centre of the artistic surface and opened up new possibilities about what art could be. These technological and chemical developments have often been held responsible for seismic changes in the course of modern art history: tired platitudes, such as the argument that collapsible paint in tubes *caused* Impressionism.[47] I aim to avoid technological determinism of this ilk by paying attention to how bases, carriers and arbiters were initially marketed and used by amateurs – Monet and the Impressionists were not the only ones to benefit from the portability of tubed paint. The reception of new technologies was uneven and varied, meaning that it was the *use* of these new technologies that determined whether a work was framed as 'amateur', 'professional', 'artistic' or 'avant garde'. Different capabilities arose out of the new tool–human relationships that emerged.

Amateurs were often beset with limitations: poor quality bases, carriers and arbiters; insufficient technical information; inadequacies of skill; and the broader social-cultural factors that marginalized their efforts. As a generalization, the amateur, beginner or student was more likely to use these newly available tools and materials to reach a level of competence or mastery according to the artistic convention of the day (through imitation). By contrast, the trained artist, more familiar with the craft of painting or the history of such processes, was more likely to stretch the potential of new technologies, extending the possibility of material, and subverting conventions of art through tool misuse. This self-conscious treatment of arbiters, carriers and bases – the elucidation of the medium as message[48] – became a recognizable trajectory within *avant garde* practice, identifiable in works from Paul Gauguin's use of jute in his canvases in the 1890s, to Andy Warhol's appropriation of the paint-by-number canvas in the 1962 *Do It Yourself* series.

Accounts of individual interaction with the things that facilitate surface intervention are important, but the analysis below has an especial focus on what uses were suggested by each base, carrier or arbiter, how they were made, how they simplified a process, and the different configurations of practice that resulted from their use. By no means is this a comprehensive history, the effort is to strengthen our understanding of accessible tooling, its commercial provision, and its impact on artistic production in order to challenge the limiting fiction of a clear divide between professional and amateur surface intervention.

Bases: the blank surface

Bases provide the surface on which amateur dreams can unfold. The prepared canvas or blank page is a raw material, but in the context of the nineteenth century and beyond it already constituted a readymade that had passed through multiple stages of production. Before the industrialization of art supply firms, bases were prepared by apprentices or colourmen employed by artists to undertake a wide range of preparatory practices, such as canvas stretching and priming, mixing colours, cleaning brushes and preparing the palettes, easels and other tools.[49] From the late eighteenth century, the barriers that had previously protected craft skills and apprenticeship learning were fundamentally challenged, both by the weakening authority of guilds and free market policies ushered in by the French Revolution and industrialization. As in many other industries, merchant capitalists started to co-ordinate the production of readymade art supplies, breaking down the process of producing one item into a series of less complex tasks.[50] As with Adam Smith's famous example of the division of labour in pin manufacturing from the early nineteenth century, canvases were being produced by labour that was subdivided between a set of discrete tasks, rather than one apprentice or colourman being in control of making the entire object.[51] Benefiting from economies of scale, bases could thus be produced in increasing quantity and at ever diminishing costs, widening access to surface intervention.

This availability was due to the modernization of a number of artistic supply firms, known in their day as artists' colourmen. With their roots in the eighteenth-century trade of producing paints and supplies under guild protection, firms like Reeves, Ackerman and Rowney in Britain, and LeFranc in France, grew to produce artistic supplies on a larger scale. The growth of Winsor & Newton from its founding in 1832 is particularly reflective of this trend. The firm set the precedent for rationalizing the production of artistic supplies, particularly in the manufacture of synthetic colour, and for re-locating manufacture to sites out-of-town: the firm established a factory in the fields of Kentish Town, North London in 1844 equipped with a chemical laboratory and mills that simulated the motion of grinding pigment by hand, and Reeves followed suit with a steam-powered factory built in Dalston, East London in 1868.[52]

Among the many products these firms sold, was an array of bases, prepared and ready for use. For example, in London, Winsor & Newton, Reeves, George Rowney & Co. and J. Barnard sold 'prepared' canvas in rolls, as well as a selection of pre-stretched, framed canvases from the 1830s.[53] In France, LeFranc et Cie and Bourgeois Aîné also marketed similar products, meaning that use of the self-primed canvases by French artists in the 1840s was 'the exception rather than the rule', according to the art historian David Bomford.[54] The commercial availability of prepared canvases might not have entirely stamped out traditional forms of production – some artists continued to prepare their own canvases and a niche market for canvases produced by artisanal labour persists to this day – but from the nineteenth century this process was no longer essential to the artist's craft. The very fact that well-known nineteenth-century artists Camille Pisarro and

Berthe Morisot used prepared canvases[55] highlights the ubiquity of this readymade form and how its use signalled the re-configuration of artistic labour away from preparing the base.

In other instances, entirely new bases were introduced to the market, the result of experimentation and increasingly sophisticated chemical knowledge. James Whatman developed new forms of paper in Britain in the late eighteenth century. His 'wove' paper replaced the 'laid' technique – an existing process of paper production that involved setting paper pulp on a wire sieve, resulting in sheets of paper on which you could see the grid pattern from the wire mesh. Whatman's paper provided a uniform surface without such imperfections and watermarks, and could better absorb watercolour paint, leading to a surge in the popularity of the medium in late eighteenth- and early nineteenth-century Britain.[56] By the end of the nineteenth century, Whatman paper sketchbooks of various sizes were ubiquitous, with advertisements (as shown in Figure 1.4) commonplace. There were opponents to this increasing standardization – Peter Bower claimed that certain artists were disappointed that firms no longer made paper to their specific needs.[57] However, the diverse range of techniques for producing the blank surface, previously the domain of colourmen producing idiosyncratic exemplars, was obscured or forgotten, ancillary to the production of 'proper' art. Prepared surfaces were just there, ready and waiting.

SOLID   SKETCH   BLOCKS,

WITH   AND   WITHOUT   CASES.

The Blocks consist of a number of sheets of paper, compressed so as to form a solid mass, each sheet of which is to be separated by inserting a knife underneath the uppermost one, and passing it round the edge.   The cases contain a pocket for carrying the sketches and place for pencil.

MADE OF WHATMAN'S ROYAL 70LBS. AND IMPERIAL 90LBS. PAPERS.

FIGURE 1.4 *Sketch block. G. Rowney & Co supplement in Henry Seward,* Manual of Colours: Showing the Composition and Properties of Artists' Colours, with Experiments on their Permanence *(London: Rowney, 1889). Image courtesy of Colour Reference Library, Royal College of Art.*

Carriers: action on the surface

Carriers are the goods that make surface intervention possible. They take two forms: the substances that facilitate the impression of creative faculties, such as ink, brushes, pencils and paints – made from a mixture of pigment and a binding substance (or 'vehicle') – and the units that contain these items as prepared invitations to art, such as paintboxes and art kits.

Accessibility to ready-mixed paint was limited up to the late eighteenth century, as preparing colour, like making bases, was the preserve of the specifically trained apprentices or colourmen, protected by guilds and pursuing their own irregular and secretive procedures.[58] Watercolour was the first paint medium to be produced on a wider scale in Britain, with the firm Reeves developing moist watercolour 'cakes' in the late eighteenth century. William Reeves, the firm's founder, applied the training he received as a member of the Worshipful Company of Gold and Silver Wire-Drawers to conceive of the idea that paint might be 'extruded and chopped into oblong cakes'.[59] Through experimentation, and the use of honey, Reeves produced small blocks of colour embossed with their logo, which, when moistened, would provide a reliable vehicle for watercolour surface intervention (Figure 1.5). These cakes were a vital part of the company's development in the late eighteenth and early nineteenth century but, as with the invention of Whatman paper, they became widely available by the 1850s when most of Reeves's competitors produced and marketed a similar product.

FIGURE 1.5 *Reeves & Sons watercolour paintbox. Reproduced courtesy of The Museum of London. Photograph by author.*

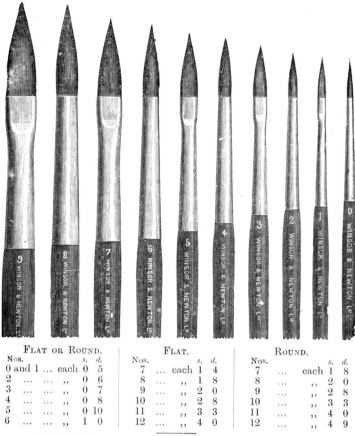

FIGURE 1.6 *Winsor & Newton brushes for oil painting. Winsor & Newton supplement in Henry Murray,* The Art of Painting and Drawing in Coloured Crayons *(London: Winsor & Newton, c.1900). Image courtesy of Colour Reference Library, Royal College of Art.*

In the nineteenth century, the production of artistic supplies was subject to 'extensive commercialisation'.[60] Catalogues selling a range of equipment were appended to the end of instruction manuals aimed at artists, students and drawing-room amateur alike (Figure 1.6). The growth of these companies was aided by the invention of collapsible metallic tubes for oil paint, invented in London in 1841 by American portrait artist John G. Rand and initially marketed by the London colourman Thomas Brown. Winsor & Newton, who had been experimenting with their own tubed paint that operated like a syringe, sensed an opportunity and bought the patent for Rand's invention in 1842. Although pre-mixed oil paint did exist before this date, packaged in pig's bladders,[61] mixtures were susceptible to dry or to spoil in contact with heat or moisture; problems that were eradicated by Rand's airtight tubes. By the 1850s this technology was widely advertised in the catalogues of art supply firms marking a key moment in improving access to surface intervention in oil (see Figure 1.7).[62]

The development of paint technology and, in particular, the introduction of oil paint in tubes, is often held responsible for the start of modern art. The argument seems to make sense: portable paints allowed artists to travel to their subject rather than sketching it and finishing it in the studio, previously 'a technical impossibility' as the art historian De Duve states.[63] De Duve places the tube of paint in the centre of his analysis of the development of an *avant garde* tradition, which offsets the declining importance of craft as a barometer of a painter's skill with the development of an internalized language: for the Impressionists this involved the 'industrialization' of the painter's hand through the fragmentation of the image, a bitmap that only manifests itself pictorially in the spectator's eye.[64] De Duve's argument that tubes of paint

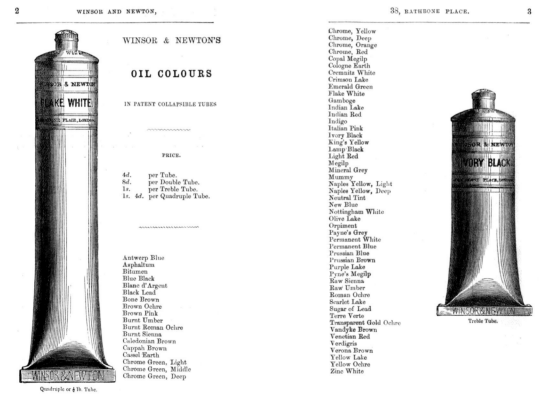

FIGURE 1.7 *Winsor & Newton oil colours in patent collapsible tubes. Winsor & Newton supplement in Thomas W. Salter,* Field's Chromatography: or, Treatise on Colours and Pigments Used by Artists *(London: Winsor & Newton, 1869). Image courtesy of Colour Reference Library, Royal College of Art.*

are readymades helpfully backdates the concept beyond Duchamp's urinals and snow shovels. However his assertion of a direct link between the introduction of new technology and the practices of *avant garde* artists not only overlooks how Impressionists continued to do most of their painting within the confines of the studio, but how amateur artists constituted the main market for pre-mixed paint and other art supplies.

Oil paints in tubes were designed to be odourless, making them suitable for domestic use and drawing room leisure. As Anthea Callen states, the *plein air* painting encouraged by their introduction had a 'greater immediate impact on the amateur than on the professional painter'.[65] Amateur reception of art supplies needs to be placed alongside the well-known response among artists of the canon, to create a greater sense of awareness of technological and social contexts. Reception of new technologies was uneven, each product entered complex hierarchies of use. The claim that readily available tubes of paint had a greater impact in the hands of amateurs than as the carrier of choice in the Impressionist's trousseau is strengthened by the fact that established artists often decided to patronize trusted colourmen using traditional methods; people like Père Tanguy, who supplied many of the Impressionist artists.[66] Jean-François Millet, Paul Gauguin, James McNeill Whistler, Vincent Van Gogh and Armand Guillaumin were known to have used commercially manufactured paint in tubes, but only during times of financial duress, when nothing else was available, or in the case of Gauguin when he was still a Sunday painter.[67]

Among artists and critics in France there was concern that new paint technologies would usher in material degradation within the arts – proof again of the generally negative way critics responded to the greater accessibility of art supplies (as seen in the later case study on paint-by-number). In the 1890s the French artist and pedagogue, Johan Georges Vibert, lamented the invention of industrially produced paint as an example of the 'pacotille' (shoddy goods) of amateur equipment.[68] Chief among Vibert's complaints, however, was not the technical inadequacy of commercially produced paint in tubes but the decline in the artist's technical knowledge that their introduction had ushered in. Fellow educationalist and writer, Karl Robert, in *Traité pratique de la peinture à l'huile* (1891), echoes Vibert's concern:

> The colour merchants and makers of chemical products have stamped out the primary job of the painter for he buys his oils without worrying about the grave consequences of such unforgivable carelessness. Such disillusion and mistrust results from the use of this new material, and what hopelessness awaits the artist when he sees each day his work, the fruit of his hard labour and pain, become little by little subject to the damage of time.[69]

Vibert proposes regulatory measures to counter this demise of the artist's technical knowledge: listing the chemical composition of paints on the packaging of tubes and proposing a centralized *Société des Artistes Françaises* that would grant a seal of approval to products tested by an in-house chemist.[70] This concern also probably explains the appearance of Gabriel Déneux's small pamphlet, *Un procédé de peinture inaltérable. La peinture à l'encaustique* (1890), in which the author praises the 'happy' times of Pericles and Egyptian portraiture 'where there was no awareness of oil paints, varnishes and siccatives, where colour was still not yet falsified'.[71] Similarly, in Britain there was a concern that the commercial provision of oil paint would threaten the integrity of artistic surface application. The paint company George Rowney & Co. was concerned enough to employ Henry Seward to write a short publication that compared pigments of the Old Masters with modern equivalents, Seward stating that permanence of colours 'has attracted considerable attention'.[72]

Vibert, Robert, Seward and Déneux all attempted to convince artists that they should pay attention to the chemical composition of commercially produced paints and sought to revive the pre-nineteenth-century notion that artists should acquire a technical understanding of their own production. Yet their assertions mostly fell on deaf ears, for although artists might not have directly used commercially produced paints, as I explained above, by the late nineteenth century they certainly no longer considered the skill of grinding paints to be an integral part of their practice. Former means of preparation, manual grinding and mixing, were no longer socially valued as artistic skills of note. As British artist, J. M. W. Turner, stated to his friend and supplier, William Winsor (of Winsor & Newton), in response to a comment about his selection of colours: 'Your business Winsor is to make colours . . . mine is to use them.'[73]

Paintboxes

Collapsible tubes of paint also prompted an expansion in the number of paintboxes manufactured by art supply firms, joining the plethora of watercolour paintboxes already on the market. Pages and pages of different sized paintboxes in Winsor & Newton and Reeves catalogues provide the strongest indication of the amateur audiences these firms were keen to appeal to. This is because paintboxes were entire invitations to art, suitable for domestic confines, containing all the basic elements needed for artistic practice in an ergonomic, portable and inexpensive form. In his manual *The Art of Landscape Painting* (1855), Henry Murray advises beginners that:

> The most convenient and advantageous mode of proceeding will be, to obtain from any respectable dealer one of the usual tin oil-painting boxes, fitted completely with the necessary articles. It will contain beside colours, a set of brushes – comprising hog-hair, sable and badger brushes, a palette, a knife, port-crayons, chalk, oil, and varnish.[74]

Paintboxes not only contained the most important carrier – the colours that were needed to make a mark – but everything else. Paintboxes were produced in ever increasing quantity from the 1850s with smaller, more convenient and cheaper models introduced, such as the Japanned tin paintbox (Figure 1.8), a portable carry case for watercolour paints. These hardy paintboxes were very popular: eleven million of them were sold between 1853, when they were introduced, and 1873.[75] These were far more attractive as an invitation to art than their cumbersome, heavy forebears.

Nineteenth-century artist supply catalogues contain large ranges of portable watercolour paintboxes suitable for *plein air* practice with titles such as 'Tourist', 'Pocket' and 'Compact', containing between 10–12 blocks or watercolour cakes with enough room for a brush and space for mixing. Alongside its Japanned tin models, Winsor & Newton sold the 'Water Bottle Moist Colour Box' for ten shillings, a handy model with compartmentalized space for colour mixing, all designed within the confines of a regular bottle that doubled up as helpful water storage and sat conveniently atop one's hand (Figure 1.9). Firms produced small paintboxes that appealed due to their convenience, the thumb-hole paint box in Figure 1.10 suggesting greater hybridity between hand and tool. French artist and manual-writer, Armand Cassagne, railed against these small paintboxes as a viable introduction to art in his *Traité de l'aquarelle*, stating that firms:

> made an excessive quantity of these small boxes, the largest among them the size of two fingers squared, others with the dimensions of a five franc coin; these are charming playthings, but offer nothing to the serious practitioner.[76]

WINSOR & NEWTON'S

" Patent Spring " Japanned
Tin Boxes,

FITTED WITH

MOIST WATER COLOURS IN CHINA PANS.

The pans of colour are fastened by the employment of a V spring in each partition of the Box (which method was secured to Messrs. WINSOR & NEWTON, Limited, under Letters Patent in Great Britain, the principal Kingdoms in Europe, and in the United States of America); they are thus held firmly, and the long-felt inconvenience of cementing the china pans *to the box*, and of removing them when empty is avoided.

The improvement is a valuable one to Artists, as any colours in a box can be at once changed to suit their requirements, and the pans can be moved from one position to another at pleasure.

FIGURE 1.8 *Winsor & Newton's 'patent spring' Japanned tin boxes. Winsor & Newton supplement in* Henry Murray, The Art of Painting and Drawing in Coloured Crayons *(London: Winsor & Newton, c.1900). Image courtesy of Colour Reference Library, Royal College of Art.*

WATER BOTTLE MOIST COLOUR BOX.

SPACE FOR BRUSHES

Containing the following Twelve Colours :—

Gamboge	Vermilion	Cobalt
Yellow Ochre	Light Red	Indigo
Raw Sienna	Crimson Lake	Vandyke Brown
Burnt Sienna	Brown Madder	Brown Pink

Price 10s.

THE ABOVE BOX CLOSED.

Size—5½ inches by 2 ; 1 inch deep.

FIGURE 1.9 *Winsor & Newton water bottle moist colour box. Winsor & Newton supplement in Scott J. Taylor,* Field's Chromatography: A Treatise on Colours and Pigments for the Use of Artists *(London: Winsor & Newton, 1885). Image courtesy of Colour Reference Library, Royal College of Art.*

WINSOR & NEWTON'S THUMB-HOLE BOXES.

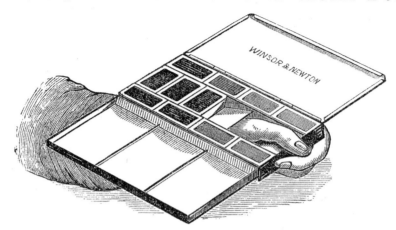

THUMB-HOLE BOX.

Empty.			Fitted with Colours.		
s.	*d.*		£	*s.*	*d.*
9	0	11 Cake Moist Water Colour Thumb-hole Box .	1	5	0
10	6	17 „ ditto	1	15	0
12	0	21 „ ditto	2	5	0

FIGURE 1.10 *Winsor & Newton's thumb-hole boxes. Winsor & Newton supplement to Thomas Leeson Rowbotham,* The Art of Landscape Painting in Water-Colours *(London: Winsor & Newton, 1878). Yale Center for British Art, Paul Mellon Fund.*

Smaller paintboxes (Figures 1.9 and 1.10) severely restricted the amount of colours that could be transported, thus limiting what the artist could depict. This reduction of art to a discrete set of colour options, exaggerated in the case of an amateur painter with a 'charming plaything', reflects the aesthetic doctrine of the Impressionists, according to De Duve, 'the act of painting as a series of choices within a standardised logic of colours'.[77] This coheres with De Duve's overall claim that, after the invention of the tube of paint, all art is reduced to making through choosing, artists merely selecting what readymade paints should be mixed together. Again, De Duve's analysis convincingly describes the narrowing of the artist's skill, encouraging the perception that there is equivalence between the artist faced with the reduced options of commercially produced colour and the novice presented with a basic palette of colours in his or her first paintbox. However, within these constraints that artists and amateurs were subjected to, there was room for considerable manoeuvre and different configurations of use. This is accentuated by certain developments in nineteenth-century paintbox design.

Winsor & Newton introduced flexibility in the design of their late-nineteenth-century paintboxes by making sure that the user could rearrange, replace and insert their own customized selection of colour. The company's 'Patent-Flexible-Division Moist Colour Box' (Figure 1.11), advertised in 1878, stressed the convenience of the divisions that ensured the mobility of colours and an improvement on previous designs where paint pans were permanently cemented to the bottom of the paintbox resulting in their obsolescence after the paint in the pan ran out.

WINSOR & NEWTON'S PATENT-FLEXIBLE-DIVISION MOIST COLOUR BOX.

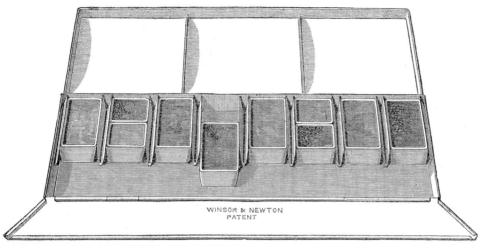

WINSOR & NEWTON
PATENT

PATENT-FLEXIBLE-DIVISION BOX OF MOIST WATER COLOURS.

(For Prices see pages 16 *and* 17.)

FIGURE 1.11 *Winsor & Newton's patent-flexible-division moist colour box. Winsor & Newton supplement to Thomas Leeson Rowbotham,* The Art of Landscape Painting in Water-Colours *(London: Winsor & Newton, 1878). Yale Center for British Art, Paul Mellon Fund.*

Similarly, the firm's 'Patent Spring' device, using a 'V' spring in each partition, introduced in 1885, further expedited the process (Figure 1.8). The creation of a colour palette specific to each user exemplifies the self-manipulation of commercially produced paintboxes after initial purchase. As Murray states, 'It is very rare to find two painters working with precisely the same colours and tints.'[78] The infinite array of colour combinations for watercolour or oil practice is evident from the manuals, each suggesting a different palette dependent on medium or subject.[79] Choosing one's colours is an example of post-purchase individualization of an object, but this is far from an unbridled, Nietzschean moment of autonomous agency: the paintbox owner is limited by the design of the paintbox and the select number of colours that comes with it. Individual choice is exercised within clearly demarcated boundaries. The design of the paintbox, allowing infinite variations within a pre-arranged readymade form, is a material metaphor for the constrained freedom of artistic expression that both amateur and professional are subject to. Paintbox design and other constraints that resulted from the industrialization of paint still permitted significant differentiation.

In addition to the small, portable paintboxes, Winsor & Newton manufactured larger, more expensive and conspicuous objects that not only facilitated art, but are advertised as art objects in their own right. The models, such as 'Lock and Drawer', 'Superior Large Caddy Lid, Brass Bound' and 'Handsome' all had the same basic materials and range of colours within them, the price differing solely because of the amount of extra compartments, drawers, accoutrements and fittings and whether the boxes were made in Spanish mahogany and French polished (Figure 1.12). Winsor & Newton's elaborate products show how the paintbox had become an item of conspicuous consumption in its own right.

"HANDSOME" BOXES.

					£	s.	d.
12 Cake " Handsome " Box,	with first class fittings		.		3	13	6
18 Ditto	ditto	ditto	.	. .	4	14	6
24 Ditto	ditto	ditto	.	. . .	6	6	0
36 Ditto	ditto	ditto	.	. .	9	9	0
12 Cake " Extra Handsome " Box,	with choice fittings		.		4	14	6
18 Ditto	ditto	ditto	.	. .	5	15	6
24 Ditto	ditto	ditto	.	. .	8	8	0
36 Ditto	ditto	ditto	.	. . .	12	12	0
50 Ditto	ditto	ditto	.	. .	21	0	0

FIGURE 1.12 *Winsor & Newton 'Handsome' boxes. Winsor & Newton supplement in Henry Murray,* The Art of Painting and Drawing in Coloured Crayons *(13th edn) (London: Winsor & Newton, 1880). Image courtesy of Robert B. Haas Family Arts Library Special Collections, Yale University.*

The paintbox is a miniaturized, reduced version of an artist's studio. It epitomises Susan Stewart's hypothesis of miniaturization – the domestication of material culture through containment and the obscuration of predominant modes of production.[80] The paintbox represents a reduced form of artistic production with various parts of the image-making process contained and compartmentalized: the reduced range of colours, the mixing palette, the requisite diluters and brushes. But, however miniaturized or compartmentalized, the reduced dimensions of art still facilitate some form of artistic production. Unlike the other objects that Stewart analyses – the doll's house, the model, the souvenir or the toy – the paintbox invites its user into the artist's craft and the ability to create individual narratives based on physical engagement. There is an expanded range of choice in both the purchase and self-construction of paintboxes – for all artists, amateur or otherwise – that facilitates the possibility of a break from these miniaturized confines. You just have to pick up the brush and paint.

Arbiters: how to do it

The final thing required for surface intervention is guidance: instruction as to what to do with these bases and carriers. If all art were reduced to choosing from a set of readymade bases and carriers, as De Duve states, then arbiters communicate the infinite gamut of options within this constraint, from selection of method, medium or colour, choice of image and aesthetic standards. In the nineteenth century, advice was communicated through an abundant supply of handbooks, manuals and treatises, churned out in increasing number thanks to advances in printing technology in the latter half of the century, and the development of half-tone printing that made it cheaper for printers to place images alongside texts.[81] It is an abundance we are familiar with today across all design, craft and art mediums. Like their contemporary equivalents, nineteenth-century 'how-to' provided hints and tips that were specifically targeted at diverse audiences of amateurs, from penny handbooks to encyclopaedic, academic tomes. Alongside textual arbitration, mechanisms also helped the amateur artists in the task of representation. These are the mechanical arbiters, the contraptions external to the work of art that helped deconstruct and reconstruct the image, landscape or scene to be depicted.

Textual arbiters

Henry Peacham's guidebooks on gentlemanly conduct, *The Art of Drawing With the Pen* in 1606 and *The Compleat Gentleman* in 1622, are early examples of textual arbitration that seek to encourage and guide artistic practice, and they demonstrate all the hallmarks that are integral to this literary genre (Figure 1.13). The layout is based on methodical and simple explanation of various procedures, leaving no doubt in the mind of the reader as to how to *do* something. Drawing is taught through a series of lessons, starting with shapes, lines and basic forms, then progressing to later chapters on portraiture, anatomy, shading, landscapes, depicting drapery, and how to mix colours correctly.[82] The language employed in the manual is deliberately uncomplicated, Peacham explaining that his work is 'fit for the capacity of the young learner'.[83]

The general assumption is that Peacham's manual, like all manuals, presents a neutral account of how to engage in something. However, the pedagogic language clouds societal, aesthetic and political judgements espoused by authors who are communicating the 'better way' of doing something. In *The Art of Drawing*, for example, Peacham legitimizes his advice by stating that

FIGURE 1.13 *Francis Delaram, title page from* The Compleat Gentleman *by Henry Peacham (London: John Legat, 1622), engraving. Yale Center for British Art, Paul Mellon Collection.*

it is more trustworthy than anything provided by the 'shops'.[84] Peacham's derisory comment on shop-floor knowledge is an early example of how advice literature primarily attempts to set out an ideal form of practice according to the opinions of someone in a position of authority.

By the late nineteenth century, instruction manuals and various forms of guidance were commonplace and published in large quantities thanks to improved printing technologies. Domestic advice literature of the period is a part of this phenomenon and has attracted particular attention from several design historians, who highlight the disparity between the dispensing of advice, often by middle-class writers, and its reception among a varied audience.[85] These historians, including Grace Lees-Maffei, who edited a 2003 special issue on the subject in *The Journal of Design History*, have problematized instructional literature as a neutral and reliable source of information about how life was actually lived in the past, and have alerted us to the political, aesthetic and social messages that were communicated through step-by-step instruction.[86]

The tension underlying nineteenth-century art manuals concerned their dual (and contradictory) function. The manuals had to provide accurate information for the earnest learner in line with the culture of information exposure (what Adamson termed the 'Age of the Reveal'), while arbitrating amidst the blurring distinctions between professional and amateur, reifying certain standards of production to defend against vulgarization. As might be expected, authors of manuals used their 'assets', such as their knowledge of historically validated procedures, to draw distinctions between genuine and poor quality production, fitting in with Pierre Bourdieu's notion of symbolic distinction. However, in the context of the amateur surface intervener who engages in production, the questions of 'how is something made?' and 'what is it made with?' became important new ways to compete for what Bourdieu termed the 'exclusive appropriation of legitimate cultural goods and the associated symbolic profits'.[87] Once a differentiated mass of makers of varying skill levels have some knowledge of a process, the politics and aesthetics of taste become very difficult to regulate.

Manual authors attempted to maintain the precarious balance between promoting access while reifying existing norms in artistic production. This can be seen in instructional literature across different mediums, but as an example for this brief analysis I have focused on nineteenth-century watercolour manuals, one of the most accessible art mediums of the century. One strategy of differentiation within manuals was the implementation of a hierarchy of cachet based on the subject depicted: for example, painting still life in watercolour had less potential than landscapes to convey artistic skill, because of its mimetic nature.[88] Epitomizing this hierarchy are the manuals of George Brookshaw, who in the 1810s introduced treatises on painting flowers, fruits and birds specifically targeted at young women. The author promises the female readership that they are 'sooner to arrive at perfection than men' because their faculties are more attuned to 'exact' representation and depiction of detail.[89] Imitative tendencies are aligned with the female practitioner who is marginalized through her assumed inability to comprehend perspective and express an original interpretation of nature. A hierarchy of artistic credibility was a way to channel the skills of the female amateur towards genres that were marginalized and associated with the domestic, helping to 'remasculinise the public sphere of high art'.[90]

If Brookshaw explicitly stated the remit of his manual, defining a specific branch of practice as feminine and undertaken for amusement only, most manuals were aimed at the upwardly mobile 'learner', a progressive archetype with no theoretical limit to achievement. According to these manuals, the learner was distinguished from those who only wanted amusement by higher levels of patience and hard work, which were deemed necessary in the pursuit of proficiency in watercolour. As manual writer Francis Nicholson notes: 'By doing quickly he will never learn to do well, by doing well he may learn to do quickly'.[91] This acquisition of skill and experience, however, was only available to those whose financial security or access to free time afforded them the ability to improve.

The most compelling way in which manuals accommodated the paradox of disseminating information, yet maintained conventional notions of artistic excellence, was by insisting on standards of aesthetic beauty, a conveniently elusive standard of judgement. As Joshua Reynolds, cited in John Clark's *The Amateur's Assistant*, states:

> When the arts were in their infancy, the power of merely drawing the likeness of any object was considered as one of its greatest efforts: the common people, ignorant of the principles of art, talk the same language even to this day; but when it was found that every man could be taught to do this merely by the observance of certain precepts, the name of genius thus shifted its application, and was given only to those who *added* the peculiar expression, grace, or dignity, or in short, such qualities and excellences, the production of which could not then be taught by any known and promulgated rules.[92]

Reynolds's words, placed in the manual's introduction, inform the amateur that even if he or she masters the skill of watercolour, there is still some intangible extra quality to art that is required for true excellence: the 'learner' has to express something beyond mere representation. As Nicholson notes, one must perfect the skills of a practice before subverting or re-inventing them.[93] By propagating the idea that the true artist has skills that cannot be contained by words or rules alone, arbiters of taste can maintain a distance between aesthetic excellence – which is privy to a small number freed from the rubric of instruction and valorized by arbiters of taste like Reynolds – and technique, which can be understood by growing numbers of amateur practitioners.

A brief survey of these watercolour manuals demonstrates the limitations of this literary genre's ability to provide comprehensive explanations of practice due to the inherent limitation of words in describing physical processes. On the whole, manuals are 'ideological texts', not direct accounts of actual practice, but rather suggestions. The subtext and meaning beneath presumably neutral instruction have been highlighted by a diverse array of writers, including the British author, artist and designer Graham Rawle, who directly cut and pasted the clearly gendered 'how-to' advice from 1960s women's magazines into his novel *Woman's World* (2005) and lifted texts from photography guidebooks for his *Diary of an Amateur Photographer* (1998) that barely conceal the subtext of repressed sexual desire in the tips on how to photograph live models.[94]

Yet it is Gustave Flaubert's novel, *Bouvard and Pécuchet* (1881), that issues a fundamental (and philosophical) critique of the manual as a vessel for the provision of knowledge or capability. The novel's title characters continually and desperately attempt to seek mastery of various disciplines from gardening, exercise, anatomy, religion and ethics through the use of guidebooks. In a comedic parody of bourgeois notions of knowledge, Flaubert's protagonists fail to excel in any of their innumerable endeavours because they rely too heavily on the constant presence of a manual or an encyclopaedia and its proscriptive explanations, leaving them disillusioned with received information and the impossibility of arriving at a 'correct' answer.[95]

Generally speaking, nineteenth-century manual authors were aware of the inherent weakness of their step-by-step instruction: they alerted their audiences that their advice could not provide all the answers, providing a pre-emptive warning against Bouvard and Pécuchet-style obsession. For example, art manual writer Thomas Rowbotham concedes in his 1855 treatise on sketching that 'the power of painting a picture is not to be acquired from books alone',[96] and in the task of mixing colour, Thomas Coleman Dibdin encourages procedures that depart from his advice, stating that the practitioner should 'not strictly be confined to . . . any other formula of colours, but use any pigment or combination of pigments which appear to work better'.[97] Textual arbiters, due to their distance from direct processes of making, were pliable in their arbitration, their authors aware that their readers need at some point to put the book down and get on with it.

At first glance, the intentions of a manual seem neutral, fulfilling the function of telling the reader 'what to do' and corresponding with Peter Dormer's concept of education as the 'honest' development of skill and gradual accumulation of tacit knowledge.[98] It is worth noting that pioneers of twentieth-century studio craft in the UK – Edward Johnston, Bernard Leach, Christopher Whall and Ethel Mairet – wrote craft manuals with this 'honest' intention in mind.[99] Works like Johnston's *Writing, Illuminating and Lettering* and Leach's *The Potter's Book* have become icons in the twentieth-century literature on craft, but this is chiefly because of the ideological content of these works that is appreciated by trained makers, rather than as their role as technical guides for the amateur. Despite the attention to 'honest' instruction, these works show clear bias against industrial processes and favour practice within the studio environment, with use of local materials, the veneration of the handmade and, in the case of Leach, a material philosophy heavily influenced by his trips to Japan and Korea. The learner is guided through craft practices but within a very specific ideological context.

Manuals have a clear democratic aspect, but as the analysis above has indicated, the nature of dispensing advice is imbued with symbolic meaning. Even when a practitioner has the skill to overcome the difficulty of hard work, the elusiveness of representing beauty remains ambiguous enough for critics to separate works of merit from those of mere technical proficiency. The manual negotiates this porous terrain between amateur and professional identities, allowing upward mobility for practitioners through explanation of skills and processes, but constantly reminding readers of the barriers that prevent all from being 'genuine' artists.

Mechanical arbiters: providing a shortcut

Though equipped with a certain degree of know-how, mass amateurism also depended on the fragmentation of complex tasks by mechanical arbiters, devices that made it easy to engage in surface intervention. Among the many products, gadgets and contraptions that deconstruct various facets of surface intervention for the amateur, the devices that helped frame a scene are the main focus. All artists use some form of mechanical arbitration. David Hockney's book, *Secret Knowledge: Rediscovering the Lost Techniques of the Old Masters*, and Martin Kemp's influential work, *The Science of Art*, draw attention to this fact.[100] But while artists claim a degree of autonomous control over the implements being used, the amateur is presumed to be more dependent on its instruction. In the following analysis I hope to quickly test the stability of this boundary, suggesting a greater degree of crossover between 'artistic', 'amateur' and 'correct' use of mechanical arbiters.

Long before the proliferation of devices specifically targeted at amateur artists, Renaissance artist Leonardo da Vinci noticed the threat that certain optical devices posed to original invention:

There are some who look at things produced by nature through glass, or other surfaces or transparent veils. They trace outlines on the surface of a transparent medium. . . . But such an invention is to be condemned in those who do not know how to portray things without it, nor to reason without nature in their minds. . . . They are always poor and mean in every invention and in the composition of narratives, which is the final aim of this science.[101]

According to Da Vinci tracing, mirrors, glass and optical devices were considered a hindrance to the artistic process if the user was unable to practise without them.

The use of a mechanical arbiter to mask a practitioner's lack of skill became increasingly prominent from the late eighteenth century with a number of devices that made it easier for artists, whether amateur or otherwise, to break down, frame and copy an image from nature. One device that was particularly popular among landscape artists wishing to depict a scene of nature was the Claude Glass, a black mirror that miniaturized the scene of nature through a darkened convex lens that enclosed the subject within a frame, retrospectively named after the famous French landscape artist, Claude Lorrain.[102] The mirror was portable and reduced the glare of luminous features in order to enhance the visibility of middle tones. William Gilpin's use of the device to transform nature into a succession of picturesque scenes encouraged wider use by artists and amateur tourists wanting to capture moments from their various excursions.[103] In the discussion as to its worth as a tool for the genuine artist, Gilpin had a clear opinion: its status as a mediator of nature depended on whether it was considered an optical, or rather an intellectual aid, as Gilpin noted.[104] If the Claude Glass was used to copy nature through direct optical translation, then it played a more direct role as mechanical arbiter, in between the subject and the object of depiction; if it was just a guide, then the artist's subjective intention was not inhibited. The way the device transposed 'reality into a more melodious key'[105] meant that its use often fell into the category of a suggestive intellectual aid, not reproducing nature directly. Its general acceptance as a valid mediation of nature among artists in the late eighteenth century depended on theories of perception in which mirrors were considered to be honest mediators between the individual subject and objective reality.

However, the cultural understanding of perception shifted in the nineteenth century, Jonathan Crary outlining how, from the 1830s onwards, there was increasing epistemological uncertainty over the nature of vision.[106] The new age lauded the 'innocent eye' – direct optical experience – as containing more 'truth' than filtration through a device, as reflected in the aesthetics of John Ruskin.[107]

By the mid-nineteenth century, the number of different devices mentioned in manuals that directly translated a scene of nature to a two-dimensional image grew. Amateur artists were given guidance in understanding perspective in manuals, and specialized devices increased the ease by which these lessons could be learnt. The minor French artist who wrote several artistic manuals, Armand Cassagne, was one of the proponents for democratizing the rules of perspective, writing in 1886: 'Today, the understanding of perspective is infinitely more widespread than in previous centuries: the unchanging principles of this science have been sufficiently simplified so as to be accessible to beginners.'[108]

To achieve the democratization of this skill, Cassagne recommended the use of perspective frames, including the 'perspectoscope' and the 'cadre-isolateur' – a portable grid device to break down the viewed image.[109] Cassagne's instruments required very little training to understand and could be simply made by the amateur artist from easily accessible material. Compared with the Claude Glass, which merely reflected nature in softened tone and line, Cassagne's perspectival aids reduced and segmented nature to composite parts, rendering the outline of the subject into a series of lines. Cassagne disseminated these educational techniques and urged the use of mechanical arbiters in a series of exercise books for beginners to be used by teachers and even fathers who were encouraged to nurture the artistic talent of their children.[110]

Any mechanical arbiter can be implicated in both amateur and professional procedures of artistic production. For example, Van Gogh followed the advice of Cassagne's manuals to build his own perspective frames in an imagined affinity to the artisanal trades of the past.[111] However, as access to devices like the cadre-isolateur became widespread in the nineteenth century, linear perspective and the mystery of depiction were democratized and decentralized into the bourgeois home. Even if individuals did not directly use Cassagne's perspective aids, they were becoming increasingly familiar within conventions of artistic practice. Arbitration through perspective devices, fragmenting a scene into bite-size chunks, demystified the process of depiction, allowing a diverse range of amateurs the chance to produce technically proficient drawings.

Mechanical and textual arbiters led the aspirant artist through the process of building up and producing an image, from subject selection and producing an outline, to finite detail.[112] They form the vital third component of a trio that includes bases and carriers, which facilitated amateur surface intervention in the nineteenth century. By the twentieth century these discrete object categories increasingly coalesced as producing a picture became easier and easier for the amateur. This trend is epitomized by one thing in particular: the all-in-one, pre-mixed, pre-designed conglomeration that is the paint-by-number kit.

Paint-by-number kits: popularity, production and appropriation

As the quintessential 'invitation to art', the paint-by-number kit represents the logical endpoint of the story of art's democratization. Produced commercially from the early 1950s in the USA, paint-by-number kits contained all the things that were needed for surface intervention in one easy-to-understand, inexpensive art kit. A readymade canvas board (or rolled canvas) provided the base, the small capsules of paint and cheap brushes were the carriers, and crucially the arbitration was not provided through the suggestive means of the manual but through the more rigid guidelines of an outlined image printed on the canvas, with numbered segments representing blocks of colour that corresponded with the colours in the capsules (Plate 1). There were earlier incarnations of paint-by-number kits before the 1950s,[113] but their commercial expansion took place in this decade when companies like Palmer Paint produced kits in large quantities. The kits meant that the amateur painter could produce an original copy each time – as the tagline went, 'Every man a Rembrandt'.[114]

Unsurprisingly, critical reception of paint-by-number kits in the 1950s was hostile. A New York art educator, Robert Kaupelis, stated: 'These kits cannot be considered as art for they are totally lacking in esthetic, expressive and creative qualities essential to artistic endeavour.'[115]

In thrall to the dominant neo-Kantian aesthetic critique of Clement Greenberg, the artistic establishment marginalized paint-by-number. They were seen to epitomize the category 'kitsch' that, according to Greenberg's definition, 'uses as its raw material the debased and academicized simulacra of genuine culture'.[116] The kits tugged at the heartstrings with their predictable ranges: sugary images of idyllic pastoral scenes, popular biblical stories, well-known masterpieces from the history of art, and cutesy portraits of domesticated animals. Their form, subject and colour combination depended on the designer of the kit and they relied on sentimentality for their appeal. It was all too easy compared with the indifferent, contemplative distance needed to appreciate *avant garde* production.

Despite a resurgence of popularity of paint-by-number kits after their decline in the late 1960s and 1970s, reflected by a growing interest among collectors and a major exhibition held at the Smithsonian National Museum of American History in 2001,[117] the Greenbergian critique of the kit-form has stuck. Indeed, recent attention among collectors has only served to strengthen Greenberg's initial marginalization of paint-by-number, as vintage canvases are primarily valued for their epitomization of 1950s American kitsch.

Out of all the scholars, journalists and artists who have commented on paint-by-number, from wholehearted admiration to downright derision, only one has seriously attempted to insert the medium into the story of Western art history. Michael O'Donoghue (1940–94) was an American writer (the first head writer of *Saturday Night Live*) and performer but also a paint-by-number aficionado, collector and co-organizer of the first gallery exhibition of paint-by-number held at the Bridgewater/Lustberg gallery in SoHo, New York, in 1992. His posthumously published article on paint-by-number in 2001 makes a sustained attempt to extend analytical reception of the medium beyond its denigration or celebration as a piece of 1950s pop culture. Due to the brevity of the article format he was unable to elaborate on the various provocations he made, but his arguments provide a structure for my analysis below. Like O'Donoghue, I attempt to account for the impact of this all-in-one invitation to art on the history of modern Western art, as an example of how tool access has an impact on modern artistic production.

His article makes three key claims. First, he explains that paint-by-number was a 'frontal assault on elitism',[118] a democratic challenge to conventions of artistic education. O'Donoghue then elaborates on paint-by-number's status as 'assembly-line' art, which instead of lamenting like many other critics, he celebrates both for its honesty ('If the subject is a covered bridge, it tries to depict the perfect covered bridge') and for the central fact that it exposes its own production process.[119] The rigid lines of a paint-by-number canvas are the result of the labour of others – the designers, colourmen, and entrepreneurs who made and disseminated the kits – and they do reveal their commercial origins, but O'Donoghue's arguments can be developed further through closer attention to the materiality of its surface. The paint-by-number kit might constitute the complete fragmentation of the process of painting, but the individual painter is still responsible for finishing it off and adding the final layer, the personal touches, the colour and the modifications.

This recalls one of this chapter's main arguments: how modern artistic labour, amateur or otherwise, is increasingly characterized by the application of the outermost layer, on top of surfaces that have been appropriated, adapted or modified after their production by others (whether manual or technological production). Duchamp highlighted this underlying truth beneath all modern art by scrawling 'R Mutt' on *Fountain* (1917) and modifying the Sapolin tin-plate advertisement in *Apolinère Enameled* (1916–17): these works did not try to conceal the readymade origin of the artwork. By default, paint-by-number has a similar revelatory quality, as the labour of others unavoidably shows through the final layer.

Finally, O'Donoghue explains how the paint-by-number phenomenon was: 'a potent and unique movement with clear historical antecedents and an obvious impact on subsequent movements.'[120] Ranking among the antecedents he places major artists – Auguste Renoir, Claude Monet, Maurice de Vlaminck and many more – all of whom express an interest in optical fusion of separate blocks of colour. We could include Maurice Denis, Paul Gauguin, and other Nabis artists of the late nineteenth century in this list because of their interest in surface flatness. However, the emphasis for the final part of this case study is on the 'subsequent', and the appeal of paint-by-number to artists from the 1960s onwards, attracted by the kit's humorous, ironic, trivial or abject status within the pantheon of art. These include Jasper Johns's *Do It Yourself (Target)* (1960), Andy Warhol's *Do It Yourself* Series (1962), Damian Hirst's *Painting By Numbers* (2001) and Jeff McMillan's *Possibility of an Island* (2009). Rather than a chronological run-through of when paint-by-number has appeared within an artist's *oeuvre*, I will approach this survey thematically and outline the different ways that the medium has been appropriated. On one side are various appropriations that flatten paint-by-number's complexity, either by emphasizing its difference for nostalgic, ironic or comic effect – thus continuing Greenbergian strategies of marginalization – or by treating paint-by-number as simple raw material. On the other are more strategic appropriations of paint-by-number, where the medium serves as a means to interrogate post-war paradigms of co-authorship, the nature of artistic skill, audience participation and the anthropology of the painted surface.

A democratic art form: paint-by-number in the 1950s

As an accessible, commercially produced, inexpensive art kit, paint-by-number reflected a particularly American model of participatory consumerism of the 1950s, in which individuals were invited not just to exercise taste in the acquisition of goods but to use their free time to do-it-themselves. The social historian Karal Ann Marling describes the self-building practices as a means of negotiating the standardization of professional life through physical labour, describing how 'DIYism . . . was the last refuge for the exercise of control and competence in a world run by the bosses and bureaucrats.'[121] This do-it-yourself art chimed with notions of American self-reliance and productivity that was defined by a resistance to idleness, a refutation of passive consumerism and a need to counter-balance professional life with useful tasks.[122] American psychologist and marketing expert, Ernest Dichter, both observed and harnessed the potential of products that left something for the consumer to do, stating in his 1964 *Handbook of Consumer Motivation* that: 'A sculpture, a painting, or a poster is better if it is somewhat incomplete, if the onlooker is invited to fill in, to do his own creative sentence completion.'[123]

The paint-by-number kit is a perfect example of a product that is left incomplete, encouraging the individual consumer to 'finish' the painting according to their whim. The role models for this new breed of artists, however, were not the representatives of the New York *avant garde* art scene but Sunday painters like Winston Churchill and the American president Dwight Eisenhower, as well as American 'folk' artists like Grandma Moses and the ever popular Norman Rockwell.[124] This was a popularization of art that did not disseminate the image of the romantic artist suffering for his work or the heady theoretical abstraction of much modern art, but instead positioned art as an engaging pastime. Eisenhower popularized the paint-by-number medium by giving canvases to his cabinet, and allegedly sought help from a professional artist in preparing the images he wanted to paint, providing an outline for him to 'fill in', paint-by-numbers style.[125] This philosophy of proactive amusement chimed with the broader context of American consumerism, amateur painting offering a cathartic 'safe' release of tension from one's everyday reality.[126]

Although paint-by-number is similar to countless other consumer products of the 1950s that left some form of customization or labour for the individual to undertake – from self-fitted kitchens to convenience food – it invited the consumer into the more complex terrain of artistic production. The conveniently packaged tools and materials ceded enough productive power for the kit to become a pedagogic tool, especially for individuals who had little or no other means of artistic education. Many paint-by-number painters recall how this cheap, accessible art form constituted their chief experience of art in the 1950s, Carol Belland explaining how her father's painstaking labour on an Emmett Kelly portrait was the only 'art' to be found in her home.[127] Another paint-by-number practitioner describes the more desperate contexts of her paint-by-number education, recalling how her drug- and alcohol-dependent parents were initially unwilling to buy her a kit. After she had bought the kit herself they then refused to buy linseed oil for her to keep the paints from drying. Determined to finish, she glued on the dried pieces of paint to the canvas and gave the finished picture to her grandparents.[128]

This tale of courage is a heart-warming example of the broader educational impact of paint-by-number kits. The kit provided the first step to something greater. For this woman, her encounter with paint-by-number anticipated her eventual employment as an artist, a pathway to a career in art followed by many other paint-by-number painters of the 1950s.[129] The story might be exceptional, conforming to the 'rags to riches' trope in American popular culture, but viewing paint-by-number as the 'first stage' in a teleological development of skill, leading to school, university education and success in the market, constitutes a defence of the medium – a way to refute claims of the medium's pointlessness and superficiality.[130] When the kit was marketed in France, it was these pedagogic ideals that were emphasized (Figure 1.14).

Paint-by-number enticed the consumer through a simple promise: that he or she would be able to produce something that looked good hung up on the wall. Yet in the course of mimicking the labour of the artist in this miniaturized, constrained form, the consumer became familiar with painterly surface intervention, which had significant consequences for both the person engaged in such activity and wider artistic production. As Peter Skolnik observed, although the ability to purchase fine art remained difficult, 'now anyone could come home with a genuine DIY-ketchup-bottle-squirt-paint-cardboard creation'. And anything became art in the 'happening'.[131] Empowered through the interaction with the physicality (or craft) of artistic production, the paint-by-number practitioner has more ammunition to counter the aesthetic expectations of cultural elites and confuses established hierarchies of taste. For example, the businessman who boasts of his artistic success and empowerment through paint-by-number even though he is completely aware of the presumed 'philistinism' associated with the medium.[132] It is no surprise then that the democratic potential of the paint-by-number was described as an 'affront to elitism', as O'Donoghue states: its marginalization a symptom of an upper middle-class strategy to 'rough up the legitimate aspiration of middle to lower-class hobbyists'.[133]

Applying the outermost layer

Hostile critical reception often overlooked the material depth of the paint-by-number surface, associating its flatness with processes of mass printing. As Elizabeth Moeller Geiken of the Davenport Municipal Art Museum stated: 'Those numbered paintings evade artistic development completely . . . A person might as well stamp a pattern on a canvas and call it their own piece of work.'[134]

Geiken's association between paint-by-number and mechanical processes suggests equivalence between stamping and painting, a parity that is not manifest in practice because each kit was completed by hand. Yet the association with mass production is hard to avoid. Even the sympathetic O'Donoghue described paint-by-number as 'assembly-line French Impressionism' in his effort to ally its mechanical look with the artistic movements that brought painting into the industrial age.[135] I accept O'Donoghue's claim that paint-by-number effectively exposes modern realities of artistic production, but these realities are different from the classic view of assembly-line manufacture he sets out. Paint-by-number is not akin to Walter Benjamin's definition of mechanical reproduction (as defined by printing and photography), but closer to manual reproduction.[136] With the help of a readymade base, the individual can complete or

FIGURE 1.14 *Publicity material for French market, 1950s. Paint by Numbers Collection, Archives Center, National Museum of American History, Smithsonian Institution.*

modify the outermost surface layer and participate in, rather than be alienated by, mass production and homogeneity.

Geiken's claim of the paint-by-number's mechanistic nature can be contested from the point of view of its early commercial production, when manufacturing processes were particularly haphazard. The success of Palmer Paints relied on the ingenuity of the both the company boss, Max Klein, and the employees, including the young designer Dan Robbins, who first mooted the idea of making paint-by-number kits. Robbins describes the laborious process of making the first paint-by-number kit, which depended not on mechanical reproduction but on an arduous process that included making preliminary sketches, painting the subject from a limited range of paints, tracing its outline and numbering it on clear film, and finally testing the colour combinations on canvas (Plate 2).[137] Paints were mixed using a combination of shop floor science and human judgement. The first paint capsules were made out of plastic pill capsules and to produce the kits in larger quantities Klein invented a 'Rube Goldberg paint filling machine' to fill them, an improvised device that depended on the dexterity of the female workers in the factory to operate it.[138] On one occasion, in the haste to secure a large order from the retailer Kresge, palettes for one kit, *The Fisherman*, were put in *The Bullfighter* kit and vice versa, leading to a wide recall and losses for the company.[139] In the early years, the production of paint-by-number initially depended on the ingenuity and perseverance of its producers and was far from being a smooth, efficiently produced product.

The risk involved in the early production of paint-by-number kits contradicts the argument that it was mass-produced art, what craft theorist David Pye characterized as the workmanship of certainty. Pye draws a distinction between 'risk' and 'certainty', clearest in his comparison between handwriting and printing: the latter process removes risks associated with the former through the preparation of jigs that ensure a predictable output each time. There are continued risks in printing, as Pye argues, but 'the N's will never look like the U's'.[140] The paint-by-number kit might accord with our ideas about the workmanship of certainty, ensuring a predictable outcome each time, as Geiken claimed, but clearly the paint-by-number's readymade outline image, prepared paints and paintbrush constituted a permeable jig that is weak in its attempt to impose certainty. The individual who adds the final layer is free to contravene the kit's outline, which is only ever a loose suggestion.

Many of the paint-by-number practitioners of the 1950s did follow their own rules and William Bird suggests that it is the attitude to 'going over the lines' that marks the moment when amateur hobbyist becomes artist: 'The real art began at the moment the hobbyist ignored outlines to blend adjacent colours, added or dropped detail, or elaborated upon a theme.'[141] Raetha Wilkins was among the many paint-by-number painters who disobeyed the rules in the 1950s: she was so despondent at the prospect of producing the equine subject as specified by the instructions that she decided to paint her own composition in the same 'horse colours'.[142] Bird describes such rebelliousness as the moment when 'real art began', conforming to longstanding codes of aesthetic judgement that prioritize autonomous decision-making as a barometer for creativity.

However, even if the rules are strictly adhered to, each paint-by-number cannot fail to be a unique copy due to the inherent idiosyncrasy of the hand. This claim is substantiated by analysis of identical paint-by-number canvases, as shown in Plate 3. These two paint-by-number paintings of the same 1969 Craft Master kit *Old Sadface* demonstrate the diversity that arises even if individuals follow exactly the same rules. There is no attempt in these paintings to 'go over the lines', to obviously rebel against the constraints of the kit. Nevertheless, variety emerges: the colours are mixed differently, they are put into different places, and the upturned smile suggests different degrees of sadness. On perusing Trey Speegle's collection of paint-by-number in his Brooklyn house, art critic Lawrence Rinder also commented on the inherent uniqueness of each paint-by-number image: 'One version of the classic, full length portrait *Pinkie* possesses all the elegance and allure of Sir Thomas Lawrence's original, while in another, the poor maiden's lipstick looks as if it had been applied with an automobile buffer.'[143]

Instead of suppressing individuality, paint-by-number actually accentuates difference between one maker and the next. Perhaps the most self-conscious means of ascribing individual authorship to the paint-by-number canvas is to author it, as shown in the version of *Old Sadface* that is signed 'Lynn' (left-hand side image on Plate 3). This signature is a self-conscious act of ownership, a *poncif* in imitation of conventions of artistic authorship as referred to earlier, an example of a person attempting to wrest authorial control from all the labour that took place underneath the outermost layer. We could stop at the conclusion that these marks merely reflect the behaviour of the creative capitalist consumer taking charge of his or her own 'sentence completion', as Dichter stated, an example of mass individualization. Yet the completed paint-by-number painting cannot help but reveal the labour of other authors, due to its fragmented quality, its reduction of painting into bite-size chunks, and its specific materiality. Lynn's signature is not only an act of personal authorship, it is the outermost surface layer of a complex readymade object – sharing the same qualities of Duchamp's own act of hastily marked authorship in *Fountain* (1917), albeit in a less self-conscious manner.

Paint-by-number kits are instantly recognizable, no matter what the surface intervener decides to do. In this sense they are unique among commodities, and indeed artworks, for their power to expose depths of production on the surface. They lay bare the labour of the paint-by-number painter – what Pye would call the workmanship of risk – *and* the labour of others, people like Robbins, Klein, and the technologies that facilitated their commercial production. This is a reciprocal relationship between individual authorship and the infrastructure of bases, carriers and arbiters, which situates the amateur surface intervener as the one who 'finishes off' someone else's plan. This does not result in homogeneity, as one might expect, but plurality: the individual painter is invited to play a proactive role in the modern world of image superfluity.

Intervening-by-number: appropriation and paint-by-number as art

Artists have long been interested in paint-by-number, attracted by its status as a lowly, abject, marginalized art form. From Andy Warhol to Damian Hirst, the paint-by-number has a strong appeal. But the question for the concluding part of this chapter is whether artists recognize paint-by-number's power to elucidate productive realities of artistic production, as outlined above. Are artists interested in how distributed authorship is contained within the final surface layer? Or do they merely use the kit as raw material, evidence of an ironic sense of humour, or a device to trigger 1950s nostalgia for 'the good old days?'

Artists have a strong track record in appropriating the cast-offs, second-hand things and unwanted objects of modern material culture. Authorless, and seemingly insignificant, they are like putty in the artist's hands. As art historian Dario Gamboni has stated: 'recognised artists have felt no qualms about damaging or destroying objects whose value was impaired by anonymity, seriality or low status, such as paintings purchased at flea markets and overpainted by Asger Jorn from the late 1950s onwards'.[144]

The manipulation of amateur material is particularly evident in artists' appropriation of completed paint-by-number paintings, found in thrift stores in ever increasing number after the decline in their popularity in the 1960s and 1970s.[145] The art historian John Welchman observed this trend in his book *Art After Appropriation: Essays on Art in the 1990s*, giving several examples of how artists in the late twentieth century have proved adept at conflating 'taking' and 'making', especially 'when the scene of re-presentation is claimed as "subversive" or "undecidable"', adding, 'the violence of the cut is accompanied by the aggravated wound of separation'.[146]

Materially altering paint-by-number is an overt example of 'the violence of the cut'. Chicago-based artist Don Baum, in the late 1980s, and Trey Speegle, in the 1990s, used paint-by-number paintings as material in their own compositions: the former inserting them into collages and the walls of his kennel sculptures, turning our 'disdain for such banal material into wonder', according to Sue Taylor;[147] the latter by using silkscreen, collage and painting techniques with Ruscha-like boldness to combine use of the medium with his other interest in words and aphorisms (Figure 1.15). In both instances the paint-by-number canvases are cut and pasted into arrangements that defy the intentions of the original authors. The 'aggravated wound of separation' is palpable. In the case of Speegle there is conscious effort to suppress these original

FIGURE 1.15 *Trey Speegle,* Can You Imagine *(2008).*

features of the paint-by-number. He states: 'The paint by numbers might be a hook but the work isn't *really* about them so much . . . it's about transforming them and saying something different than was originally intended.'[148]

Speegle wants his viewers to recognize that these works are not 'about' paint-by-number, but more about his own modifications and transformations. However, the paint-by-number 'hook' constitutes a strong lure (the outlined image, the segmented blocks of colour, the banal imagery). In a more recent interview, Speegle acknowledges how paint-by-number, unlike most paintings, democratically reveals its sources:[149] this is the 'architecture' or, more fittingly, the archaeology of the painted image. However, there is a tension between Speegle's own authorship, the past interventions undertaken by other labourers, and the paint-by-number format that remains unresolved. It is unclear whether his material alterations bring attention to the many levels of authorship inherent to paint-by-number and whether the full complexity of the multiple layers is revealed through his material transformation of the surface.

The display of paint-by-number in the museum or gallery might suggest a more sympathetic treatment of the medium as an art object in its own right. Since the growth of interest in collecting paint-by-number from the 1980s, there have been many exhibitions in America devoted to the medium. The 'first ever' exhibition fully devoted to the medium, *The Fortieth Anniversary of Paint-By-Number Paintings*, which Speegle co-curated with O'Donoghue, took place at the Bridgewater/Lustberg Gallery in SoHo, New York in 1992 and attracted much interest.[150] Equally popular was the 2001–2 exhibition at the Smithsonian National Museum of American History curated by William Bird entitled *Paint-By-Number: Accounting for Taste in 1950s America*, which laid greater emphasis on the position of paint-by-number within American cultural history. These well-known exhibitions reflect the wider interest in these eminently collectible forms of vintage Americana, particularly popular among baby boomers nostalgically recalling their childhood interactions with the kits.[151]

Whereas too much material alteration of the paint-by-number surface is in danger of reducing the art kits to the status of a raw material, their display within the rarefied contexts of the gallery or museum arguably does not intervene enough. Through presumably neutral placement within the gallery walls, with the requisite amount of white space between each painting, the paint-by-number is isolated: it becomes an historical entity, in danger of being objectified and rendered static, and its dynamism as a layered deconstruction of painting is overlooked. The paint-by-number revival in recent years, led by collectors, curators and art galleries, has mostly served to reinforce Greenbergian categorizations of the medium as kitsch. The kit's economic and cultural value mostly derives from its camp associations – 'it's good because it is awful', as Susan Sontag states.[152] This ironic play with the kit's abject status characterizes Damian Hirst's encounter with the medium in his 2001 *Painting by Numbers* where he produced a kit of his dot paintings. The artist was more than happy with the news that after the opening night the whole exhibition (and not just the cigarettes and beer cans he deliberately brought into the gallery for the event) was mistaken for rubbish and thrown out by the cleaner.[153]

Museums and galleries have regularly been criticized for their appropriation of kitsch, outsider or abject art. In the year 2000 Jim Shaw displayed a whole collection of amateur art in *Thrift Store Paintings* at London's Institute of Contemporary Arts.[154] Shaw put the 'continual conceptual inventiveness' of amateur work on show, according to art critic Julian Stallabrass, but he also pushed the collection 'away from its origins and towards the art elite'.[155] Reduced to organizing and re-naming the canvases, the restraint of Shaw's intervention accentuated the paintings' displacement from their original contexts. The naivety and unusual technique, the unconventional materials used and bizarre choices of subject matter, were projected forward as patently 'other', for the art audience who were flattered for their ability to appreciate the eccentricity of these unusual paintings. At the same time, Shaw strengthened the rigid and outdated dichotomies between amateur and professional, high and low, insider and outsider.[156] There were no paint-by-number paintings in Shaw's exhibition, but his treatment of this selection of amateur art serves as a warning against adopting the same conventions of 'white cube' display when showing artworks that were intended for different contexts. Hanging paint-by-number in an 'unshadowed, white, clean' space 'devoted to the technology of esthetics' would only serve to emphasize their otherness for knowing intellectual degustation.[157]

There is a clear connection here between the display of paint-by-number as found art and the controversy surrounding the 'discovery' and exhibition of outsider art, the subject of a comprehensive monograph by Colin Rhodes.[158] Like outsider art, amateur art (including paint-by-number paintings) was rarely produced for the gallery, and has different intentions: as domestic decoration, a gift, or a 'first step' in the development of artistic skill. Promotion to the walls of the gallery threatens to overlook the intentions and environment of paint-by-number painting. Seattle's Official Bad Art Museum of America does revel in the otherness of amateur painting, but its methods of display – with canvases hung above café booths within an environment of heady Americana – might offer a more sympathetic contextual setting for such works.

Appropriation of paint-by-number is often caught between heavy-handed intervention that subjugates the medium to the status of raw material, and the hands-off approach of museum display that conversely serves to confirm the marginalization of the medium as 'kitsch' art. However, two earlier appropriations of paint-by-number offer something completely different. Jasper Johns's *Do It Yourself (Target)* (1960) and Andy Warhol's *Do It Yourself* series (1962) utilize paint-by-number as a way to interrogate artistic labour, the paradigms of co-authorship, and how the medium suggests an alternative means to negotiate modern (capitalist) image superfluity.

Warhol's oeuvre can be fairly summarized as the exploration of surface superficiality and reproduction.[159] He was a notorious celebrity, famous for his silk-screen portraits produced in vast quantities during the 'Factory' years, and he paraded the quintessential surface medium – wallpaper – as fine art when he covered a room in the Leo Castelli Gallery in New York with cow wallpaper in 1966.[160] Critics have observed the originality in his artistic approach: 'By erasing himself from his creations minimizing the artist's responsibility, the significance of talent, and the value of originality, Warhol challenged what art is supposed to be and how one is to experience it.'[161]

Warhol's *Do It Yourself* series of 1962 can easily be read into this narrative of increasingly impassive celebration of brand, celebrity and reproduction, and his critique of originality (Plate 4). Completed just months before the famous *32 Campbell's Soup Cans*, Warhol's first depiction of a static capitalist commodity, the *Do It Yourself* series has been interpreted as the last gasp of Warhol as a painter, after his early career in which original composition still featured. Heiner Bastian argues that the series represents the logical endpoint of painting and the one essay fully devoted to analysing the *Do It Yourself* series by Meredith Schiff, comes to a similar conclusion, situating the work more biographically, as the 'turning point' in the artist's career, marking the shift from his early work when Warhol still deployed his skills as a painter.[162]

These readings rely on the assumption, contested above, that paint-by-number kits do entirely remove skill from painting. Warhol's interventions were far from compliant; there was a material dynamism to his approach to the paint-by-number surface not dissimilar to those rebellious paint-by-number painters who went 'over the lines'. For a start, the work in the series was not 'an exact replica of the actual merchandise'.[163] Warhol made several amendments to the Venus

Paradise kits that formed a base for the work: he used paint instead of crayon (for which the kits were intended), left large sections of the paint-by-number blank, exposed the outline and numbered sections, printed letters over completed sections of colour and used Letraset – the commercial means of applying type to surface.[164] Moreover, there is evidence that in *Do It Yourself (Seascape)* Warhol deliberately changed the colour assignation suggested by the kit makers, and in *Do It Yourself (Violin)* the artist used crayon in the work, a nod to the initial medium the kits were intended for.[165] Compared with paint-by-number practitioners who followed the rulebook, Warhol took many shortcuts – Patrick Smith commenting that dutifully completing the paint-by-number as intended by the Venus Paradise designers would have been 'too much trouble' for the artist.[166]

This attention to small details helps illustrate the fact that Warhol was not completely removed from the production of these paintings: there are little hints, minute flourishes that demonstrate how Warhol is still involved in the application of the outermost layer. Arthur Danto stated that 'with Warhol there are no accidents'[167] and it is hard to ignore these casual, irreverent and witty interventions in his paint-by-number surfaces. They suggest a tension between Warhol's subjective agency as the artist, and Venus Paradise's lingering authorial voice that resides in the layers of production underneath the surface, a tension that the artist was happy to keep alive.

Warhol draws attention to his role as a surface intervener involved with manipulating and applying the outermost material layer. He sends a subtle message to his audience that infrastructures of artistic supply (represented by the paint-by-number kit) facilitate individual pathways through capitalist image superfluity based on participation. Perfect reproducibility was not a major concern for Warhol. As Danto stated, Warhol emphasized a point through hand-made reproduction.[168] The *Do It Yourself* series accentuates this idea that difference arises out of repetition: how you, as the painter, decide to finish the painting. He simultaneously situates the kit as a prime metaphor for the conditions of modern artistic production – defined by the impossibility of autonomous authorship and the reliance on other labourers – whilst exposing how the artist's skill is still required in the production of the outermost layer.

Johns's earlier appropriation of paint-by-number *Do It Yourself (Target)* (1960) also celebrates the potential of audience participation at this important juncture of post-war American culture. In the painting Johns explicitly invites the viewer in, providing a brush, three circles of solid paint, and an outline of a target. In additional to these materials Johns has pre-signed the work and left a space for his future collaborator to sign alongside. Once again, co-authorship and the re-configuration of artistic labour is centre stage. Arguably Johns's appropriation of paint-by-number more potently reaches out to the viewer in comparison with Warhol's *Do It Yourself* series due to the fact that materials are provided, the entire outline is left blank and that there is a space for a signature, or *poncif*. It is a radical challenge to the notion of singular authorship within artistic production.

In addition, the work gives an obvious indication as to what constitutes artistic labour in the era of the readymade. Johns, quite openly, is playing a game with his audience, directing them by inviting them to hit the target he has made for them. As art critic Max Kozloff said of the painting in 1964: 'the viewer, conventionally enough is left with the task of completion itself, but unfortunately with the insufficient visual clues to discharge it.'[169] The audience is clearly prevented from taking Johns up on his offer to paint the target on account of its presentation as a work that cannot be touched. But even if one was able to participate, there is a difficulty in discharging the responsibility of surface completion – 'How do I fill it in?', 'Can I go over the lines?' – the same questions that face the paint-by-number painter who opens the kit for the first time. Johns asks the viewer to imagine themselves as artists, not only as the person wielding the brush but also as the artist living in an era when painting can be reduced to a ten-dollar kit.

Through the paint-by-number concept, and its open invitation to engage in artistic labour, Johns, like Warhol, presents a fairly optimistic assessment of artistic practice.[170] The use of the paint-by-number is not an ironic joke – the projection of a readymade as art in the conventional Duchampian mode – nor does it provide confirmation of the death of the craft in painting. Instead its use by these artists suggests an alternative, less pessimistic attitude towards artistic production where audience members can get involved. However, this is not a re-definition of art as performance or social encounter, as pronounced by Nicolas Bourriaud and his concept of 'relational aesthetics',[171] but a re-negotiation of the meaning of art based on an engagement with the material surface and tackling the task of adding the outermost layer, finishing off the labour of others. The art demands the audience's labour, not just their sociality.

Jeff McMillan's *The Possibility of an Island* (2009), exhibited at the PEER Gallery, provides a convenient bookend to this story of paint-by-number's appropriation by artists (Plate 5). McMillan organizes a large number of paint-by-number landscapes, which depict snow-capped mountains, waterfalls, birch, tundra and even a few deer, into one amorphous mass, spanning two walls to create an installation that evokes the traditions of landscape painting. He confines his intervention to arrangement, reversing some canvases or placing them upside down, avoiding the more aggressive material alterations of Speegle and Baum, and his own earlier experiments of dipping found paintings in industrial paint (*Perla*, 2003).

McMillan keeps the material dynamism of the paint-by-number surface alive: the installation manages to retain the individuality of each paint-by-number painting while stopping short of cruelly presenting them in the same manner as most gallery art, with a white border or frame. Instead each canvas is flush with another. This form of presentation highlights the notion of individuality within a mass. As art critic Richard Noble states: 'Each image is the product of a significant expenditure of labour, and would seem to have a certain claim on our respect because of this. Yet at the same time they are very similar and banal as individual paintings, reflecting the fact that they originated in a process of mass production.'[172]

This strategy of display in *The Possibility of an Island* accentuates what Noble refers to as 'painting as anthropology'.[173] Canvases reflect both individual creativity, and the social collectivity of this mass-produced art kit. As such, they alert us to the humanity of the signs of artistic aspiration and endeavour inherent in each painting, while at the same time pointing to the advanced post-war infrastructures of artistic supply and entrepreneurial commerce that made the mass production of such kits possible.

Paint-by-number is unique as a form of amateur surface intervention. Historical narrative, social relations, artistic skill and material anthropology are embedded within its layers, but unlike other amateur art forms they are also palpably present on the final surface. The paint-by-number canvas – whether produced by amateur painters in the 1950s or self-consciously appropriated by artists – draws attention to what Alfred Gell referred to as the entire nexus of social relations within the art object, whereby subjective 'agency', or distributed personhood, is disseminated throughout. Defining an agent as 'the one who has the capacity to initiate causal events in his/her vicinity', Gell's anthropology of art is one in which amateurs clearly feature.[174]

Amateurs, sufficiently tooled, clearly impart a sense of productive agency in their 'vicinity', within Gell's notion of a network, but their labour has a certain honesty, highlighting at the same time as the insertion of the *poncif*, the importance of other agents: from John G. Rand who invented paint in tubes, to Dan Robbins's role in the paint-by-number boom, to the words of countless manuals offering various forms of advice. It is this dependence on other labourers and technology, and the fact that the amateur's labour is rendered transparent by its technical or conceptual naivety,[175] that conversely offers a way of inscribing amateurs into the annals of art history. Their practice exposes the repressed truth that all art, particularly since Duchamp's experiments with the readymade, is dependent on the labour of others. This demystification, however, reminds us, more acutely than ever, that the artist's skill is still needed in the application of the outermost layer.

The history of the paint-by-number craze and its strategic appropriation by Warhol, Johns and McMillan, marks the culmination of the two narrative arches of this chapter: the history of widening access to an infrastructure of bases, carriers and arbiters, and the impact these tools and materials have on modern paradigms of artistic production. Amateur surface intervention – a flat, expressive layer on top of a productive base of disseminated authorship – is the lens through which these repressed truths about artistic production can be exposed: a continuity that runs through the 'ismism' of canonical Western art.

2

Space

In his 2007 work, *Shed*, James Rigler explained how he 'spliced together the signifiers of two very different building types – the super-humble and the super-significant' (Plate 6).[1] The shed – made with panels of timber, with a door, a lock, a small window and an apex roof – is ubiquitous, a common sight in any suburban garden, available from any out-of-town hardware store. Rigler's installation of a church spire, made in wood and covered in roofing felt, atop the shed, transforms its meaning, inviting comparisons to the significance, religiosity and grandeur of ecclesiastical buildings. However, in fusing these seemingly opposing building types, a more curious parallel emerges. Structures of religion represented by the church spire and the backyard productivity of the amateur craftsperson represented by the shed share a similar tangential relationship to forms of organization that structure modern everyday life. Both offer some form of departure from regularized, standardized conditions of capitalist existence – one in the form of spiritual nourishment, the other in the form of autonomous control over one's labour-power.

This chapter is about the latter form of release, the space of amateur craft. The key argument is that once equipped with bases, carriers and arbiters, an amateur creates highly personal and idiosyncratic spaces that demonstrate particular and unusual relationships to production that nonetheless link back to the economic and societal reality from which the practice departs. Just as regular attendance at a church has an effect on the attendee's everyday experience of life, production that takes place in the shed shapes an individual's understanding of work and labour.

There is a temptation to characterize amateur space as a zone of personal self-fulfillment and 'measurable accomplishment': an escape from systems of efficient mass production, smooth technological perfection, commercial facelessness and homogenous mass culture.[2] This is certainly how amateur space is often perceived, as exemplified by Matthew Crawford's 2009 book, *The Case for Working With Your Hands*, in which he describes manual tasks, such as motorcycle maintenance, as an opportunity for individuals (mainly men) to attain a 'greater sense of agency', providing an antidote to the regularity, boredom and technological touchscreen smoothness of modern work.[3]

However, in line with this book's intention to contest the individualistic discourse that surrounds recent commentary on amateur craft practice, I will situate amateur space within broader frameworks of society and insist on the importance of the many links between amateur space and other spaces of everyday life. Amateur space is not unimportant or superfluous – a permitted triviality within context of alienation as codified by Theodor Adorno – but neither is it an anti-modern space, a secure refuge from the idea of capitalist dominance and homogeneity.[4] Instead, it is integral to and embedded in the experience of daily life, particularly in relation to modern labour and production, in a number of surprising and unexpected ways.

This chapter contains many examples of the tangential links between amateur space and various configurations of everyday socialized space, from self-built, portable workstations that reinforce notions of efficiency to the late-nineteenth-century suburban chicken keeper who managed the backyard with an eye for profit. Amateur space is complex and ambiguous: it seeps into other categorizations of space and cannot be easily sidelined as the marginal, unimportant, trivial aside to everyday life. It is a space of critical thinking and allows forms of practice that are freer than most forms of labour or work organization, yet at the same time does not constitute a blatant threat to the interests of capital. The challenge of this chapter is to demonstrate how amateur space is a permeable category *within* capitalist production, and examine how it draws off and feeds normative modes of production whilst essentially demonstrating unique characteristics.

To lay the theoretical foundations for this analysis requires an analysis of studies of everyday life that have long privileged the superfluous or unimportant and, in particular, the work of French sociologist, Henri Lefebvre. Lefebvre's conceptualization of space is integral to this chapter, particularly his notion of 'differential space' – a space of production (that is both linguistic and material), which departs from the normal 'abstract' conditions of everyday life, yet tangentially relates to, and depends upon, its structures.[5] What is crucial about amateur space, and the labour that inhabits it, is that it relates to other spaces of capitalism like professional space and the spaces of everyday life. Amateur space needs these other sites, but in a fashion that is beyond mere antagonism. In this theoretical opening of the chapter I account for the particular quality of amateur labour and situate it within the intellectual traditions of Marxist and phenomenological thinking.

Academic traditions that marginalize the alternative forms of productivity that arise from amateur space overlook the curious relationships between amateur labour and other forms of labour organization. One manifestation of this that I cover in the chapter is the 'professionalization' of amateur space. With its roots in nineteenth-century self-help, the 'professional amateur' represented a new model of productive leisure, using free time to engage in tasks that were deemed morally, functionally and socially worthwhile, such as repairing windows, building bookshelves, or home decoration. An overview of this phenomenon is followed by two case studies – one on amateur tool organization in Britain and America, the other on the history of suburban chicken keeping in Britain between 1870 and 1920 and its subsequent revival today, not so much by suburbanites but by the British artist Simon Starling. The case studies enable a description of complex, surprising, diversionary and unusual characteristics of the labour that harnesses the slack capacity within the highly structured systems of modern capitalism – for example, the conflation of ornament and function when building and maintaining a chicken coop. I aim to emphasize how amateur space is inherently subversive, albeit with a small 's'.

Before proceeding with the chapter it is necessary to clarify the distinction between amateur space and amateur time, as amateur labour – a key subject in this chapter – has both spatial and temporal properties. This chapter's prime focus is on amateur differential methods of production, whereas Chapter 3 moves from the realm of production and output to the experiential aspect of being an amateur labourer and the temporal modalities that arise from practice, such as 'switching off', obsession or 'killing time'. Broadly speaking, labour in amateur time relates to phenomenological experience, while labour in amateur space, on which I now will focus, is contingent upon production methods and what is produced. The relationship to Chapter 1 is more obvious, moving from the impact of tools that enabled material marks and their reception, to the social and political space that is inhabited in the course of amateur making.

Amateur space and everyday life

There is a dichotomous tradition in modern Western thought of dividing space between the phenomenological-social – the realm of the sensual, experienced and lived – and the conceptual-mental – where humans are able to abstract their ideas into realms that cannot be directly perceived. Each side of this dichotomy maps on to further stereotypical oppositions: the conceptual is male, public, rational and scientific; the phenomenological is female, private, irrational, poetic and closer to the everyday. Henri Lefebvre is one twentieth-century thinker who takes these bifurcations as the starting point of his attempt to construct a theory of social space that challenges the assumption of an 'abyss between the abstract mental sphere on the one side and the physical and social spheres on the other'.[6] For example, Lefebvre critiques the language and practice of town planning for the way it reduces the full complexity of social space to rational description through the use of scientific methodologies that create an extra-ideological space ('in an admirably unconscious manner'[7]). For Lefebvre this scientific interpretive framework offers only one potential 'reading' of a space among many others.

Lefebvre's sensitivity to plural readings of space was linked to his lifelong project to understand and conceptualize everyday life. Everyday life – the habitual, the ordinary, the mundane – contains within it registers of space entirely different from scientific measurement of the rationalization of bureaucracy. Whether poetic, psychological, sensual or irrational, everyday life is complex and highlights how space can be understood in many different ways beyond the rational. Lefebvre was not alone in this intellectual pursuit: Michel de Certeau, Sigmund Freud and Gaston Bachelard can all be grouped as theorists of the everyday that were sensitive to the alternative readings of space. In an effort to elucidate a theory of amateur space, this particular inter-disciplinary intellectual tradition proves invaluable.

The study of everyday life offers a departure from the meta-narratives common to the humanities and social sciences that often reduce multifarious experiences into recognizable social movements, canonical lineage or major events. Writing privileges the 'imaginative fiction' of everyday life,[8] the unexpected and the ignored, like Walter Benjamin's commentary on Parisian street names and gas lights in the Passages des Panoramas in the *Arcades Project*,[9] or, more recently, Joe Moran's study of how the British take breakfast, queue or experience office architecture.[10] Yet in creating a theory of amateur space, everyday life is not primarily useful for alerting us to the richness of ordinary experience. Instead, the sub-discipline provides solutions to the methodological challenge of how to write about the everyday. To throw light on the trivial, mundane, ignored and overlooked elements of everyday life requires a distinctive methodological approach. As cultural theorist Ben Highmore notes: 'the everyday might be more productively grasped if the propriety of discourses is refused'.[11]

Studies of everyday life face a dilemma. There is a tendency to position or describe the everyday within the humanities or social sciences as an 'object', making claims for it under the banner of 'gender', 'race', 'the domestic' or 'nation'. But by creating such narratives the very 'everydayness' of the subject is lost. The everyday, as a concept, offers its advocates the chance to bypass existing realms of discourse, but with the significant difficulty of not surrendering to the 'propriety of discourses' as Highmore states. Amateur space needs to be studied with the same sensitivity as everyday life. We cannot just describe amateur space and expect its full richness to be revealed; the goal is to develop a sensitive theory that encapsulates its essence.

The space of everyday life, like amateur space, is like old, dried paper that threatens to fragment as soon as it is touched. So what can be learnt from how established thinkers conceptualized this sensitive terrain, and in particular the methodologies they have used to study it? Gaston Bachelard's methodology involved abandoning scientific and rational analysis altogether in his famous 1958 work, *The Poetics of Space*. Bachelard advocates a geographic psychology that invests the concept of the home and its spaces with poetic potential: 'You don't live in houses positively but with all the partiality of the imagination.'[12] Bachelard constructs a philosophy of poetry that suggests coherence between the psyche of the human mind and the home. In the context of amateur space, which often (but not exclusively) overlaps domestic space, his work could be deployed to highlight the poetic power of amateur making: he infuses cleaning and waxing with poetic quality and talks of boxes as inherently signalling the 'need for secrecy'.[13] As an emancipatory framework that attributes poetry to domestic space, Bachelard draws attention to forgotten acts of the everyday; a research methodology that is particularly useful when empirical information is scarce.

Bachelard's work also references Sigmund Freud, who thinks about the everyday that lurks and murmurs underneath the civilized veneer.[14] Highmore, with reference to Freud, applies psychoanalytic models to the everyday: the unconscious, like the everyday, exists behind dominant discourses and derives from concrete experience and is not 'made up'.[15] However, drawing a parallel between Freud's cryptology of dreams and the everyday results in countless possible narratives, which although creative, disturbing or beautiful, are overly elemental and do not reflect the totality of everyday life. In the case of Bachelard, is the happy household always a 'flourishing nest', is the wardrobe a 'centre of order', do locks always conceal something hidden? The poetical is present in the everyday but studying the rhetoric of the daydream is not enough to establish a comprehensive concept of amateur space. Each poetic image, as Bachelard admits, suggests no cultural past or future. To search for space purely in the poetic or in the literary text, Lefebvre states that you will 'find it everywhere, and in every guise, enclosed, described, projected, dreamt of, speculated about'.[16]

Poetic articulations of space are valuable but are only part of the way towards an effective theory of amateur space. In addition, we need to pay attention to what Lefebvre terms the 'practico-social realm',[17] the socio-economic conditions that surround poetics, requisite infrastructure (as outlined in Chapter 1) and, most importantly, how language and poetics are inextricable from production and materiality.

Like Lefebvre, De Certeau attempts to grasp the 'unreadable' of the everyday that forever eludes 'analysis or interpretation', and both draw attention to direct forms of practice.[18] De Certeau uses examples from everyday phenomenological experience; what he describes as strategies and tactics. The former is an expression of a definitive power structure, the latter constitutes the 'art of the weak', as epitomized by De Certeau's well-known phrase *la perruque*, the idea of working within work, such as 'a cabinetmaker's "borrowing" a lathe to make a piece of furniture for his living room'.[19] De Certeau's examples of 'antidiscipline' could feasibly be an example in Lefebvre's work as a space of everyday resistance, but De Certeau imbues such activity with a sense of conscious, overt political resistance: ' "putting one over" the established order on its home ground'.[20] For De Certeau *la perruque* develops into a polemic, an underground network of diversionary practice against the bosses, which overlooks the closer links between the everyday and other less antagonistic experiences such as compliance (for example, borrowing the lathe after asking the boss). Moreover, his focus on tactics of resistance is primarily read through 'an inventive language that will register the inventiveness of the everyday'.[21] Again, as with Bachelard, rhetorical articulation of everyday experience is given primacy over its practice in a social and material world.

Lefebvre's argument that space is produced is a significant point of departure from other theorists of the everyday and is critical when constructing a theory of amateur space. For Lefebvre it was not language, logic or even the Hegelian notion of the spirit of history that amounted to a universal, abstract code lying behind all experience, but instead 'production' and 'the act of producing'.[22] Space had been perceived and conceived by thinkers for centuries, but Lefebvre, building on the ideas of Karl Marx, insisted that space 'cannot be detached from the material preconditions of individual and collective activity . . . whether the aim is to move a rock, to hunt game, or to make a simple or complex object'.[23]

The importance of Lefebvre's argument in constructing a theory of amateur space derives from his insistence that 'material preconditions' are intrinsic to our understanding of space. And when he used this term it was not just base materiality he was referring to – how the wood a shed is made of contributes to its spatial existence – but instead the productive forces that shape 'material preconditions' such as technology, social knowledge, the social division of labour, state infrastructure, etc.; the entire apparatus behind production and producing. Amateur space can be poetically described or related to the realm of abstract space – just think of the wistful description of a declining handicraft, or the geometric plans for a customized, self-built kitchen – yet these descriptions do not reflect how wider systems of socialized production have an effect on individual activities. Amateur space amounts to individual, voluntary acts of production embedded within 'material preconditions' – wider structures of capitalist production that determine the type of making taking place.

Amateur space possesses this illusive quality. It facilitates moments of individual production free of the constraints associated with capitalist production, yet it entirely depends on these systems for its survival. In this respect it shares the characteristics of Lefebvre's notion of 'differential space', the so-called 'enemy within its gates',[24] which is not an alternative to homogenous, techno-bureaucratic abstract space that Lefebvre identifies with state power, nor a mirror image of conventional modes of its production, but a space that tangentially relates to its norms. Lefebvre's examples include local resistance to central authorities, but primarily cluster around the act of leisure. He endows leisure with quasi-revolutionary potential, stating: 'The space of leisure *tends* – but is no more than a tendency, a tension, a transgression of users in search of a way forward – to surmount divisions: the divisions between the social and the mental, the divisions between sensory and intellectual, and also the divisions between the everyday and the out-of-the ordinary (festival).'[25]

Lefebvre was aware of the inherent susceptibility of leisure to succumb to capitalist relationships of production – exemplified by package holidays, the commercialization of camping or the standardization of sport. However, lazing on a beach, organizing a carnival or manning the cake stall are examples of the diverse, self-directed activities that occupy the slack space of leisure, which have the potential to transgress conventions of production. Leisure is not openly revolutionary – it is managed and usually organized under the auspices of bourgeois power – but Lefebvre placed 'some hope' in the pluralism it facilitated.[26]

Discussion of Lefebrvre's conceptualization of 'differential' space provides a way of understanding amateur space within everyday life – a means, drawn from everyday life, of bringing unity to that which abstract space partitions and breaks up. However, Lefebvre stops short of analysing the craft practices that take place within the slack space of leisure. Later on in the chapter I will recall the histories of various productive leisure-time activities, namely suburban chicken keeping, but for now it is important to establish a definition of amateur labour and see how it shares the 'differential' characteristics Lefebvre ascribed to his most radical of spatial categories.

Amateur labour

Amateur labour constitutes a productive inhabitation of Lefebvre's notion of differential space. It can be primarily characterized within Marxist theory by its 'non-necessity', corresponding with the notion of 'surplus labour': labour-power that produces more than is needed for basic subsistence 'which, for the capitalist, has all the charms of a creation out of nothing'.[27] Surplus labour existed in pre-modern societies but the division of labour that both Karl Marx and Adam Smith described exponentially increased the productivity of labour-power from the late eighteenth century onwards.[28] Marx and many of his followers have studied surplus labour extensively, interested in how it is channelled to ever more sophisticated means of capital accumulation, while labourers themselves are kept distant from the means of production.[29] This narrative is well known. However, less has been said about how excess productivity is channelled through amateur labour, certainly within Marxist theory at least.

Marx makes very few direct references to amateur labour. He used the word 'amateur' in an 1871 letter to New York socialist Friedrich Bolte to describe and condemn various socialist sects that were threatening the unity of the International, the body set up in 1864 to consolidate left-wing groups in a worldwide working class movement. Marx labelled these groups as 'amateur experiments', as well as denouncing the Russian libertarian intellectual Mikhail Bakunin who opposed Marx's authoritarian political opinions, as 'a man devoid of theoretical knowledge'.[30] Marx aligned the word 'amateur' with disorganized, ramshackle political organization, using the term pejoratively and in contrast to his own professionalized doctrine, backed up by his scientific method of historical materialism. Marx's use of the word 'amateur' seems to confirm its unimportance in his wider theories of human labour – a distraction from the macro-level socio-economic convulsions of different classes and the destiny of world history.

Amateur labour did become a concern for twentieth-century Marxist scholarship, even if it was relegated to the sidelines. Scholars of the Frankfurt School subjected popular culture, art and many other realms of cultural experience to Marxist analysis, and on occasion this raised the spectre of amateur labour, albeit in a roundabout, indirect way. The negative characterization of amateur labour was most clear and comprehensive in Hannah Arendt's theories of work, as outlined in her book *The Human Condition* of 1958, a work that critiqued Marx's study of labour, work and productivity. Central to her theories of labour is the division between two categories of work: the *animale laborans* who is occupied with the endless satiation of everyday needs, or the labour of the body, and the *homo faber* the 'fabricator of the world' whose ideals are 'permanence, stability, and durability'.[31] It is no surprise that Arendt classified amateur labour, or 'hobbies' within the former category, claiming: 'The spare time of the *animale laborans* is never spent in anything but consumption, and the more time left to him, the greedier and more craving his appetites. That these appetites become more sophisticated, so that this consumption is no longer restricted to necessities but, on the contrary, mainly concentrates on the superfluities of life.'[32]

This characterization of the *animale laborans* is very different from the idealism of Marx expressed in *The German Ideology* whereby individuals freed from the necessity to work voluntarily opt to fish in the afternoon and criticize after dinner.[33] It is reflective of Arendt's belief that she was living in a 'labourer's society' where man was in thrall to the 'theoretical glorification of labour', unable to discern the difference between work – allied to the *homo faber* – and working – the biological repetition of the *animale laborans*. For Arendt, the *homo faber* added 'new objects to the human artifice', while the *animale laborans* 'produces objects only incidentally and is primarily concerned with the means of its own reproduction'.[34] Objects that result from amateur labour could not be considered genuine additions to the human artifice according to her schema, but were at best incidental, the unimportant detritus of an individual's cycle of perpetual consumption and production.[35]

Arendt's pejorative understanding of amateur labour within scholarly discourse is further exacerbated by an inter-connected intellectual discourse that has built up around the adulation of the *homo faber*. This positive estimation of the skilled maker who makes genuine additions to the human artifice has its roots in the Arts and Crafts romanticism of John Ruskin and William Morris. Ruskin's prescriptions on how to combat the degradation of work in the nineteenth century anticipate Arendt's later bifurcation between *animale laborans* and *homo faber*. Ruskin pronounced in *The Nature of the Gothic*: 'never' encourage manufacture beyond what is necessary, copy (except for the purposes of education), or 'demand an exact finish for its own sake'[36] – three stipulations that amateur labour often falls short of. In the twentieth century the veneration of the *homo faber* is further cemented: from Martin Heidegger's philosophy of 'thingness' that endows the maker with the power to 'bring forth' material presence[37] and Bernard Leach's veneration of the studio potter as the bearer of centuries-old skill, cultural tradition and tacit knowledge,[38] to Richard Sennett's recent praise of the *homo faber* (in his widely read book, *The Craftsman*) who combines head and hand to respectfully treat materials in the world.[39] The skilled maker is seen to possess all the characteristics that are lacking in fast-paced modern capitalist production: the consideration of material, appropriate and respectful use of tools, and working within a comfortable environment. The term has political clout too, the British Chancellor George Osborne recently invoking the values of the *homo faber* in his 2011 budget, when he expressed a desire to see Britain 'carried aloft by the march of the makers'.[40]

This elevation of the ideals of the *homo faber* that inherently marginalizes the imperfect configurations of amateur labour is largely dependent upon object analysis: whether the result of labour is considered an authentic addition to the material world or not. The celebration of the *homo faber* in dominant cultural discourse has served to marginalize amateur labour, ever since the nineteenth century when technologies of artistic supply broadened the base of amateur craft practice. Talia Schaffer and Jennifer Harris have written on the gendered dimension of this exclusion in the context of the late-nineteenth-century Arts and Crafts: William Morris and his circle did not much appreciate the dilution of their socialist message and hopes for craftsmanship when it spread to the messy realm of part-time, domestic, handicraft undertaken by women who posed a 'threat' to their 'fragile artistic insurgency'.[41] The seemingly innocuous results of amateur labour – whether it is nineteenth-century imitation coral made in wax (the example that starts Schaffer's book on domestic handicraft, *Novel Craft*), the perfect lasagne or a self-built spice rack – seem trivial when compared with other forms of production. Yet the differential qualities of amateur space are elucidated in their full richness when analysis focuses not on the final object but on the process of making. This is what has been overlooked.

I contest this marginalization of amateur space. I argue that the cyclical repetition of Arendt's *animale laborans* does have the potential to be productive and add to the human artifice: scholars have hitherto simply failed to register the non-conventional, differential forms of productivity and ways of working that take place. As Lefebvre stated, we might bemoan the 'poverty of vocabulary and a clumsiness of expression' that results from people's inhabitation of everyday life, but that does not preclude 'the relevance of the testimony'.[42] We must be alert to the characteristics of amateur labour – its idiosyncrasy, its uniqueness and how it stretches conventional notions of work, even if the final product contravenes notions of quality or seems unimportant. It is useful to heed the words of mid-twentieth-century Danish artist Henry

Heerup, who wrote in 1944 as a part of his defence of folk expression in his country (anything from cake decoration to junk models): 'One Must Refrain From Judging Too Hard This Common Love of Labor'.[43]

Framing amateur labour as differential helps us to move away from Arendt's clear-cut distinction between the purity of the *homo faber* and the slavery of the *animale laborans*.[44] Amateur labour is certainly consumptive and dependent, yet crucially provides an opportunity for the unleashing of the *homo faber*, even if such interactions lack the purity that Ruskin, Arendt and Sennett would preserve for direct, 'honest' engagement with raw material. Fascinating configurations of labour result: amateur space is not just the clear opposite of 'professional' space, characterized by regularized and standardized systems of organization, there is a greater sense of 'mixture'.[45] Amateur space replicates and refracts these forms of organization in unexpected and unusual ways, and mimics and stretches its aesthetic codes. As shown throughout the chapter, the efficiency, portability, profitability and innovation of voluntarily undertaken labour feed into the structuring of professional spaces and broader socio-cultural notions of work. The entrenched polarity between amateur and professional space, dating from the early nineteenth century onwards, has served to mask these strong affiliations in everyday, practised reality.

One of the most striking manifestations of this mixture is the so-called professional-amateur hybrid. The term has been conceptualized in a myriad of different ways, but perhaps Charles Leadbeater and Paul Miller's 'Pro-Am' is the most well-known recent characterization, describing in their publication *The Pro-Am Revolution* (2004) 'innovative, committed and networked amateurs working to professional standards'.[46] Leadbeater and Miller argue that Pro-Ams undertake activities for the love of it but with a 'professional standard' in mind, and they invest a great deal of power in this categorization, stating that Pro-Ams can destabilize 'large hierarchical organisations with professionals at the top' through 'distributed organisational models that will be innovative, adaptive and low-cost'.[47] Leadbeater and Miller do not critique the parameters of their categorization, or question how they infuse amateur space with a goal-orientated, competitive model of productivity. They do not emphasize the differential quality of amateur practice. Going back to an earlier moment of professional amateurism in the late nineteenth century when individuals were encouraged to engage in various tasks of home maintenance and construction, provides a compelling evidence of the differential status of amateur space: how it replicated and reified dominant notions of an emerging Victorian ethos of productive, honourable work, while offering various forms of departure from it.

The late-nineteenth-century 'professionalization' of amateur practice

In the second half of the nineteenth century the burgeoning middle classes were increasingly encouraged to become more self-reliant. As Francis Chilton-Young stated in his 1886 self-help manual, *Everyman His Own Mechanic*:

The changes that have gradually come over things during the years that have passed since The Great Exhibition of 1851 have rendered men far more inclined to regard and consider the signs of their times than they were wont to do during the first half of the present nineteenth century, and anyone who will do this earnestly and searchingly cannot but come to the conclusion that the field of a man's knowledge must be far wider, his education far more general, his self-reliance far stronger and the power to help himself far greater than was either thought to be necessary some fifty years ago or even less.[48]

For Chilton-Young this 'wider', 'more general' education included work that conventionally fell within the remit of tradesmen. He proclaims: 'Yes reader, mend your broken chairs and crippled furniture; put fresh panes of glass into your broken windows; do your own repairs as far as practicable, make your own garden plants and appliances.'[49]

Chilton-Young's call for a legion of self-reliant men able to tackle everyday tasks of repair and construction was part of a late-nineteenth-century flourishing of 'amateur carpentry' or 'amateur mechanics', what we would today probably recognize as 'do-it-yourself'.[50] Journals such as *Design and Work* (1876–81), *Illustrated Carpenter and Builder* (1877–1971) and *Amateur Work* (1881–96) edited by Chilton-Young (Figure 2.1), encouraged invention, repair, model-making, building and home improvement through a series of instructional articles, information about new tools and materials, and reader-to-reader counsel.[51] These publications invited the amateur to engage with a variety of tasks, from building desks, chairs, rustic garden furniture and organs, to house plumbing, and even tennis court construction,[52] challenging the stereotype that the Victorian home was purely a site of passive leisure or sentimentalized aesthetic display.[53]

Philosophically, self-reliance represented a reaction to the pressures of modernization – mass production, larger firms, rural depopulation, business fraud and an increasingly politicized working class demanding higher wages. The doctrine's bible was Samuel Smiles's mid-nineteenth-century bestseller *Self-Help*,[54] which championed the honour, virtue and merits of one's own labour and intellect rather than relying on external bodies, such as the state or paid labourers. Smiles argued that society should be made up of individuals who use their common sense, hard work and motivation to overcome problems and excel in the world, relying on that which is within rather than without.[55] The American transcendentalist writer, Ralph Waldo Emerson, in his 1841 book *Self-Reliance*, had set a precedent for this anti-statist political philosophy, influencing later anti-capitalist, anti-civilization initiatives, from Henry Thoreau's experiment in self-sufficiency in a small wooden hut in Walden, Massachusetts to Stewart Brand's *Whole Earth Catalogue* (1968–72).[56] Smiles's work is less individualistic given the centralization of political, economic and social life of Britain at the time (compared with America), but he does advocate the idea that things are better when done under one's own volition through processes of self-education. His book allowed middle-class readers to imagine themselves in the same light as the pioneering young Michael Faraday, William Shakespeare or Bernard Palissy, whose biographies Smiles used to illustrate how obstacles and failures can be overcome in the course of a successful life.

For Smiles and Chilton-Young, self-reliance was not just a quirky, entertaining aside to everyday life, but integral to an individual's moral virtue and social standing. Their project involved the re-configuration of what it meant to be a 'gentleman'; Asa Briggs notes how Smiles's work attempted to sever the word's link to ideas of superfluity, rank and inherited wealth, towards moral worth and virtue in labour.[57] Another author of several self-help manuals of the era, Ellis Davidson, stated in *The Amateur House Carpenter* (1875) that the 'refinement' of 'men of education' should not be at odds with the ability to pick up tools and undertake manual labour oneself.[58] According to these authors, gentlemanly work did not exclude manual labour.

At the same time, notions of the amateur also underwent a shift, reflecting this new bourgeois paradigm of self-sufficiency. In an article for the 1881 edition of *Design and Work*, an anonymous

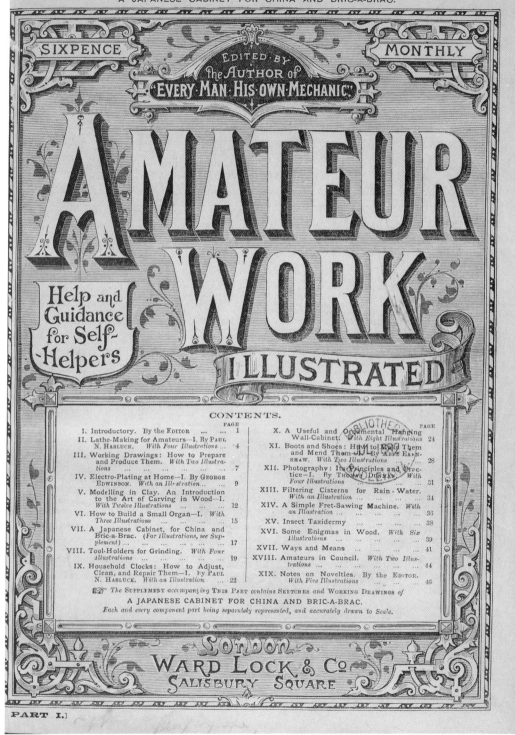

FIGURE 2.1 *Cover of* Amateur Work *(1881). Courtesy of Bodleian Libraries.*

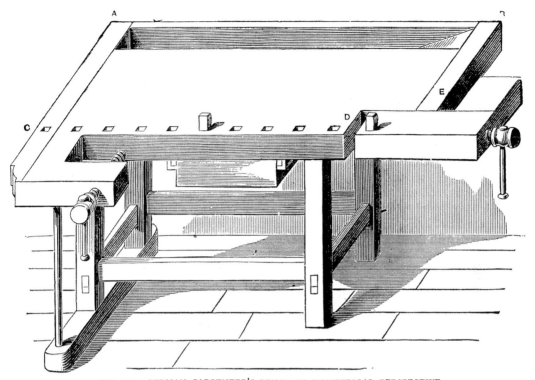

FIG. 21.—GERMAN CARPENTER'S BENCH IN ISOMETRICAL PERSPECTIVE.

FIGURE 2.2 *Carpenter's bench from* Amateur Work *(1881). Courtesy of Bodleian Libraries.*

writer suggests that there is no reason why the amateur 'should remain the "careless whistling boy"' but instead could 'become the skilful mechanic, and in every sense of the word the "professional amateur"'.[59] An editorial that appeared in the same journal later in the year further characterized this new trope of the 'professional amateur' stating that 'the entire kingdom of amateurism' was not exclusively populated by those whose attention passed from one fad to another, but also included 'many hard working students who set themselves to accomplish one thing at a time, and overcome its difficulties first, ere they attempt to plunge into the mazes of another'.[60] Within this culture of Victorian self-help the amateur became associated with forms of devoted practice, more akin to the 'student' or 'improver' than the dabbler or dilettante, able to mirror the practices of skilled handymen, and even sharing similar tools: this impressively equipped 'German Carpenter's Bench' (Figure 2.2), sold by the firm Messrs. R. Melhuish and Sons of Fetter Lane, was deemed suitable for 'professional joiner and amateur woodworker' alike.[61]

Honing skills of self-reliance was not just a moral undertaking; there were clear practical benefits. For a start, doing it yourself avoided the need for external labourers who, according to self-help manual authors Davidson and Phillis Browne, had a reputation for laziness, betraying their client's trust and for eking out as much money as possible from the simplest of tasks through underworking.[62] Then there were the financial benefits. Chilton-Young claimed to his readers in 1886: 'you shall find yourself in pocket at the end of the year merely through resorting to self-help',[63] and one reader, 'F.M.', agreed with the economic rationale for self-help, describing the savings he made after following instruction as follows:

Your paper has I reckon saved me about £1 for each number. I mention one case. Through the articles 'Gilding on glass' I was enabled to paint my own fascia in gold, measuring 25 feet by 2 ½ feet, at a cost of £6 10s. It took me thirteen days to do and the lowest estimate I could get for the same thing was £18 10s.[64]

As with more recent booms in do-it-yourself home improvement projects, there was a clear economic rationale that underpinned voluntarily undertaken labour in the Victorian era. Smiles, Chilton-Young and other authors were keen to insist on the moral virtue of developing skills for self-reliance, but these lofty ideals went alongside ideas of social and financial advance, moral standing and even notions of social Darwinism, the maxim of the survival of the fittest transposed on to everyday life.[65] If middle-class individuals were to survive more effectively – socially, economically, politically and morally – then getting better at manual tasks and engaging in a spot of amateur carpentry was one clear solution. This necessitated ever more 'professional' attitudes to amateur work.

The call to professionalize voluntarily undertaken activities by Chilton-Young, Davidson and others is an example of the blurred line between professional and amateur. In this instance, notions of efficient self-sufficiency, honourable labour and financial acumen key to the Victorian work ethic had an impact on how amateurs practised in their free time. Although I have focused on the advocacy of self-help among the Victorian male population, an equivalent cultural force prevailed upon middle-class women too. Literature scholars Kyriaki Hadjiafxendi and Patricia Zakreski recently coined the notion of the 'industrious amateur' to refer to female domestic work of the nineteenth century that 'offered opportunities for women to develop and refine the skills that were needed to participate in commercial enterprises and the public world of work'.[66] We could argue that this encouragement to self-help and better standards of work represented the spread and dominance of a capitalist ideology of work, evidence of how Smiles 'hymned the virtues of capitalism', as Marxist historian Eric Hobsbawm has claimed.[67]

However, this spread of the Victorian work ethic does not amount to a complete capitulation of amateur space to professionalization, the subsumption of all production to ideals of capitalist work. This chapter's hypothesis is that amateur space was and is 'differential' within capitalism. This means that the late-nineteenth-century professionalizing amateur does not simply mirror the practices, conditions and structures that characterize norms of work, but departs from them in various, and often idiosyncratic, ways. There is a greater dialectical relationship too. Efficiency, regularization, standardization and other qualities associated with professional (and capitalist) notions of work and labour often derived, at least in part, from amateur craft practice itself.

An illustration of this can be found in a very unlikely source: Frederick Winslow Taylor's *Principles of Scientific Management* (1911). At first glance, Taylor's seminal work concerning productivity and efficiency in the factory seems at odds with amateur labour: he advocates a shift from systems of labour organization based on encouraging individual worker initiative through incentives, to management rooted in the scientific method.[68] This work has come to epitomize the values of capitalist labour organization; however, in his work, Taylor co-opts the idea of the self-reliant, competitive individual who shares a resemblance to the 'professional amateur' to inform his theories of factory management. He cites the example of the American baseball players or English cricketers who 'strain every nerve to secure victory' in order to avoid being branded as a 'quitter'.[69] Taylor recognized the importance of harnessing individual motivation for the pursuit of greater efficiency in the workplace, explaining how one of his subjects of analysis – a non-skilled worker called 'Schmidt' – walked to and from work at the same healthy pace because he was keen to complete a day's work and return to making his garden wall at home.[70] Both examples demonstrate the productivity, determination, willingness and moral character that were demonstrated in work undertaken outside the regulated, supervised realm of 'professional' space. The former shows the will to succeed in competitive sports that Taylor wants to map onto work practices, the latter shows how Schmidt's self-built 'garden wall' drives his enthusiastic attitude to work during the day. Taylor's work ethic, often thought to be typical of professional space, derives from his observations of amateur self-reliance.

It is dialectical relationships like these between categories of amateur and professional space that I will explore in the case studies below. I will start with the workstations; the kinds of spaces from which amateur work commences, whether garages or foldaway tables, and in particular how tools are organized within such spaces. This is mainly achieved by comparing British amateur carpentry manuals from the first era of 'professional amateurism' – the late nineteenth century – with similar handyman advice manuals from the United States in the 1950s and 1960s, echoing the chronological parameters of the first chapter.[71] DIY enthusiasts like David X. Manners – 'one of America's leading "how-to" authors', according to the editor of a series of handyman publications, Ray Gill[72] – repeat the same arguments made by Davidson and Chilton-Young decades before: how domestic construction, maintenance and repair has a beneficial effect on the worker, can improve quality of living and save money.

The comparative framework is narrow, primarily theoretical, and lacks adequate historical contextualization. But the intention is not to describe various craft practices in detail but to reveal the broad differential qualities that characterize amateur space across these periods and beyond. I continue to build on the chapter-wide hypothesis that amateur space is differential within normative structures of capitalism, reifying the prevailing middle-class ideology of work while consistently stretching its boundaries. From self-reliance onwards there are many salient characteristics of amateur tool organization that demonstrate affiliations with comparable systems in retail, factory and other settings not usually associated with amateur craft. These might seem self-evident, yet they attest to the differential quality of amateur space within contexts of increasing societal and market pressures to regularize such practices.

The malleability and invisibility of amateur tool organization

Decisions pertaining to the organization and set-up of an amateur workstation are unique to each maker and depend on the particular things being made. However, there are key structural characteristics of the amateur workstation that reflect differential qualities.

For a start, the supplemental nature of amateur practice means that the workstation has to be malleable enough to 'fit around' other commitments. In terms of physical space for tool organization, this often means that the materials and tools have to disappear, or at least be stored in an unobtrusive manner. This characteristic is epitomized by the portability of certain crafts such as knitting and needlecraft, which have rarely been allotted a permanent place within the home. Cheryl Buckley uses interviews with her female relatives to show how these crafts – more specifically, dressmaking – took place in spaces that were not fixed according to 'the frozen space of patriarchal mythology' with a room exclusively devoted to specific gendered tasks, but instead took place alongside other forms of domestic work (and continue to do so) within a 'fragmented place', where tasks of maintenance, repair, decoration and even paid work, happen in the same space.[73] This lack of a permanent home for much amateur craft practice is a reflection of its supplemental status in relation to everyday life and subsistence.

Buckley's concept of the 'fragmented place' usefully dismantles the idea that amateur tasks are confined to a particular room or area, common in histories of the modern home, and instead highlights how amateur workstations are often so portable and easy to put away. This is a pan-amateur phenomenon: from late-nineteenth-century amateur china decorators who were encouraged to add an armrest to a normal dining table to support careful painting,[74] to Sunday painters of the same era making use of Winsor & Newton's portable sketching easel, or their easel chair hybrid (Figures 2.3 and 2.4). As the figures show, Winsor & Newton marketed these products on their ability to be packed away into a confined space, suitable for the 'fragmented place' in which the activity was situated within everyday life. These portable workspaces suggest that leisure could be easily accommodated within the limited spaces of the bourgeois home, brought out during the weekends, opened up, only to be put away again when other less supplementary activities of life take over.

Shifting attention to the late-nineteenth-century amateur carpentry, one might expect the amateur workstation to occupy a more permanent location within the home, due to both the processes inherent to the craft that require more space – the manipulation of large pieces of wood, use of dangerous, bulky tools and the need to leave projects half complete – and the gender associations of the activity. This would conform to our nineteenth-century stereotypes of gender, with the more 'expressive' craft of carpentry requiring more space than the ephemeral handicrafts.[75] However, in this era, carpentry benches were often sold on their ability to be concealed and transformed, possessing the same malleability and invisibility of tools needed for so-called 'softer' labours.[76]

For example, Melhuish's substantial 'German Carpenter's Bench' shown in Figure 2.2 was easy to take apart, with the top and stands all-collapsible, meaning it could easily be tucked away.[77] In Leo Parsey's step-by-step instructions on the tools required for amateur wood-carving, published in *Amateur Work* in 1881, the author also comments on the ability for the amateur's workstation to temporarily disappear, stating that his design of a wood-carver's workbench could easily be covered to look like an 'ordinary table'; adding that a standard household table would suffice for carpentry if resources were even more restricted.[78]

In the context of 1950s America, space was less of an issue for amateurs due to the large size of garages, basements and sheds. However, it was from the United States that one of the most ingenious solutions for portable carpentry tool organization was found. As in the late nineteenth century, limitations on space did not necessarily discourage practice. As Manners put it, 'Remarkable things have been done only with a closet in a crowded apartment'.[79] Sam Brown's work, *Planning Your Own Home Workshop*, published by the Popular Mechanics Press, provided readers from the cities with an unlikely solution to spatial limitations, explaining how to build a workshop that transforms into a couch, with all the space needed for necessary tools (Figure 2.5):

> Even in a small city apartment, a homeshop is perfectly possible! And not by the usual expedient of trying to carry on craftsmanship using the kitchen table as a workbench and having to put everything away at every meal. Instead you can have a portable, self-contained and practically complete workshop that folds up to become a usable studio couch.[80]

Brown's cunning device provided an adequate space in which domestic amateur carpentry could flourish without getting in the way of other household tasks. This sofa workshop attempted

38, RATHBONE PLACE. 23

WINSOR AND NEWTON'S
SKETCHING EASEL.

This Sketching Easel possesses those qualities most required by the Sketcher and Tourist. It is of the simplest construction, very portable, and of extreme lightness, its weight, in deal, being 1¾ lbs. The adaptation of a joint or collar of novel construction, allows the legs to be placed in any position most suited to the Sketcher.

			s.	d.
The Easel in Deal .	. .	5 feet 4 inches high . .	5	6
Ditto Polished	. .	ditto . .	7	0
The Easel in Mahogany	.	ditto . .	10	6
Ditto Polished	. .	ditto . .	12	0

COMPANION SKETCHING EASEL.

Similar to the Sketching Easel, but with socket joints so as to be more compact for carriage.
The Easel in Mahogany, 12s

FIGURE 2.3 *Winsor & Newton's sketching easel. Winsor & Newton supplement in Thomas W. Salter,* Field's Chromatography: or, Treatise on Colours and Pigments Used by Artists *(London: Winsor & Newton, 1869). Image courtesy of Colour Reference Library, Royal College of Art.*

Gentlemen's Sketching Seat and Easel **combined.**

FIGURE 2.4 *Winsor & Newton seat easel. Winsor & Newton supplement in Thomas W. Salter,* Field's Chromatography: or, Treatise on Colours and Pigments Used by Artists *(London: Winsor & Newton, 1869). Image courtesy of Colour Reference Library, Royal College of Art.*

to confine do-it-yourself activity to a separate realm in order to reduce its interference with other domestic spaces, epitomizing the phrase 'hidden in plain sight': one can see the sofa, but its true properties remain concealed from view until it is opened or when its use as a chair is accompanied by the jingle-jangle of loose tools. This phrase has also been used to characterize the marginalization of the female embroidery worker in the context of patriarchal dominance within the home – women could be seen but the expressive content of their work and organization was hidden from public attention.[81] Brown's sofa workshop, as well as a plethora of other fold-away tool box solutions and workstations on wheels,[82] demonstrates how the character of 'putting away', or concealing, one's tools was infused with expressive potential by the 1950s: the impromptu and creative transformation of an apartment to a handyman's workshop demonstrating the resourcefulness, efficiency and guile of a keen amateur.

   The marginal role that amateur practice occupies in everyday life has been reflected in the limited physical space granted to such activities, and the transformable, collapsible, concealable workstation has responded to this need. The portable and invisible workstation fits around other commitments, expressing its differential status within everyday life in much the same way as Lefebvre's construction of the carnival. This association alerts us to the potential productivity that emerges from mobility, evident in Brown's workshop sofa and in the toolkits of female embroiderers throughout the centuries. The impermanent, concealed and convertible workstations are conduits of expression that allow the amateur practitioner to temporarily become the *homo faber*: productive in their own mobile and idiosyncratic way.

FIGURE 2.5 *'Make a studio-couch "workshop" '* in Sam Brown (ed.), Planning Your Home Workshop *(Chicago: Popular Mechanics Press, 1949), p. 48.*

Everything in its right place: security and possession

The toolbox is another example of a portable, concealable workstation that also imposed a degree of tool organization. Davidson and Chilton-Young gave their readers instructions on how to build toolboxes,[83] insisting that compartments were needed to contain specific materials or facilitate easy access. Like the paintbox, the toolbox miniaturizes processes of labour, establishing a tool order, with a view to encourage productivity. However, as I covered paintboxes in depth in Chapter 1, the focus here is on the exterior compartmentalization of tools, through racks and brackets used to store tools on walls.

The most obvious rationale for keeping tools in some kind of order, as Davidson and Chilton-Young pointed out, was that it helped the amateur undertake a task more effectively. Put simply, workshops were arranged so as to best accompany the task at hand. This is epitomized by the proverb 'a good workman is known by his tools', a message as relevant to late-nineteenth-century amateurs as it is today. As Black states in *Saxon's Everyday Guide to Carpentry* (1898):

> The good workman obtains 'good' tools in the first instance, and then by constant care keeps them in a state of 'goodness' that he has never occasion to row with them. He does not keep plane, iron or chisel in such a condition that it turns round and barks at him, and he has to 'cuss' it in return.[84]

Maintaining tools required essential surface interventions such as polishing, sharpening, grinding and cleaning. Yet a tool's 'state of goodness' also depended on the arrangement and storage. Davidson's explanation for why it was important to build a tool rack, like the one shown in Figure 2.6, seems obvious: 'If each set of tools is kept at a particular part of the rack, it will save much time, for the eye will soon become accustomed to the positions, and will at once seek the tool required in its right place, instead of being compelled to travel along the entire rack.'[85]

Within reach, easily accessible, and allowing tools to be organized according to size, Davidson's tool rack made practical sense. If an amateur was attempting to make anything, to have the tools clearly displayed and within reach rather than cluttered on the floor would ease construction. But the common sense approach to organization also highlights the important of safety. Davidson even recommended installing a lock and key mechanism on his tool rack in order to prevent the likelihood of injury to curious infants or clumsy adults.[86]

Securing a tool rack in the manner that Davidson suggested was not just common sense – merely rational, neutral or safe – it hints at a relationship to personal property and a desire to protect tools from theft or misuse. Davidson bemoans the tool abuse that ensued if tools were not adequately safeguarded:

> and who, on being questioned as to some missing tool favour the amateur with the information that it has only been used for a few minutes (long enough to destroy a dozen chisels) in the kitchen; or that the axe is in the coal cellar, the proper coal-hammer having been 'lost' long ago even in the days of their predecessors.[87]

Davidson's words recall his experiences with domestic servants who used tools against the function for which they were intended. More than just a safety precaution, the concern to secure one's tools reflects a particular amateur relationship to tool organization, one based on a strong personal relationship with them. Outside agents – in Davidson's case domestic servants – were unlikely to be aware of the particular reason for which an amateur keeps a tool, and by using it to fulfil an immediate need might unintentionally damage it. For the amateur, the tool was selected, arranged and maintained with a specific use in view and was more likely to be cherished for this reason.

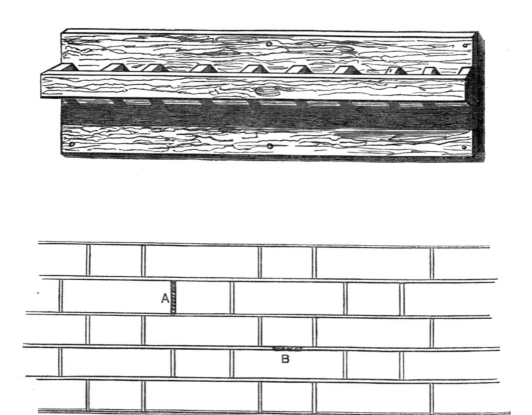

A TOOL-RACK.

(Fig. 12.)

FIGURE 2.6 *Tool rack in Ellis Davidson,* Amateur House Carpenter *(London: Chapman and Hall, 1875), p. 26. Image courtesy of Science and Society Picture Library.*

The need to keep tools safely stowed away that is manifest in late-nineteenth-century manuals is mirrored by Manners's mid-century US handyman literature.[88] He recommended a practice of tool organization that demonstrates a heightened degree of care, security and possessiveness: drawing an outline of a tool on a wall in pencil, pen or paint, a strategy that has since become a common solution to tool storage (Figures 2.7 and 2.8).

In his 1955 book, *How to Plan and Build Your Workshop*, Manners recommended that pegboard – a recently developed artificial hardboard with pre-drilled holes – was the perfect solution to tool storage, even providing natural ventilation for the tools to protect them from rust (Figure 2.9).[89]

More than merely keeping tools secure and within reach, a succession of outlined tools made it easier to ascertain whether a tool was missing or lent out (a feature within amateur workshops

FIGURE 2.7 *Handyman board and tool rack. David X. Manners,* How to Plan and Build Your Workshop *(New York: ARCO Publishing, 1977), p. 46.*

FIGURE 2.8 *Tool wall with tool outline at Lock 7 Cycle Cafe, Broadway Market, London (2010). Photograph by author.*

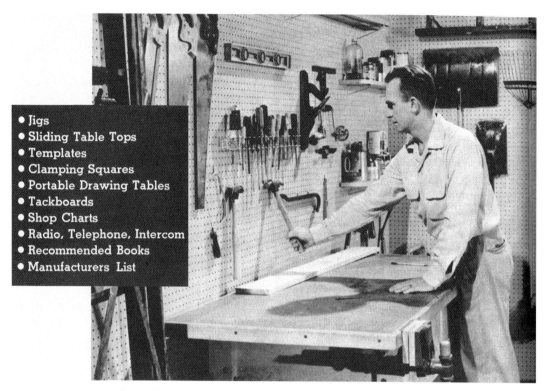

- Jigs
- Sliding Table Tops
- Templates
- Clamping Squares
- Portable Drawing Tables
- Tackboards
- Shop Charts
- Radio, Telephone, Intercom
- Recommended Books
- Manufacturers List

FIGURE 2.9 *Man placing hammer on pegboard workshop. David X. Manners,* How to Plan and Build Your Workshop *(New York: ARCO Publishing, 1977), p. 136.*

that is similar to strategies of retail stocktaking that I cover in more detail below). The outline encouraged the sense of possession over tools, even when they were not there. In addition, the outlined tools create the effect of 'work-readiness', or 'standing reserve' to use Heidegger's term for latent technological energy, a testament to what these tools could foreseeably achieve.[90]

Like Davidson's solutions to guard against tool misuse through lock and key, the tool outline suggests a degree of possessiveness common to amateurs who have sentimentally invested in their tools or developed highly specific functional demands of them. This relationship to tooling encourages the forms of protection outlined above, showing how amateur space stretches the expectation of a purely functional relationship between man and object into the differential category.

Everything in its right place: efficiency/comfort

Given the lack of accountability to any paymaster, a concern to economize and be efficient might seem irrelevant for amateur craft practice. However, the reverse is true. As Davidson notes: the 'amateur has want of time, and annoyance of missing, misplaced, or inconveniently stored tools deters activity'.[91] Contrary to expectation, an efficient relationship between body and tool is at the heart of amateur craft practice. As amateur practice is supplemental there are limited resources of time to spare, therefore it is key that the tools are immediately ready to hand. Manners, in 1955, chimed with Davidson's sentiment: 'What sense is there wasting half an hour looking for a particular nail or a mislaid tool? . . . Make the shop as efficient as a good kitchen, and it will pay off by saving you time, sparing your nerves'.[92]

Efficient organization of workshops, putatively to save frustration for the individual, leads to a particular type of hyper-management where space is specifically tailored to the precise needs of the amateur. Unlike the professional who would have to work despite tool disorganization, the amateur can make sure his or her mini-factory suits particular needs. In their quest to encourage self-reliance, Davidson, Chilton-Young and other late-nineteenth-century manual authors urge a level of workspace efficiency that shares strong parallels with later modern theories of systematic domestic management, in particular Taylor's *Principles of Scientific Management*. In this book, Taylor sets out a plan to 'professionalise' systems of management to iron out inefficient practices and, in particular, singular, aberrant bodily movements. He quotes the example of one of his fellow labour reformers, Frank Gilbreth, and his study of the 'rationalisation' of the process of bricklaying: 'He developed the exact position which each of the feet of the bricklayer should occupy with relation to the wall, the mortar box, and the pile of bricks, and so made it unnecessary for him to take a step or two toward the pile of bricks and back again each time a brick is laid.'[93]

Taylor includes this case study to advance his argument that efficiency derives from the spatial management of tool and body. As with the example above of the enthusiastic cricketer or baseball player, Taylor co-opts a feature of amateur labour – in this case workspace organization completely tailored to an individual worker – for his own philosophies of management. Taylor's interpretations of body-motion analysis, however, epitomize a rational, scientific understanding of space, just one possible 'reading' of space, as Lefebvre states. The efficient relationship between tool and body in amateur space is driven by a different cause – a lack of time that derives from its supplementary status. Positions of readiness in relation to tools were important, as poorly organized workstations would stultify any pet project.

The other key attribute of efficient amateur workstations is that they were customized according to the comfort of individual makers, rather than being aggregated outwards as a 'one size fits all' solution to concentrated labour. The issue of comfort provides another opportunity to stress the differential status of amateur space. Efficiency that resulted from keeping tools and materials within reach was not just about spatial proximity, which Taylor sought to systematize, but from the differential status of amateur space. In other words, Taylor did not fully recognize that efficiency was not just an issue of scientific space and distances, but social space. The way in which amateur space is arranged has a more acute relationship to the labour that takes place thereafter: efficiency derives from the individual's ability to have a closer, more autonomous relationship with their tools. The professional ethos that Taylor's work came to exemplify did not stress the importance of this individual comfort and thus came to be associated strongly with worker alienation, from Harry Braverman's critique onwards.[94]

Consuming one's own tool organization: amateur and retail space

The differential quality of amateur workstations can also be seen in the parallels between retail organization and the workspaces of judicious amateurs. Both spaces were arranged to exaggerate the availability and ease of use to the user/consumer.

In the late nineteenth century the ironmongery store was the principal site for the purchase of supplies and tools for tradesmen as well as for the amateur enthusiast.[95] One textual aid to the ironmonger – *The Complete Ironmonger* (1895), written by G. A. Hardy – urged effective compartmentalization and organization of storefronts in a manner similar to contemporaneous amateur carpentry manuals. Hardy stated that the appearance of goods is improved 'when all of one kind are kept together', adding that 'the test of good arrangement is that the salesman can find goods easily, and thus serve the customers expediently'.[96] Hardy gives several other tips to store managers: such as encouraging them to keep their stock on show to impress customers, categorizing similar object or material types and keeping them together, replenishing window displays frequently, and placing goods within easily navigable display cabinets. This advice constitutes an alternative retail strategy to department store organization. Rather than overwhelm the consumer with spectacle, hoping that in the confusion the individual will be more likely to consume,[97] the systematic management advised by Hardy, with its outward presentation of available stock that alerts the shopkeeper when any particular item is running out, appealed to an audience that values efficiency.[98]

Workspace management in the domestic environment differed from store management in that the amateur did not have to appeal to a broad range of consumers. However, one could argue that various manuals' models of the 'ideal' tool rack positioned the amateur maker as the consumer of their own tool organization, attracted by the conspicuousness of perfectly ordered tools; an image that had market appeal.

Amateur workstations were not immune to commodification, particularly in the context of the market-driven post-war DIY boom in the USA. In this environment Manners's proscriptive advice to his readers on workspace organization reads as veiled support for consumerism. He advised his readers to take an inventory of essential tools, discard any that are deemed unnecessary and draw on experience from past projects to predict which tools would be necessary for the future: 'Put a price beside each item you'll have to buy'.[99] The strategy of outlining tools on a wall is a system of organization – an automatic inventory – similarly highlights tool absence. This lack, of course, could be remedied by finding the tool, but it also could be resolved through further consumption.

The accentuation of absence in amateur tool organization and the encouragement to fill in the gaps, chimes with values of consumption, retail and efficient stock management. This sense of lack was exacerbated by post-war advertisements that exaggerated the extent of plenty in the ideal construction of a fully kitted-out workstation, an example of the emerging aesthetics of efficiency upon which the commodification of the workstation relied – a subject to which I will now turn.

The aesthetics of the workstation

So far analysis has focused on how the organization of workstations reflects the differential quality of amateur space, and the dialectical relationship between amateur forms of tool organization and those of the factory or shop. But emptied of any concerns about a workstation's function, the beauty of tool organization as an entity in itself was one reason for its appeal amongst amateurs. As Manners stated in the context of pegboard-lined workshops, 'an orderly arrangement of good tools is a joy to behold'.[100]

Pegboard is the perfect material through which to explore the aesthetics of amateur workstations. Pegboard is the common name for perforated hardboard, an artificial hardboard with pre-drilled holes arranged in a grid structure (Figure 2.9).[101] The material, developed and marketed from the 1950s onwards, provided a simple means of fastening brackets, fixtures or hooks to the wall, making it the perfect solution for tool organization as tools could be displayed within an easily accessible grid. Manners was a particular fan of the versatile qualities of pegboard. He provided reader instructions in his various works on how to use the material for fencing, wall partitions, corner storage units, even a boot bin where the small holes in the board functioned as efficient ventilation.[102] Most importantly, pegboard automatically made walls into 'prefinished' tool racks, according to Manners.[103]

The aesthetic appeal of pegboard's potential to bring order to amateur work was accentuated in the Masonite Corporation's advertisement of its new range of Presto Pegboard, which appeared in various editions of *Popular Mechanics* and *Popular Science* in the early 1960s (Figure 2.10).

The company had developed a range of hardboards since its founder, William H. Mason, patented a particular process of exploding and steaming woodchip into panels.[104] In the Presto advertisements, the modern solution for tool organization was favourably presented against past models of 'cramped, old-fashioned mess' and offered the promise of transforming rooms into neat and tidy units that were 'eye-pleasing', 'attractive' and 'handsome' with a 'tracery' design.[105]

The allure of a workshop with perfectly new tools, attractively arranged in a systematic display, evokes the aesthetic wonder of regulated order that Siegfried Kracauer observed in mass synchronized dance. In *The Mass Ornament*, Kracauer describes the de-sexualization of the Tiller girls (a group of synchronized dancers who toured Europe throughout the 1920s) that accompanies their subjugation to a rationalized, symmetrical, linear choreography, demonstrating how their performance reflects contemporaneous capitalist realities.[106] Their dance dispassionately reflects a demand for 'calculability' and the 'abstractness' of modern capitalist thinking as a subject for audience contemplation. It also constitutes a situation where the mass ornament, of which audience and performers are both part, assumes an authority beyond individual subjectivity: 'The human figure enlisted in the mass ornament has begun the *exodus* from lush organic splendour and the constitution of individuality toward the realm of anonymity to which it relinquishes itself when it stands in truth and when the knowledge radiating from the basis of man dissolves the contours of visible natural form.'[107]

Kracauer's analysis of how the dancing girls' bodies lose their visible natural form, and become subsumed into a rationalized unity, can be mapped onto the woman ordering the shelf in the Masonite advert (Figure 2.10). She loses her organic composition, accentuated by her floating position above the ground, and dissolves into the rationalized grid system. She becomes the transparent and anonymous operator rather than a subjective agent, much like the telephone operator in Hollywood films of the era.

Beyond the figure, the grid in itself possesses characteristics of the mass ornament, rendering space calculable. Although grids are thought to be the epitomization of modern order, the art critic Rosalind Krauss echoes Kracauer's words by explaining their mythical potential: grids convince onlookers of their rationality, while remaining an aesthetic construct.[108] Krauss explores the exposition of the concealed internal dynamic of the grid as myth in De Stijl artist Piet Mondriaan's paintings but, like Kracauer, her arguments are surprisingly relevant in this analysis of the Masonite pegboard advert. The order of the garage has the guise of rationality, neutrality, as if this systematic form of organization is the uncontested method of how garages *ought* to be organized absent of any aesthetic partiality. However, the opposite is the case. The organization is aesthetic, and the apparent neutrality only serves to accentuate this. It is no surprise that the dishevelled pre-pegboard garage mess is a drawing, whereas the solution achieved by Masonite's product is presented in the form of a photograph, increasing its 'truth' claim through the medium's presumed ability to be a more accurate representation of reality.

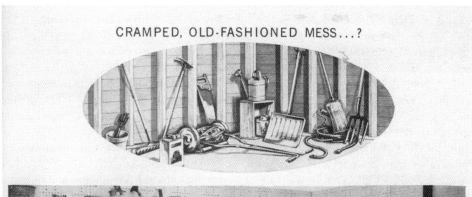

Organize your garage with

PRESTO PEG·BOARD

New Presto Peg-Board by Masonite makes it easy work to transform children's rooms, garages, utility rooms into neat, well-organized areas.
No need to paint Presto Peg-Board. It comes to you all prefinished in an eye-pleasing pattern.

More good news: this strong, heavy-duty Presto Peg-Board is priced so low it will amaze you.
Why not start from the plans we'll send you? Just fill in the coupon.

MASONITE *shows the way!*
Masonite and Presto Peg-Board are registered trademarks of Masonite Corp.

SEND FOR
FREE
PLANS BOOKLET
AND
LITERATURE

Masonite Corporation, Dept. PM-10, Box 777, Chicago 90, Illinois
Send me plans booklet and literature for Presto Peg-Board.

Name_____

Address_____

City_____ Zone_____

County_____ State_____

OCTOBER 1962   219

FIGURE 2.10 *Presto Peg-board advertisement,* Popular Mechanics *(October 1962), p. 219.*

Kracauer and Krauss problematize the presumed neutrality of the grid by showing that it has an autonomous aesthetic appeal that exerts a 'mythical' power over those who look upon it, much in the same way as the discovery of perspective in early modern art. In the context of post-war America, the aesthetic appeal of an ordered workshop mirrored the extent of order in modern kitchens and bathrooms that emerged as 'a surreal conflation of the organic and the mechanical: its seamless skins are fluidly curved yet impervious to dirt and moisture', according to Ellen Lupton.[109] Masonite's image of a pegboard garage crucially allies domestic aesthetics with the 'workshop' that has to be managed to cohere with rigorous standards illustrated in magazines and advertisements, constituting 'a laxative for hastening the flow of goods through the economy'.[110] Lupton convincingly argues that streamlining in kitchen and bathroom design reduced these rooms' functions to a series of knowable choreographic steps that help guard against the perils of dust and improve efficiency along Taylorist lines. Underneath all these modifications is the drive to sanitize cluttered, unhealthy interiors, considered hallmarks of Victorian living: in the context of the garage, the sweat, failure and mess of a functioning workshop.

The garage kitted out with Presto Pegboard, with the tools placed in a delicate symmetry, suggested the inexhaustible potential of domestic labour, its 'work-readiness'.[111] The advertisement appropriates the allure of the latent energy inherent in tools themselves and the fact that all these tools could be employed in a multitude of domestic labours. The advertisement does not depict a workstation that shows obvious signs of labour or human activity, like the drawing in the oval frame of the garage in a pre-pegboard state of mess, but instead a streamlined absence of messy work. The woman in the advertisement is not deploying her labour to make something, modify, clean or repair, but rather to organize and manage a vast array of consumer goods in an attractive, ordered pattern. Taylor's principles of scientific management applied to the garage reduce it to an aesthetic of 'work-readiness' or an indication that work *has* taken place but has subsequently been finished and cleaned up, with the tools that performed the process put back into their correct place within a rational grid structure.

The affective relationship between tool organization, labour and aesthetics prompts a reminder that there is flexibility within the pre-arranged systems of tool organization. Amateur workstations do not completely capitulate to abstract supra-human models, whether they use pegboard or not. Brown's encouragement to build quirky little devices in his how-to book, using discarded car pistons to hold nails and building a sectional rack for small parts, which swivel and are arranged according to the specific needs of an individual's practice, are an illustration of non-uniformity in workstation management.[112] Tools are made and tailored to the body of any one maker and there is infinite uniqueness.

In addition, usually home workshops are dirty and messy, the opposite of what is presented in the pegboard advert. After giving detailed proscriptions on how to organize a workshop according to the same logic manifest in the Presto Pegboard advertisement above, Brown states:

> Usually it takes three years for the average crafter to acquire a full setup of the needed tools. By that time you know your tools and you know what you want – remodelling and rearranging come easy. And you may never get above the slap-happy stage with tools scattered haphazardly and junk everywhere. Some of the best, most enjoyable and most productive homeshops in the country would never take a blue ribbon in a picture contest.[113]

Brown's observation that some workshops never get beyond the 'slap-happy' stage and remain disordered challenges the thesis that amateur makers followed the 'rationalizing' advice of manual authors or the systematic layout offered by Masonite's Presto range. Individual subjective agency can of course be exercised within the structures of the grid.[114] Creating mess, not following didactic advice and following one's own rules demonstrates the inherent flexibility inherent to amateur space. Yet this individual action constitutes a mediation of meta-structures, such as Taylor's principles of scientific management, through the course of everyday practice/labour.

As this background grid is often lost beneath the presumption that amateur practice is inherently individualistic and subjective, the attempt in this section has been to show its links to other spaces of capitalism – the factory, the retail environments, or the spectacle of the mass ornament. However, if the grid is a part of an aesthetic in which the rational and calculable takes centre stage, its appropriation by amateur practitioners constitutes its miniaturization and thus a form of quasi-control. There is a greater degree of flexibility for amateurs to operate within the confines of the grid than Kracauer imagined. The amateur maker constructing a tool wall or buying Masonite is the manager of his own de-cluttering aesthetic, existing both within the grid, and outside as its operator.

Making suburbia productive: poultry keeping, 1870–1920

The rest of this analysis of amateur space moves from amateur workstations that are organized, to the types of spaces that amateurs create. Again I challenge the notion, articulated emphatically by Hannah Arendt, that things produced in free time are largely superfluous, unnecessary and unproductive. Like amateur workstations, the spaces that amateurs create are also differential: they mirror other spaces of everyday life while simultaneously stretching or quietly subverting these structures.

The selection of the history of suburban chicken keeping to exemplify the stretched or differential characteristics of amateur space is deliberate. Chicken coops and runs, built in increasing number from the late nineteenth century onwards, were unavoidably productive, showing how occupying amateur space is not passive or unproductive, as we might think. The egg, itself a metaphor for bringing forth life, constituted the valuable and unavoidable 'end goal' that resulted from turning one's garden from a site of leisure or display into a site of production. The chair, table, musical instrument or shelving unit built through amateur labour also demanded levels of diligence, standards of management and a determination to achieve an 'end goal'. Yet the fact that chicken keeping required constant management and produced an easily sellable product with economic value highlights the relationship with normative capitalist rules of production. Success in keeping chickens involved several tasks – building a house and run, cleaning, collecting eggs, preparing hens for exhibition, etc. – that compelled the suburban chicken keeper to be 'more or less a Jack-of-all-trades'.[115] In this instance amateur space constituted a type of training ground for principles of good management, rehearsing and sharpening the skills useful in everyday capitalist life. There was no doubt that keeping chickens was in every sense, the epitome of the productive hobby.

However, chicken keeping only ever verged on total capitulation to structures of commerce, economic efficiency or Taylorist ideas of the rationalization of everyday life, due to the fact that labour-power was retained within the hands of the individual worker, rather than the external capitalist.[116] The division of labour is not replicated but 'miniaturized' within the context of the suburban garden, resulting in distortions of normative modes of production.[117] These are the differential characteristics that I will explore in the historical analysis below: from the tailor-made solutions to managing a brood and the ambivalent attitude suburban chicken keepers often had towards making a profit, to the aestheticization of productive hens.

Context

Chicken keeping became a widespread means of putting the suburban garden to productive use in the late nineteenth century, as shown by the volume of advice manuals, treatises and other publications on the subject that specifically targeted amateur audiences.[118] Several factors contributed to the popularity of keeping hens in confined spaces at this time. For a start the infrastructure that had previously been in place to breed poultry for cock-fighting was re-deployed after the practice was criminalized in 1848, primarily towards breeding hens for exhibition, commonly known as pursuit of 'the fancy'. This practice was already established by the 1850s but by the 1870s rearing hens for exhibition experienced its 'heyday' amongst suburban chicken keepers.[119]

There was also a clear economic rationale for keeping hens. By the latter half of the nineteenth century the costs of maintaining a brood on a confined run no longer outweighed the gains as egg output from a healthy brood would cover the expenses of building a run, with the potential to even undercut the prices in grocery stores.[120] Such contributions to the household economy were particularly attractive given the impact of widespread urbanization that reduced the supply of eggs while demand rose. At this time Britain was relying on imports to satiate the demand for eggs, adding an extra (patriotic) impetus for keeping a brood in the garden.[121] However, the most important contextual factor contributing to the rise in suburban chicken keeping was the growth of suburbia itself and the development of suburban culture.

The pastoral ideal drove the popularity of suburbia from the late nineteenth century onwards; a home at the end of a train line was far away from the poor sanitation, disease, noise, industry and proximity of individuals within the city centre, yet still within reach of its work opportunities. The suburban garden was an important part of this dichotomous construction, setting the 'distinction between public and private spheres' with the areas out front used for display and the backyard used for vegetables and relaxation.[122] The historian Susie Barson hints at the productive potential of the back garden as a place for growing vegetables but not enough scholarly attention has been devoted to the suburban garden as a site of amateur work, reflective of a tendency to forget that a pastoral idyll needs to be maintained during free time.[123] By paying heed to this phenomenon we can start to more fully understand the aestheticization of suburban labouring in the garden, as shown for example in Stanislaus S. Longley's (1933) London Underground poster depicting a city worker's joy in mowing his lawn (Plate 7).

Suburban chicken keeping represented a productive use of one's garden, as one prominent author of late-nineteenth-century practical poultry manuals, Lewis Wright, stated: 'It has been a great gratification to observe the immense increase of this kind of domestic poultry keeping [for eggs] during the last 20 years, as seen especially from any railway, in the small London suburban gardens.'[124]

The poetic image of spotting chicken coops from the train carriage perfectly encapsulates how chicken keeping was a part of suburbia's emerging pastoral ideal. The green patch of land attached to each home[125] was not just a garden for decoration or ornament but a place of industry; a 'backyard' worked productively to produce a specific end with quasi-economic, quasi-aesthetic qualities. The backyard provided the middle classes the chance to engage in husbandry, to exercise Victorian self-help, and be virtuous stewards: a trial run in playing the role of the capitalist manager within a miniaturized realm.

Designing a chicken coop

The smallest area required for the rearing of poultry is cited by most late-nineteenth-century authors of chicken advice manuals as between 4 to 6 feet square and a height of 5 to 6 feet for the house, with an extended separate run (10 to 20 feet long and 4 to 8 feet wide).[126] The average suburban backyard could accommodate such a unit, providing the spatial structure for the creation of a mini farm. In no source is the link between poultry rearing, amateurism and suburbia more explicit than in Chilton-Young's manual *Every Man His Own Mechanic*, where he describes to his readers how to construct the 'Amateur Suburban Fowl House' – an all-in-one do-it-yourself chicken coop construction (Figure 2.11).

Chilton-Young urged backyarders to use their garden's back wall to create one side of a chicken coop,[127] which epitomizes the intrinsic relationship between suburban space and the space of amateur chicken keeping in particular.

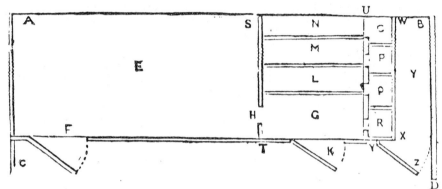

FIG. 506. PLAN OF AMATEUR'S SUBURBAN FOWL-HOUSE.

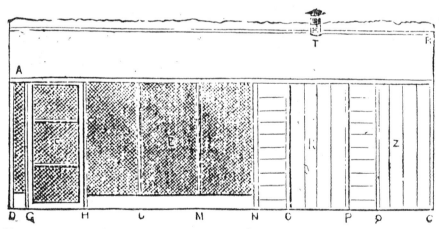

FIG. 507. ELEVATION OF AMATEUR'S SUBURBAN FOWL-HOUSE.

FIGURE 2.11 *Francis Chilton-Young, Plan of Amateur's Suburban Fowl-House. Francis Chilton-Young,* Every Man His Own Mechanic: A Complete and Comprehensive Guide *(1880–1). Microfiche collection of the Hartley Library, University of Southampton. Images reproduced from microfiche of the original source, with permission of ProQuest LLC.*

FIGURE 2.12 *Boulton and Paul advertisement for readymade poultry units. Advertisement at the end of William Bernhard Tegetmeier,* Poultry For The Table and Market Versus Fancy Fowls. With an Exposition of the Fallacies of Poultry Farming *(London: H Cox, 1893).*

Within the suburban plot, the construction of the chicken coop could take many forms. Readymade chicken coops were available from firms like Wrinch and Sons and Boulton and Paul for keepers unwilling to make a coop themselves (Figure 2.12).

These units provided a shortcut to practice but they were criticized for their expense and poor quality.[128] Manuals regularly encouraged amateurs to make chicken houses and runs themselves, insisting that the costs would be much less than buying a fabricated readymade.[129] Constructing one's own chicken house also meant that it could be tailored to the immediate environment, taking into account specific spatial irregularities.

The amateur had to keep three essential requirements in mind when designing a chicken coop: the construction should face south-southwest, both to catch the sun and to shield it against cold northerly winds; the unit should be designed with good ventilation; and should facilitate easy access to all areas to assist regular cleaning. Several how-to manuals suggested that detachable fittings within the chicken house – from the perches to the floor areas – provided the most effective means of ensuring cleanliness.[130] Poor sanitation and draughty houses resulted in sickly hens that were unproductive.[131]

Authors already mentioned in the chapter – Ellis Davidson, Francis Chilton-Young and Lewis Wright – all gave detailed instructions of how to build the efficient comfortable chicken house and run that was easy to clean. Their models were very similar to the one submitted by 'Amateur Woodworker' in an 1882 edition of *Amateur Work*, a wooden skeleton made of lengths of timber connected by butt, tongue-and-groove and various types of halving joints, upon which weatherboarding or wooden panels would be attached (Figure 2.13).

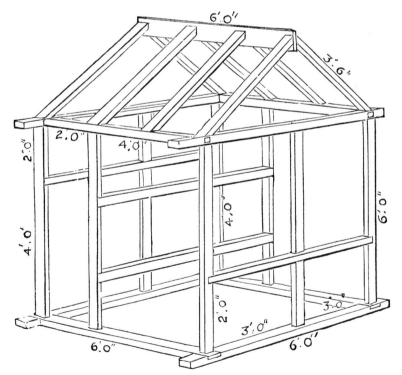

FIG. 2.—SKELETON OF BUILDING, SHOWING LENGTH OF PARTS.

FIGURE 2.13 *Skeleton of chicken hutch in* Amateur Work *(1882). Courtesy of Bodleian Libraries.*

Structured solutions to chicken house construction, like those proposed by 'Amateur Woodworker' were only ever suggestions and belie the variety of approaches to this craft. Many authors encouraged a more *ad hoc* approach, insisting on the importance of tacit knowledge and using what is to hand.[132] Chicken coop construction was far from being an exact science. The words of J. Roach of Kensington reflect a particularly 'bottom-up' approach. To ensure ventilation for a chicken house Roach felt there was no need for specially made (or bought) 'ventilation crowns', holes in the wall or roof would suffice; and in constructing a chicken house he urged his readers to use whatever resources were to hand, explaining that an old out-building, a coal-shed, everyday items of packaging (such as egg or orange boxes from grocery stores), and even a barrel would suffice as accommodation comfortable enough for chickens to live and lay eggs.[133] Chickens clearly did not require sumptuous quarters – Wright observed in the 1880s how chickens were even being kept on flat roof spaces or in attics.[134] From this evidence it is clear that suburban chicken keepers departed from ideal models of construction and developed a variety of different spatial practices for accommodating their broods, from the scientific to the idiosyncratic and impromptu, that treated instruction more as a framework than as the precise answer to particular needs.

Management of the chicken coop

Whatever the motivation for keeping hens, whether for eggs, meat, feathers or breeding for exhibition, enclosing them within confined spaces required constant management. As a bare minimum, manuals stressed the need for routine feeding and a thorough clean two or three times a week.[135] This was often beyond the resources of one individual, compelling the chicken keeper to rely on the labour of others, perhaps another family member, domestic servants or paid outsiders. As a result of this range of tasks involved in keeping chickens, suburban amateur chicken keepers found themselves implementing a miniaturized division of labour with specific tasks allocated to different individuals.

The question of 'who does what' in suburban chicken keeping provides an opportunity to elaborate on the role of men and women in this activity. In line with the stereotypes of pre-enfranchisement gender roles and the concept of Victorian male patriarchy, one might expect the labours of chicken keeping to be broadly in line with the 'sexually polarized way' in which the household was organized, accrediting the man with the more physical 'hard' job of building the coop, leaving the everyday 'soft' maintenance of the dwelling to wives or dependents.[136] However, the phenomenon of suburban chicken keeping reveals subtler permutations of Victorian gender roles.

Advice manuals with sections on chicken house construction were mainly targeted at male amateur carpenters.[137] Yet this did not mean that the job was considered difficult. Chicken house construction afforded the male amateur carpenter the opportunity to test his skills on a project that, even if it failed, would not result in grievous calamity. Davidson stated that making a dwelling for animals is a good starting point for an amateur 'even though he may not yet have acquired the power of making a good mortise joint'.[138] It was a task suited to the enthusiastic novice, a thing to make before attempting more 'important' works, according to Davidson, such as a desk, table and chair, it only required the knowledge of how to use a hammer and nail. Perhaps because of this ease and lack of importance, the chicken coop also offered women the opportunity to learn and utilize certain carpentry skills: Wright stated that he knew certain 'blooming damsels . . . who could perform incredible feats' in the realm of poultry production and maintenance.[139]

There is limited direct evidence, however, that women engaged specifically in chicken house construction: Wright implies that these 'blooming damsels' might have had the resources to employ other labourers. Nevertheless, there are many accounts of successful female management of backyard coops. Miss Edwards was one poultry enthusiast, who rose to prominence and won many prizes in the early 1900s, having only started with twenty hens in her country cottage that she moved into in the 1890s.[140] Other famous female poultry figures included Lady Gwyder who in 1880 had the largest farm of exhibition hens in the whole of Britain at Stoke Park in Ipswich, and Mrs O'Grady from Cork in Ireland who managed to breed 100,000 chickens a year on an acre of land.[141]

These famous examples of female managers of poultry farms are exceptional cases, yet their stories reflect the potential of women to make effective managers of poultry smallholdings. As good management often depended on the labour of others, managers had to delegate, mimicking the behaviour of company bosses. Edith Park, in her manual *Farming For Ladies*, recommended hiring a sharp, willing and able boy for £10 a year; a useful assistant, 'provided the "boss" be he man or woman, possesses the required knowledge, and can see at a glance that things are being done as they should be'.[142] The hiring of specialist assistants or the use of domestic servants in keeping a brood was common, positioning the manager of the coop, who was often the woman of the house, as a director of the labour of others, responsible for control, discipline and pay. This association between domestic life and management suggests the home was more like a micro-factory than a space of aesthetic display, introducing, as Elizabeth Langland states, 'class issues directly into the home . . . setting up the home as a site for the conflicts between labour and management that afflicted the nineteenth century generally'.[143]

However, in line with Davidson and Chilton-Young's message of self-help, poultry manuals did warn against over-reliance on others. As Anne de Salis states: 'I feel sure that if gentlewomen, young or old, were to look after fowls themselves – not trust entirely to servants or paid dependents – and kept good laying breeds . . . there would be no cry of "My fowls are not attempting to lay".'[144]

De Salis's message was that individuals should take it upon themselves to manage effectively, a self-reliant ethos echoed in William Powell-Owen's advice to chicken fanciers: 'Always depend on yourself. Never trust others to do what you should do yourself'.[145] Supporting self-reliant chicken keepers were a whole host of technologies and devices that allowed them to undertake tasks more easily, 'substituting the privately contracted servant for the privately purchased product', as Lupton states in the different context of early-twentieth-century kitchens.[146] Technical inventions, such as Hearson's 'Champion Incubator' (Figure 2.14), available commercially from the late nineteenth century, allowed the chicken keeper to attempt breeding and hatching hens, expanding the 'capability' of the self-reliant amateur, to adopt the language of Shove et al.

Management was a key aspect of keeping hens in the backyard. Chicken keeping provided 'a useful and instructive lesson', according to Lady Arbuthnott (a.k.a. the 'henwife'), instilling 'regularity, tidiness and perseverance',[147] values completely in sync with the Victorian work ethic. Whether harnessing technology or other labourers the backyarder was taught various principles of management, showing skills of construction, perseverance, dedication and delegation. Suburban chicken keeping was imbued with the virtue of making land productive but as a result of its demands managers of backyard coops were compelled to become soft capitalists, in imitation of farmers and businessmen who kept chickens with the specific aim of making a profit.

FIGURE 2.14 *Advertisement for Hearson's 'Champion Incubator'. Advertisement at the end of William Bernhard Tegetmeier,* Poultry For The Table and Market Versus Fancy Fowls. With an Exposition of the Fallacies of Poultry Farming *(London: H. Cox, 1893).*

PLATE 1 *Ballet Dancers '1, 2, 3'. Oil painting set, Craft Master, Palmer Paint Inc. (1955). Paint by Numbers Collection, Archives Center, National Museum of American History, Smithsonian Institution.*

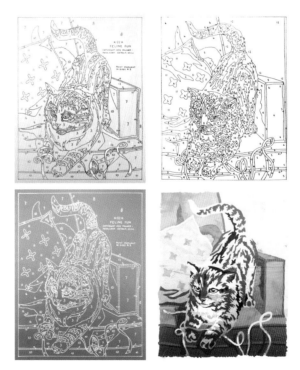

PLATE 2 *Feline Fun. Preparation prints, samples and test runs. Palmer Pann Corp (1955). Paint by Numbers Collection, Archives Center, National Museum of American History, Smithsonian Institution.*

PLATE 3 *Old Sadface Craft Master Kit* (c.1969). *Private collection.*

PLATE 4 *Andy Warhol*, Do It Yourself (Landscape) *(1962). Synthetic polymer and Prestype on canvas. 70×54″. Courtesy Museum Ludwig, Cologne. Photo: © Rheinisches Bildarchiv, Köln, Schlier, Britta.*

PLATE 5 *Jeff McMillan,* The Possibility of an Island *(2008). Image courtesy the artist and PEER. Photo: Stephen White.*

PLATE 6 *James Rigler,* Shed *at Turf Gallery, Westbourne Grove, London (2007). Photograph by James Rigler.*

PLATE 7 *Stanislaus S. Longley*, Gardening by Underground *(1933). © TfL from the London Transport Museum collection.*

PLATE 9 *Eglu Classic by Omlet. www.omlet.co.uk*

PLATE 8 *Harrison Weir, 'Golden-Spangled Polish' from* The Poultry Book *by William Bernhard Tegetmeier (London: George Routledge and Sons, 1867), chromolithograph. Yale Center for British Art, Paul Mellon Collection.*

PLATE 10 *Simon Starling,* Burn Time *(2001). C-print mounted on sintra. 76 × 98.5 cm. Photo: Simon Starling. Courtesy of the artist and neugerriemschneider, Berlin.*

PLATE 11 *Copenhagen Fields. Photograph by Craig Tiley, courtesy of the Railway Modeller.*

PLATE 12 *T. WATSON Modern Dentistry, detail of block of shops in Copenhagen Fields made by Matthew Wald (1985). Photograph by David Mallet.*

PLATE 13 *Grahame Hedges, Stoney Lane Depot (2011). British N Gauge Scale Model 1:148 based on the Southwark/Borough area of South London, during the Network Southeast Era (1986–2000) Photograph by author.*

PLATE 14 *We Work In A Fragile Material*, We Built This City *(2009). Photograph courtesy of We Work In A Fragile Material.*

Profitable but not commercial

The potential to make profit from a voluntarily undertaken activity provides a strong indication of the changing culture surrounding amateur practice in the late nineteenth century. Rather than retracting from the moral value of the amateur activity (as would have been the case for early modern gentleman amateurs), the ability to make money from an amateur activity increased its moral and social standing in the Victorian mind. Keeping chickens in the backyard was the perfect task for the suburban productively minded amateur because hens furnished households with a ready supply of eggs. And through the adoption of some straightforward procedures – such as hatching or buying hens in spring so that they would lay well by the winter when egg prices were at their highest – manual authors insisted that suburban backyarders could easily generate profit.[148]

The writer Kinard Baghot Edwards, who wrote *How the French Make Fowls Pay* (1871), recommended a particularly business-like approach to poultry keeping: 'Fowls should be looked upon as mere machines for converting one material of smaller value into one of greater value.'[149] Edwards's conceptualization of the chicken as a machine seems like a sensible tip for commercial farmers, but her call to rationalize chicken keeping was part of her wider goal to make smallholdings profitable for amateur, farmer and cottager alike. Other authors writing for suburban backyarders also insisted on a business-like attitude when keeping hens. Watts, De Salis and Powell-Owen all discouraged backyarders to look upon their fowl as pets; the latter, who wrote a stream of books in the 1910s about profitable smallholding, advising in *An Income from Backyard Fowls* (1911) that hens should not be kept alive if the costs of keeping them became inversely proportional to their output.[150] There is more evidence of this economic attitude in the world of suburban chicken keeping in this era: the marketing of Poultry World's 'Recorditte' poultry calendar to amateurs – 'the cleverest egg recording card ever'[151] – that documented output and overheads; Watts's discouragement of chicken keepers to add ornamental detail to their fowl houses;[152] and the criticism of managers who keep five to six hens in spaces and accommodation that could house two dozen without any extra expense.[153] These various encouragements from the manual literature all prioritized the need for heightening productivity and demonstrate an understanding of amateur space based on abstract, rational readings, in a similar vein to Taylor's principles of scientific management.

A productive ethos to smallholding and using land productively was clearly a concern during the First World War, which falls within the chronological parameters of this case study. Yet the call to improve the operation and management of coops was just as pressing and economically expedient during periods of relative affluence. According to W. B. Tegetmeier and William Powell-Owen, two other poultry authorities and advocates of making fowls pay, smallholdings were the economically optimum means of egg production either side of the First World War, and they insisted that smallholdings, rather than intensive farming, were the way forward for the industry.[154] Many backyarders, including manual authors Hobs, Wright and Arbuthnott, found commercial success with their backyard enterprises.

However, amateur suburban chicken keeping can be distinguished more broadly from commercial enterprise on account of the way in which the division of labour takes place within this miniaturized realm. In his analysis of Adam Smith's famous account of pin manufacturing, Harry Braverman states that with the division of labour 'not only are the operations separated from each other but they are assigned to different workers', adding that being a capitalist involves first breaking up 'the process' and then the 'dismemberment' of the worker as well.[155] In the context of suburban chicken keeping the amateur does play the role of a manager, breaking down a task into 'operations', and sometimes external labour is deployed. Yet, amateurs do not go as far to fulfil Braverman's second qualification of the capitalist: the dismembering of the worker as well. This is the crucial difference between suburban chicken keeping and overt commercialization. There is a division of labour in management, but the chicken keeper was a soft, or occasional capitalist adopting informal, idiosyncratic procedures: from the use of old barrels as chicken houses and the sentimental relationships keepers developed with their chickens, to the development of Heath Robinson style inventions designed to provide chickens with an early morning meal, and strategies for deterring egg-nappers, such as installation of electric circuits with bell alarms.[156]

The hobbyist-to-business(wo)man narrative shows how initially supplemental forms of income can come to dominate, as Powell-Owen describes in his account of 'progressive' poultry manageresses.[157] Yet the inclination to be efficient and profitable in suburban chicken keeping was not driven purely by the need to be commercially successful. In keeping with the late Victorian work ethic, chicken keepers did not necessarily want the financial gains associated with profit, but rather the satisfaction of being effective managers of resources that the generation of profit indicated. The paradigm of Victorian self-reliance incorporated profit into non-commercial and differential realms of human practice: even the presumed antithesis of amateurism can be absorbed into its psychological texture.[158]

Utility or fancy, or both

Among the diverse array of individuals who kept chickens in their back garden, there were a large number who bred and reared chickens for exhibition in agricultural fairs. Powell-Owen commented that 'countless numbers' of backyarders had taken up fancy chicken keeping since the mid-nineteenth century.[159] The practice was compact – able to fit within the confines of a backyard – and boasted a comparable infrastructure of readymade products, supplies and manual advice as witnessed in the field of utility hens. Lewis Wright's *Illustrated Book of Poultry* (1881), which included coloured plates of various breeds (Plate 8) and information about exhibition 'standards', demonstrates the popularity of the hobby; the book going through twenty editions and reaching circulation figures of 80,000 by the end of the decade.[160]

Using the backyard to rear fancy hens conforms to our expectation of amateur craft practice as a supplemental activity: unproductive, superfluous and ornamental, the complete opposite to the productivity of keeping hens for eggs (or meat). Poultry manuals usually followed this divide, including Arbuthnott who explained that rearing hens for exhibition required the chicken keeper to pour more resources into the bird than he or she would get back: 'Should the farmer be an exhibitor, he must of course, submit to some expense in carrying out his hobby.'[161] Arbuthnott's reference to the cost of keeping hens for exhibition, as well as her use of the word 'hobby', refers back to the eighteenth-century view of amateur practice as an aesthetically accomplished occupation done for enjoyment with little consideration of use or functionality. Indeed, Thorstein Veblen, in *The Theory of The Leisure Class* (1899), positioned 'fancy-bred animals' as the epitomization of a leisure activity; the 'non-productive consumption of time', 'evidence of pecuniary ability to afford a life of idleness'.[162] Alongside the cultivation of manners, learning redundant languages and domestic handicrafts, Veblen situated fancy breeding as a conspicuous display of free time (and therefore wealth). This superfluity of fancy chicken keeping encouraged an association between the practice and fine art. As Arbuthnott stated: 'a modern prize-bird almost merits the character which a Parisian waiter gave of a melon, when asked to pronounce whether it was a fruit or a vegetable. "Gentlemen", said he, "a melon is neither; it is a work of art".'[163]

Arbuthnott's comparison between prize birds and 'a work of art' suggests that the space of fancy chicken keeping is not productive (as argued above) but instead closer to the *fin de siècle* dictum of *l'art pour l'art* and Veblen's concept of conspicuous consumption. It comes as no surprise that Tegetmeier, friend of Charles Darwin, editor of *The Field* ('A Country Gentleman's Newspaper') and author of a string of late-nineteenth-century instruction books on husbandry and domestic economy,[164] criticized this aestheticization of fowls, expressing his preference that poultry keeping be a useful, utilitarian activity.[165] For Tegetmeier, the cultivation of hens primarily for show, which involved cultivating plumage, training a hen to respond to judges and experimental cross-breeding, was an extreme inversion of Darwinian natural selection, where chickens were bred not even with a 'standard of beauty' in mind, with the sole aim to 'prove the extent to which living organisms are variable under the influence of artificial rather than natural selection'.[166] Looking at the Golden-Spangled Polish fowl drawn by Harrison Weir in 1867 (Plate 8), with its feathers cultivated into elaborate bearding that obscured the chicken's vision, it is hard to disagree.

Like Veblen's split between productive labour and conspicuous leisure, Tegetmeier's black-and-white distinction between utility and fancy fowls maps onto a conventional understanding of the function–ornament dichotomy. However, as shown throughout this chapter, the differential status of amateur space complicates such binaries. I have shown how supplemental amateur space has been filled with useful and productive tasks. Similarly, activities that seem completely non-functional and aesthetic, like fancy chicken keeping, have an underlying function that is concealed by their apparent superfluity.

To make sense of the conflation of function and ornament that emerges from 'differential' amateur space, it is necessary to look again to the work of Kracauer. Perhaps the most resonant image in Kracauer's famous essay 'The Mass Ornament' is the parallel he draws between the hands of the factory worker and the legs of the Tiller Girls, as referred to earlier on in the chapter. But the dancing girls are not merely engaged in replicating the action of a machine. Instead, as Kracauer states, 'the mass ornament reveals itself as a mythological cult that is masquerading in the garb of abstraction'.[167] The 'garb of abstraction' – the rationalized bodily movements, the iteration of machinery, a mirroring of homogenous social order – conceals an underlying myth according to Kracauer, a 'rational and empty form of the cult'.[168] The modern mass ornament is no mere addition or add-on but has a crucial function: to channel the irrational, subjective and mythological drivers of human behaviour through the auspices of a reproducible, systematic dance.

What is familiar to both these cultural forms – the mass ornament and amateur labour – is that they both testify to the increasing redundancy of the function–ornament dichotomy. Instead, modern leisure that includes amateur craft practice is characterized by the 'ornamentalization of function and the functionalization of ornament',[169] as cultural theorist and translator of Kracauer's work, Thomas Levin, has stated. Production that derives from amateur labour represents the conflation of the functional–useful and ornamental–superfluous. Examples throughout this chapter have demonstrated this conflation – from Wright's aesthetic appreciation of functioning backyard coops that he saw from the carriage of a suburban train and hyper-localized, customized amateur workspaces to breeding hens for exhibitions.

At first glance fancy chicken keeping might be seen to have an air of pointlessness, but it was a practice that required significant levels of commitment and management. It was a highly constructed expression of whimsy. Fancy chicken keepers were competitive, disciplined and motivated and the exhibition fowl (the 'end goal') was not just an aesthetic object but also a demonstration of the owner's industry, a conspicuous sign of their labour. Winning medals at an agricultural fair did not reflect an abandonment of the idea of achieving a 'return' for one's fowls, but instead a reconfiguration of what this 'return' constituted. The exhibition standard, the labour that goes into preparing fowl for exhibition (including feeding the selected chicken by hand from up high, encouraging the bird to show off 'the smart and shapely appearance' of his feathers as he reaches up for the food[170]), the networks of clubs through which fanciers developed their skills, are manifestations of this functionalization of ornament.[171] Skills learnt within this amateur space were directly transferable, arming the individual to function more effectively within capitalism's structures.

Two final elements of rearing chickens for exhibition attest to its differential quality as a space between ornament and function. The crossbreeding at the heart of fancy chicken keeping that Tegetmeier so disliked for its over-prioritization of aesthetics might have produced bizarre results, but such activities also prompted a mentality of innovation, experimentation and research. Conversely, the seemingly aesthetic distraction could provide an experimental space that resulted in future productive gains – how often is the bedroom desk or amateur shed the site of remarkable discovery. The full extent to which suburban backyard chicken keeping constituted a site of experimentation is open to question, although some manual authors do emphasize these qualities.[172] This potential 'productivity' of distraction can be mapped onto amateur space in general and demonstrates another unexpected 'differential' characteristic.

The dichotomous structure that separates utilitarian egg production from decadent *l'art pour l'art* fancy equivalents can be resolutely undermined by the popularity of one particular breed of fowl: the Black Minorca (Figure 2.15).

FIGURE 2.15 *Image of a Black Minorca Bantam. Photographed by Rupert Stephenson.*

Dubbed the 'working man's fowl' by Powell-Owen, the Black Minorca was hardy, had a long life, was suitable for confined runs and apparently performed well both on the show bench and in the nest box.[173] It was the multi-purpose fowl, simultaneously ornamental and productive. The Black Minorca was the ultimate living proof that the separation between fancy and utility hens was not as entrenched as we might presume. Backyard fanciers *could* make a profit from their hens and backyard utilitarians *could* keep chicken for aesthetic reasons.

The encouragement of chicken keeping in the late nineteenth and early twentieth century – whether fancy or utility – was just one example of a socially useful occupation of newly emergent leisure time. As author Elizabeth Watts, author of *The Poultry Yard*, stated in 1893:

> that undoubted advance in wealth and leisure, which has permeated all sections of the community, and the need for relief from the cares and turmoils of daily labour or business, find its satisfaction in this direction [in suburban poultry keeping]. Hence we see the man of profession or of business, the artisan or the clerk equally in the pursuit with those who are sleeping partners in our great industrial army.[174]

Despite its reputation for alienating the worker, capitalist labour organization also offered a differential space for voluntarily chosen amateur activities of which suburban chicken keeping was just one example. I have argued that amateur space is heterogeneous, complex and should not be reductively classified as unadulterated distraction or escape from the drudgery of labouring, or as a supplemental, ornamental aside. Critical are the links to the spaces of everyday life, one's existence as part of the 'industrial army', as Watts states.

Neither is amateur space a mere reiteration of the structures that condition modern everyday experience. As shown above, amateur space in the modern era involves effective management, yet the ability to employ convoluted production processes; the aim to be profitable while resisting commerciality; applying general advice to local circumstances; and stewardship of the land in partial imitation of early modern husbandry. Far from being a passive occupation of free time, suburban chicken keeping, like other amateur craft practices, has an elastic relationship with other spaces of everyday life. It performs the function of providing a space of suspension from everyday normative capitalist alienation where an individual can direct labour-power towards self-directed goals whatever they may be. Resourcefulness, the ability to experiment, management and delegation, the separation of tasks in a miniaturized form of the division of labour, are all rehearsed in amateur space, providing the amateur the chance to better negotiate the structures of capitalist society.

Chickens and eggs, a complicated story

Out of all the amateur crafts covered in this book, suburban/urban chicken keeping is perhaps the most fashionable at the time of writing. The burgeoning ranks of chicken keepers in the UK – half a million in number in March 2011, according to the Radio 4 documentary 'Attilla the Hen' – attracted by the prospect of a productive pet have propelled the activity into the media limelight.[175] In the US, one prominent advocate, *New Yorker* journalist Susan Orlean, writing in 2000 explained how 'chickens seem to be a perfect convergence of the economic, environmental, gastronomic, and emotional matters of the moment', demonstrating how their multi-functionality endears them as much to twenty-first-century suburbanites as to their nineteenth-century forebears.[176] Similarly, in the UK, the trend has attracted media interest.[177] A rooftop chicken coop is part of a fashionable urban farm in a terraced house in Dalston, East London[178] and the activity even formed part of a 2010 BBC reality television re-enactment of 1970s self-sufficiency called *Giles and Sue Live The Good Life*.

The difference with the current interest, according to dungaree-adorned Sue Perkins, the star of *Giles and Sue Live The Good Life*, is that keeping chickens has become an 'upper middle class accoutrement',[179] part of a swathe of environmentally aware eco-consumerism in which green credentials are traded as signs of social status. While Perkins overlooks how backyard chicken keeping has long played this role as a sign of social status (as Veblen noted in 1899), her words represent the aestheticization of a productive pet. Recent designers have sought to exploit this demand for suburban chicken keeping, most notably Omlet that was formed by a group of graduating Royal College of Art students in April 2004, who developed a range of plastic, portable and ergonomic chicken hutches under the brand name 'Eglu' (Plate 9). The marketing for Omlet's ready-to-use units (sold with readymade hens if needed) plays down their bother, such as noise and smell, and emphasizes the social cachet in having chickens, stating: 'The first your neighbours will know of your pet is when you invite them round for a quiche and tell them proudly that you made it with your own home-grown eggs'.[180] Chicken keeping's entrenchment as a prominent niche within the fashionable market for eco-consumption is confirmed when a sculptural henhouse called the 'Nogg' made from English-grown cedar wood can sell for £1,950 (Figure 2.16).

These chick [sic] readymade houses seek to flatten the irregularities and quirks that arise from making a hen house from scratch. The designs facilitate the quick and easy passage to the pastoral-aesthetic ideal of roving chicken and free-range eggs: the end product is celebrated while the process of getting there and the necessity for everyday maintenance is downplayed. Besides contradicting the green message for simplicity and re-use (as we have learnt, chickens only need a dry, warm and well ventilated space to live) the creation of these easier-to-use, fashionable readymades encourages a distance between the amateur and production processes.

By contrast, artist Simon Starling's interactions with chicken keeping, in the work *Burn Time* (2000), draw direct attention to production processes within amateur space (Plate 10). He exaggerates the often convoluted paths of production of amateur practice rather than fetishizing the slick image of suburban chicken keeping that the Eglu and Nogg designs perpetuate. Of course, the destination for Starling's work is the gallery, and not the broad consumer market that Eglu and Nogg are targeting. But his evocation of hard work, time, complexity, circularity and idiosyncrasy in *Burn Time* better relates to and highlights features of differential amateur space, in particular the roundabout and idiosyncratic procedures often adopted.

Following his signature strategy – 'the very simple model of unpacking something, and then tweaking it a little bit'[181] – Starling situated a classic item of Bauhaus design, the Wilhelm Wagenfeld egg coddler of 1922, at the heart of an investigative history of production. Working down the production line from the egg coddler, Starling built his own chicken house, accommodating hens that would provide eggs for the coddler. Not content to simply use an Eglu or any other readymade suburban chicken unit, Starling's hen house was a scale model of the Ostertorwache building in Bremen built in 1829 by F. M. Stamm, a former prison incorporated into the city's town wall that was converted to the Wilhelm Wagenfeld Museum in the late 1990s. Starling built the neo-classical henhouse from wood picked up from skips near his studio in Dundee and installed the house at Stronchullin Farm in Strone, Scotland, between 31 July and 22 October, 2000. After the chickens furnished Starling with fresh eggs, the artist assembled a stove in the Camden Arts Centre made from discarded bricks from the building, on which he cooked the eggs in the Wagenfeld coddler, using the same timbers that previously provided the chickens their accommodation, as fuel.[182]

FIGURE 2.16 *The nogg. www.nogg.co – Matthew Hayward, Nadia Turan.*

Like many other works by Starling, *Burn Time* is a back-projection of the production process, fragmented and put on view. The materials for making the work were brought to light through their re-use, particularly through their consumption as fuel in the final presentation of the piece, a similar strategy to the one deployed in *Blue Boat Back* (1997) and *Kakteenhaus* (2002). This inversion of the production process is highlighted by the deliberate selection of an inefficient and farcical production process, which offers multiple interpretive pathways through Starling's work. For example, Juliana Engberg points to the association between the Ostertorwache's role as a modern prison that sought to organize nineteenth-century felons according to new methods of surveillance and management, and the contemporaneous economic imperative to develop a poultry industry that depends on the same drive to institutionalize and standardize.[183]

Starling's deliberately eccentric production procedures are redolent of much amateur practice. Amateurs have their own convoluted, inefficient and superfluous processes of production that reflect their subjectivity and freedom from the obligation to produce a defined output. Starling's interaction with chicken house construction is clearly infused with the self-reflexivity, wit and historical research that mark him apart from the average amateur chicken keeper. Yet, like an amateur who often has to laboriously explain the process behind the production of an incongruous object when insisting on its worth to others, an appreciation of Starling's work also demands patience with tentacular narratives. As Katrina Brown states, Starling demonstrates 'an empathy for known but not experienced distant sources',[184] in the case of *Burn Time* pursuing the project with the same diligent attention to process and enthusiasm for making that is central to much amateur practice. This limitless curiosity might have earned him the nickname the 'nutty professor' within the popular art press, but his is a madness shared by many amateurs.[185]

Interactions between artists and amateurs rarely expose the madness, wildness or differential characteristics intrinsic to amateur labour. Despite the increasing importance invested in participation within contemporary art, the artist, when making use of or encouraging amateur labour, rarely relinquishes their position as 'choreographer', or director of others' labour. Famous examples include Judy Chicago's feminist statement, *The Dinner Party* (1979), where the artist maintained a strong element of quality control over the porcelain dishes and embroidery that were produced by amateur hands (to the detriment of the work, according to Laura Meyer)[186] and, more recently, Jeremy Deller's various re-enactment projects from *Battle of Orgreave* (2001) to *Procession* (2009). In these, and many other appropriations of amateur labour by artists, the differential qualities of amateur space are bound by regulating frameworks often set by the artist-as-choreographer.[187]

Instead of engaging directly with amateur makers, Starling's work, and *Burn Time* in particular, reference the differential characteristics that epitomize their relationship to space. As Starling used rudimentary techniques to cobble together recycled materials to create the chicken house in *Burn Time*, it is no surprise that the final output has been described as 'professionally amateur'.[188] Francis McKee deploys this phrase to account for Starling's adept and expert (i.e. professional) use of improvised techniques most commonly associated with the amateur, in order to foreground all the ingredients and mixes that are required in the production of objects. The term has been used to describe Kieran Jones's 'Chicken Project', a Starling-esque effort to transform the leftovers of a cooked chicken (skin and bones) into a bomber jacket and an eggcup from which he eats his eggs.[189] Yet McKee's use of the term 'professionally amateur' to describe Starling is based on an artist's clever appropriation of a presumed quality of amateur practice – the rough and ready, use-whatever-there-is-to-hand mentality of the capitalist bricoleur – and is not viewed from the opposite angle: the perspective of the amateur who aspires to professional standards that I have characterized in some depth above.

While McKee positions Starling as the professional looking down on a variety of amateur practice that he dips into from the perspective of the expert, Brown places Starling on an equal footing with amateurs: 'the self-taught experimental scientist guided as much by feeling, intuition, instinct, visual stimuli and a not inconsiderable degree of pleasure'.[190] Starling is not professionally amateur, but amateurly amateur: his general interest in the ways things are made – the means of production – echoes the amateur's own emphasis on differential processes. Amateur space accommodates a myriad of trajectories of making, all of which are prioritized over the end result, which might be confusing and fail to conform to conventional ideas of a finished product. Starling pays homage to the circuitous, haphazard routes of production intrinsic to amateur space.

This is not to say that utility is unimportant for Starling. As I have argued, the 'professional amateur' describes a middle-class ethos of using time productively with its roots in nineteenth-century self-help. In these contexts, utility and functionality provide the amateur with a pretext to delve into the social lives of objects, learn about their meaning and how they were made – functionalizing ornament and ornamentalizing function. Amateur practice starts with a self-defined functional purpose, an occupation of slack time and space, which acts as a smokescreen to mask its wider economic non-necessity and the convoluted, inefficient production processes that are often pursued. But however superfluous its form or circuitous in its realization, amateur practice always relates back to broader socio-economic mentality. While amateurs mostly confine this re-building of the world to private, domestic contexts, Starling accentuates his status as a dabbler, a jack-of-all-trades, by thrusting this same productive curiosity into the realm of the art gallery.

As a consequence, Starling does more to highlight the unusual dialectics of function and ornament in suburban amateur chicken keeping in *Burn Time* than the various array of kooky, designed henhouses. Whereas the plastic Eglus reflect a trend to see amateur chicken keepers as just another passive market that needs the designer's helpful intervention, Starling's *Burn Time* references the differential status of amateur space, the drive to re-build anew in endless convoluted configurations. He also proved in the process that chicken can live in a wooden scale model of a German museum. The reference is to the amateur's prioritization of process over end product, but the functional output – the egg – continues to play an important role in anchoring practice within prominent social, economic and cultural paradigms of value. In the famous conundrum, it is definitely the egg that comes first for the amateur, but it is what follows that is of most interest.

3

Time

The hobby was often simply an extension of ordinary paid work routine with the crucial modification that routine was replaced by autonomy and choice.

ROSS MCKIBBIN, *IDEOLOGIES OF CLASS* (1990), P. 160

Amateur time is inextricably tied to the notion of 'free' time, defined as the time notionally set aside from the obligation to work. Central to this experience, as described above by social historian Ross McKibbin, is autonomy – the individual freedom to decide how time is spent. Up until now I have looked at production that arises from amateur craft practice: the infrastructures that facilitate it and the ways of producing that emerge. By contrast this chapter focuses on the experience of occupying amateur time, and how the end product that derives from the craft process is subservient to the experience of doing it. As trainspotter John Stretton describes: 'For me the over-riding joy of trainspotting . . . is the peace at the lineside. For some it is fishing, reading or even a Hamlet cigar! But put me at the side of the railway line and I am happy. Almost, there is no need for an actual train, the place is therapeutic enough.'[1]

Although the hobbies Stretton mentions – trainspotting, fishing, cigar smoking and reading – are not crafts in the conventional sense, Stretton's explanation of the near irrelevance of the final result elucidates the prioritization of process over material output that is critical to understanding any practice of amateur craft. The experience of time, in Stretton's case the therapeutic benefits of being close to the railway, is more important than the end result (a notebook containing a checklist of all the trains that pass).

Resources of time and money are poured into amateur craft in order to achieve particular temporal experiences. To analyse them we could plunge into the array of individual accounts of uplifting experiences or therapeutic benefits offered by amateur time, as many scholars have done.[2] However, as McKibbin states above, hobbies – the activities that occupy amateur time – are often 'simply an extension' of everyday work routine. Frankfurt School scholar Theodor Adorno was alert to the clingy co-dependence between free and work time, stating how 'free time is nothing more than the shadowy continuation of labour'.[3] He showed in his essay 'Free Time' (1977) how the 'otherness' of amateur time – whether therapeutic, politically subversive or physical in character – is a condition of its unfreedom. With this critical perspective in mind this chapter assesses whether freedom is possible in amateur time, and what this freedom consists of. In our contemporary environment where every media outlet is full of a thousand and one suggestions on how to spend free time, it is hard to disagree that our decisions on how we spend our free time are determined in some way. Yet I argue that there are distinctive temporal characteristics that distinguish amateur craft: even if exactly the same production procedures used under the conditions of salaried work are replicated in amateur practice, temporal differences arise from the amateur's notional freedom and the essential non-necessity of its undertaking. Amateur time is an extension of other temporal modes, echoing the differential aspect of amateur space, but by dictating the pace and conditions of labour's exploitation, amateurs can create personal, miniaturized utopias and alternative worlds, for a limited time only.

After accounting for constrained freedom of amateur time, with reference to Adorno and Marx, I seek to demonstrate the alternative temporal experiences that emerge from voluntarily undertaken labour, from play to therapy. I will then locate these experiences in the particular amateur craft of railway modelling. Analysis of the craft provides an opportunity to expand on propositions made in opening parts of the chapter, concerning amateur craft's differential status, its utopian leanings and the different ways it stretches normative temporal structures.

The distinctive temporality of amateur craft practice and its uniqueness have proved particularly attractive to artists and designers aiming to mine this fertile terrain of experience. In line with the other chapters, I conclude with case studies from contemporary art and design practice to analyse how various groups of artists and designers have occupied amateur time and the ways in which this sideways movement has the potential to rejuvenate practice. Empathetic observation of amateur time prompts a consideration of the temporal qualities of amateur craft practice and outlines why contemporary art and design practice should take heed of amateur experience in light of art's ever-increasing democratization.

Is free time free?

A key theoretical tension that helps us frame amateur time is whether it can be characterized as permitting genuine freedom. Amateur practice takes place in 'free' time, the time outside salaried labour, where Marx states the labourer feels 'at home', in stark contrast to the alienation suffered when he is compelled to make objects that satisfy others' needs.[4] Although Marx used the term 'amateur' pejoratively to describe a political opponent (see Chapter 2), there is a domestic, hobby-like quality to Marx's vision of a utopia of freely undertaken labour.[5] Once the necessity of human subsistence was taken care of by socialized forms of labour organization, an individual could 'hunt in the morning, fish in the afternoon, rear cattle in the evening, criticise after dinner, just as I have a mind, without ever becoming a hunter, fisherman, cowherd or critic'.[6]

Marx was optimistic about the fate of the labourer (Hannah Arendt's *animale laborans*), arguing in *The German Ideology* that once freed from the pressure of subsistence the energies previously spent working would be directed towards 'higher goals'. As discussed in the last chapter, Arendt and thinkers who follow her trajectory see no evidence to back up this optimistic viewpoint because amateur production was considered to be imitative and superfluous. As shown in Chapter 2, Arendt too quickly ties the quality of temporal experience with the need to produce things that, in her eyes, are genuine, valorised additions to the human artifice. The account of the trainspotter above shows how an individual might produce things of little significance, and even openly admit that fact, but the experiences that arise from such inane production can be akin to boundless freedom. This is the question though: how free is this freedom and what is its inherent nature?

Adorno's provocative assertion that 'free time is shackled to its opposite'[7] constitutes an approximate equivalent to Arendt's thesis in the temporal dimension: in the process of succumbing to the cyclical biological necessity for endless production and consumption, the *animale laborans* spends free time engaging in activity that ensures further entrapment rather than a release from conditions of capitalism. Adorno states: 'Free time depends on the totality of social conditions, which continues to hold people under its spell. Neither in work nor in their consciousness do people dispose genuine freedom over themselves.'[8] Adorno echoes Marx's thoughts on alienation as being ruled over by a totalizing inhuman power, but he directs his critique specifically against those leisure activities that are presumed to be free. Going to the gym, visiting the Eiffel Tower, making a shed in the garden, and the entire gamut of possible uses of free time all in some way serve the interest of capital, fuel a market, or commodify an activity. This is the sophistication of late capitalism, according to Adorno. The abundance of free time made possible by increased productivity is neutralized by convincing individuals that they are in control of how this excess time is used, whereas in fact their desires, wants and longings are shaped by the institutional and social expectations underpinned by capitalist production. He adds that free time is only given once the imaginations of workers are sufficiently quashed, rendering them incapable of using this time effectively. This results in boredom, the continuation of bodily labour through competitive sports that ensures the ongoing fitness of workers, or the facile pursuit of the commodity fetish (he cites the example of women going on holiday to get a tan rather than be with their fellow man).[9]

It is within this context that Adorno criticizes hobbies as an engagement with mindless infatuations that exist 'in order to kill the time' that, in classic academic style, he resolutely distances himself from ('I have no hobby').[10] Adorno, as a theorist, takes his work very seriously and refutes the conventional work–leisure bifurcation by insisting that everything he does fits in with his overall vocation – academic labour. In contrast, the hobby industry, like the leisure industry, is a 'continuation of the forms of profit-oriented social life', according to Adorno.[11] Instead of leading to a possible utopia, amateur labour taking place in free time confirms the capitalist colonization of all aspects of life as the labour undertaken in free time mimics the alienated conditions of normative capitalist work.

Despite Adorno's scepticism he does suggest that society 'cannot have it all its own way' in free time, hinting at the possibility of some form of release from capitalist structures. Yet this enlightenment in free time depends on what he refers to as 'maturity' (*Mundigkeit*), a specific ability to critique, through exacting erudition, the illusory nature of capitalism's edifice. His example is the self-critical reflection on how spectators 'consumed and accepted' Princess Beatrix of Holland's televised wedding whilst not quite believing in what they saw.[12] Adorno is clearly sceptical that amateur makers can reach such levels of criticality: 'What they [amateurs – *Freizeitler*] create has something superfluous about it. This superfluousness makes known the inferior quality of the product, which in turn vitiates any pleasure taken in its production.'[13]

Adorno's standard of maturity privileges his own conception of freedom as the self-realization of existence within the negative dialectics of capitalism, all the while bemoaning the way in which people spend their free time. Adorno's analysis, like Arendt's, too heavily weighs on the material thing produced at the end of amateur production rather than the different experiences of time that take place while making. Pleasure arises in amateur practice despite the 'inferior', slavish imitation of pre-given styles; indeed, from railway modelling to furniture restoration and embroidery the accuracy of the copy often is the barometer by which success and gratification is measured. Adorno might lament the spuriousness of hobbies based on the material content that is generated by them, but this spuriousness, marginality and political irrelevance can produce alternative temporalities within structures of modernity. As argued in Chapter 2, investigation of amateur craft demands a departure from judging the quality or content of production and a greater consideration of the alternative temporal experiences that arise in the course of making.

Adorno's identification of the constraints of free time is critical in my attempt to conceptualize the bounded freedom of amateur time. Other twentieth-century Marxist scholars also recognize such constraints: for example, Braverman's assessment of autonomy within the workplace where management 'deliberately leaves insignificant matters open to choice'[14] can be analogized to free time, where individual selection of one's hobbies is an unimportant choice that merely gives the illusion of control. Jean Baudrillard also claimed the 'ideology of freedom is the weak point in our Western rationality, including Marxism'.[15] These scholars, influenced by Marx, help critique overly optimistic assessments of the character of amateur time as an individualistic, antagonistic (and anti-capitalist) release. But there is something unique about temporarily taking control of one's labour-power and alternative experiences of time (time-states) can emerge that stretch, exaggerate or highlight everyday reality: invention, critical thought and play.

Homo ludens and *homo faber*

Chief among the alternative temporal modalities generated by amateur practice is the experience of play. One would expect that amateur time surely involves play, given the voluntary nature of its undertaking and the expectation that humans would seek to fill excess time with enjoyable, pleasurable tasks. Yet interrogation of the notion of play within the discipline of sociology helps elucidate its more complex relationship with amateur practice. Critical to an understanding of play are Johan Huizinga's four key qualifications set out in his 1950 work, *Homo Ludens*. He states that play is voluntary; essentially superfluous because it can stop at any time; is not 'real' or 'ordinary', in that it requires its participants to 'play along' or 'pretend'; and is limited to specifically ordained times and spaces, such as the playground or moments of recreation during the working week.[16] Huizinga distances play from the concept of a pure child-like innocence towards a more nuanced understanding of play as embedded in culture. Even in the purest acts play is bounded by rules, and Huizinga emphasizes the centrality of play as a social function: 'It adorns life, amplifies it, and is to that extent a necessity both for the individual – as a life function – and for society by reason of the meaning it contains, its significance, its expressive value, its spiritual and social associations.'[17]

In many respects, Huizinga's concept of play shares affinities with Lefebvre's celebration of the carnival as an interruption to everyday life that seems to depart from its foundations only to affirm the everyday more powerfully. As Huizinga states, play is 'an intermezzo, and *interlude* in our daily lives. As a regularly recurring relaxation, however, it becomes the accompaniment, the complement, in fact an integral part of life in general'.[18] For Huizinga, music fulfils the essence of play, alongside dance and other elements of medieval court culture. Lefebvre also used musical metaphors in his lifelong effort to determine a methodology appropriate to locating the freedom and wonder manifest in everyday life, whilst being aware of the very real limitations that everyday life operates under. In his last work, *Rhythmanalysis* (posthumously published in 1992), Lefebvre constructed a methodology called 'rhythmanalysis', which involved the metaphorical translation of the various activities of everyday life into musical 'presences', each with a particular rhythm that possesses its own interior logic as well as the ability to co-exist with multiple surrounding harmonies.[19] The disciple of this new science, the 'rhythmanalyst', is able to discern the co-existence of multiple rhythms, both social and biological, and read the harmonies that result. The carnival, according to Lefebvre, is the point at which these rhythms coalesce.

Huizinga and Lefebvre use these musical metaphors to foreground a temporal modality within which play and differentiality can be situated without breaking or interrupting the dominant harmony of everyday life. Both thinkers are attracted by the notion of alternative temporal experience (play and the carnival) that is bounded by rules but is never the same twice, thus providing an opportunity for individuals to deconstruct the world – the mechanics of social, political and economic reality – only to recreate them again. Henricks, in his monograph on play, emphasizes this feature: 'To play fully and imaginatively is to step sideways into another reality, between the cracks of ordinary life. . . . Like wilful children, they unscrew reality or rub it into their bodies or toss it across the room. Things are dismantled and built anew.'[20]

Play, as conceived by Huizinga, conveniently maps onto Lefebvre's notion of differential space, and seems to reflect the experience of amateur craft: both are voluntary types of performance, bound to various spatial parameters – the home workshop, shed, etc. – and are superfluous compared with other practices of everyday life. However, Huizinga resolutely denies that there is any play in the practice of plastic arts, stating that the artist's 'inspiration may be free and vehement when he "conceives", but in its execution it is always subject to the skill and proficiency of the forming hand'.[21] The plastic arts transform free, potentially playful ideals into grounded material reality. The production of objects is inherently bound to the material world and hierarchies of skill, and therefore runs counter to Huizinga's expectation that play should have an 'unreal' quality.

Friedrich Schiller, an earlier theorist of play, did not confine play to the immaterial, commenting on the play-drive inherently on view when lifeless marble is carved into 'living form'.[22] However, Huizinga's separation of play from the objecthood inherent to the plastic arts conforms to the expectation that play purely occupies the realm of immaterial human interaction, whereas craft, or the making of things, solely involves the relationship between person and object. This serves to create an abyss between constructions of the *homo ludens* and the *homo faber*. Yet amateur time often incorporates elements from both of these human behaviours. In accounting for the complexity of amateur experience of time it is right that we examine how these instincts interconnect and map onto each other. Key is the idea that play constitutes an alternative temporality within the everyday (not against it) that is bound by cultural and social rules, which individuals can voluntarily move in and out of, as well as modify and adapt. The making that takes place in this temporal zone leads to temporary and differential experiences of time.

Critique of the atemporal construction of amateur time

The main conceptual barrier to elaborating on the particular experience of amateur craft is, once again, the intellectual discourse that venerates the *homo faber*. John Ruskin, William Morris, Martin Heidegger, Arendt and, more recently, Richard Sennett, all, in their various ways, privilege the idea that making, if done properly, can lead to an unalienated, atemporal relationship between person and object. Their collective idealism surrounding the *homo faber* is perhaps best summed up by mid-nineteenth-century transcendentalist Henri Thoreau's maxim that 'into a perfect work time does not enter'.[23] Their writing has encouraged a perception that all forms of craft, including well executed amateur craft, have the potential to lead to a utopian atemporal experience. Craft's presumed affiliation with some sort of antithetical standpoint, a utopian (often pastoral) alternative to the regularized time and complexity of the modern world, has fuelled cultural expressions as varied as William Morris's *News*

From Nowhere (1890), Eric Gill's early twentieth-century neo-medieval Guild of St Joseph and St Dominic in Ditchling, East Sussex, and contemporary alternative craft fairs with their global appeal.[24] The expectation is that craft allows for a simpler, more authentic experience, closer to the uncomplicated relationship between humans and nature and pre-civilization, child-like innocence.

Recent craft theory, by Glenn Adamson in particular, has challenged these dominant anti-modern, pastoral, nostalgic and romanticized expectations that are placed on craft.[25] Amateur craft is not purely a retroactive or progressive utopian mode, either recalling a pristine past or contributing to a reformed 'brave new' future, as many amateurs might claim. The partial or temporary quality of amateur time has more in common with Fredric Jameson's conceptualization of utopia as an impulse 'finding its way to the surface in a variety of covert expressions and practices', that depends on, and feeds back into, existing social reality.[26] For Jameson, in *Archeologies of the Future* (2005), these 'covert expressions' were post-war American science-fiction novels, but his nuanced understanding of utopia as cultural expression rather than as an alternative political reality is helpful when making sense of amateur time. Yet before moving on to how this partial and temporary utopian impulse manifests itself, it is important to criticize two recent intellectual incarnations of the expectation that craft can lead to a form of atemporal release.

Utopia in a moment

Ask any craftsperson, amateur or otherwise, when they enjoy their making the most and the reply is likely to contain reference to entering 'the zone', or a state of 'flow'. The psychologist Mihaly Csikszentmihalyi famously used the latter term as the title of book in which he describes 'flow' as 'the way people describe their state of mind when consciousness is harmoniously ordered, when an individual pursues an activity for its own sake'.[27] At first glance Csikszentmihalyi's concept of 'flow' – an 'autotelic experience' of immersion, when 'nothing else seems to matter'[28] – seems to effectively describe the amateur experience of time, when an individual becomes so devoted to the voluntarily chosen activity that time flies and the tea that has been prepared becomes cold. Contemporary scholars who have studied the motivations for amateur craft often make reference to their ability to enter this 'flow' state.[29] We could describe this as utopia in a moment: an atemporal release and liberation from capitalist time and its schedules by intense concentration on an activity.

However, we need to be alert to the links between Csikszentmihalyi's praise of 'autotelic experience' and the structures that he considers such experiences to be dependent on. Csikszentmihalyi argues that, in order to achieve the meaningful benefits of flow, time has to be ordered through the imposition of rules and objectives that allow individuals to strive, achieve and start again, operating in much the same way as productivity targets in the well-oiled modern Taylorist workplace. For example, Csikszentmihalyi explains that 'mowing the lawn or waiting in a dentist's office can become enjoyable provided one restructures the activity by providing goals',[30] suggesting that the only way to inject time with meaning is to subject it to miniature, goal-driven teleologies – a competitive temporal model. His insistence on the desirability of 'optimal experience', when external factors (what he terms 'psychic entropy') are removed,[31] echoes the prioritization of securing individual isolation and autonomy from the external social world in achieving a sense of happiness. This is an existential philosophy purged of Sartrean self-doubt and acknowledgement of the social that simply serves to reinforce dominant paradigms of capitalist temporality.

Clearly this goal-driven temporal modality is evident in amateur practice, particularly in the realm of sport. It is no surprise that Csikszentmihalyi cites examples from sports and physical exertion to substantiate his concept of flow.[32] In theory, sports are akin to play, offering a parallel universe, but in the modern era they do not disrupt normative temporal modalities but serve to amplify them. The disorder of sporting activity is bounded by a framework – the rules, regulations and competitions – that facilitate the 'enjoyable and controlled de-controlling of emotions' and, as Henricks explains 'playful energy' is channelled into contests that 'seem consistent with the spirit of an economically competitive society'.[33] For all the presumed escapism of sport – the chance for physical exertion, play, camaraderie – there is a clear extension of the same temporal parameters that define everyday life: the 'sportization' of time.

Csikszentmihalyi's concept of 'flow' epitomizes the 'sportization' of time, reflecting the subtle reinforcement of competitive, capitalist notions of work by subterfuge. The dream-like 'autotelicism' of flow provides only a limited explanation of amateur experience because it is too directed towards successful accomplishment of a goal, rather than the multiplicity of temporal modes within amateur craft that include non-flow-like states, such as struggle, repetition, obsession. Flow is just one temporal modality among others and cannot claim atemporal status.

The programmatic utopia of unalienated labour

> For anyone who still remembers Karl Marx's sketch of full communism's Utopia, the amateur railway life-world looks remarkably like that dream of unalienated labour.
>
> IAN CARTER, *British Railway Enthusiasm* (2008), p. 264

If Csikszentmihalyi's notion of 'flow' reflects the seductive notion of achieving an isolated atemporal experience through amateur practice, the utopia of unalienated labour is about the attraction of a broader, social atemporality. Notional freedom from top-down structures, the voluntary nature of practice and sensitivity to local environments, has meant amateur time is often charged with programmatic utopian political potential, a vehicle through which to express a critical discursive position, whether feminist, traditionalist or environmentalist.

Ever alert to the utopian possibilities of unalienated labour, many practitioners in the fields of art, craft and design have been drawn to the presumed freedom offered by amateur time, particularly given the exhaustion of other utopian possibilities. This has led to over-optimistic appropriations of amateurism; amateur time is associated with necessarily antagonistic positions that have more to do with the programmatic intentions of the artist than the nuances of amateur practice itself. As John Roberts has noted: 'The artist claims to be an amateur or identifies with the amateurish only insofar as he or she does not want to be seen as a particular kind of professional.'[34] In many instances it is the unattractiveness of the term 'professional', with its connotations of conformity, a lack of inventiveness and doing things 'by the book', that leads artists and designers to appropriate amateurism, believing it to be representative of unalienated labour.

One example of this use of amateurism to signify a strongly discursive critical position was shown in the event series 'Masters of Amateurism' (2009), run by the Amsterdam-based Platform for Design and Fashion, Premsela. The project managers, Roel Klaassen and Bart Heerdink, outlined their goals at a conference on digital design held at Harvard University in April 2009:

We would like to argue that design as we know it has ceased to exist. As digital technology has matured and found its way into design practice, so has the public. People have begun resisting being mere bystanders and consumers of marketing messages and pre-chewed messages . . . In taking a share of design practice, amateurs are challenging the position of design professionals.[35]

Klaassen and Heerdink's prophesy of the end of 'design as we know it' is reflective of a common utopian trend, according to Jameson: a 'combination of closure and system, in the name of autonomy and self-sufficiency'.[36] Throughout the paper, Klaassen and Heerdink over-emphasize the autonomy of the amateur, positing this figure within narratives of 1960s counter-cultural subversion, DIY, punk and 'hacker' movements.[37] The intent is to marry amateur practice with the political agency of movements that operate on the 'fringes of the mainstream'.

This reading of amateur craft as subversive has been a feature of the critical discourse, particularly since the 1970s when scholars like Lucy Lippard interpreted everyday, mundane and unspectacular craft practices as sites of feminine agency. Lippard argued that feminists should be interested in domestic handicrafts and how-to books countering the presumption of their political irrelevance. She likened the grid in embroidery kits to the 'underlying grid' of modern art.[38] In *The Subversive Stitch*, Roszika Parker argued that embroidery was a site of feminine self-expression over the course of many centuries despite the patriarchal and social-cultural expectations from without that determined the framework in which the craft operated.[39]

The work of Lippard, Parker and Felski has been critical in re-evaluating amateur craft production and criticizing its presumed irrelevance within patriarchal discourse. Within the discipline of design history, 1970s feminist discourse has prompted both a reassessment of the position of women in the production of the domestic interior and their role in design reform movements, like late-nineteenth-century Arts and Crafts.[40] It also is a critical trajectory that underpins the recent 'Craftivism' movement, coined by Betsy Greer to describe how knitting, practising embroidery or a range of other handicrafts 'has become a valid and effective means to critique capitalism'.[41] Craftivism is not alone in attributing a radical quality to amateur practice: Joost Smiers and writer Aram Sinnreich, two contributors to the Masters of Amateurism series, established a critique of commercial methods of intellectual property by invoking the amateur; and London's Amateurist Network (active between 2010 and 2013) used the term to critique the notion of immaterial labour that abounds in contemporary art practice.[42] Driven by Morris's idea that craft production could be an agent of social change, amateur craft is often seen as a byword for all sorts of subversive (with a big 'S') counter-cultural trends among contemporary practitioners, from politically motivated yarnbombing to Victor Papanek-style 'real world' local manufacture, and this is despite the very clear scepticism shared by Morris and his circle of the quality and value of domestic handicrafts.[43]

These recent appropriations of the term 'amateur' often seem driven by concerns that have little to do with amateur practice itself – notably, the unattractiveness of the label professional, and new contexts of digital design technology. While it is true that the recent popularity of embroidery, knitting, crochet, etc., has served to rejuvenate artistic practice and resulted in some powerful political statements, such as Marianne Jørgensen's anti-Iraq war statement *Pink M.24 Chaffee* (2006) – a knitted cosy placed on top of a Second World War tank produced in collaboration with the Cast of Knitters[44] – they do not reflect the broad range of amateur experiences of time. 'Amateur' has become almost a byword for opposition, its power almost exaggerated by the presumption that it is twee, quaint and parochial. Nothing is more shocking than embroidery containing swear words, unsettling our expectations of the gentility of this activity.[45]

Amateur craft can contain this discursive potency as these examples demonstrate, but it can equally be about the absence of any message, individual narrative or overt self-expression. Compliance, invisibility, privacy and submission are among the temporal modes of amateur practice. For example, Jenni Sorkin has shown how the artist and friend of Marcel Duchamp, Beatrice Wood, assumed the guise of a 'coquettish amateur' by under-emphasizing the worth of her artistic talent and stressing her position as the female among the group of *avant garde* artists: a 'wilful subordination', Sorkin describes, that offered 'freedom precisely through diminishment'.[46] In a more everyday context, Alice Walker celebrated the invisibility of her mother's amateur craft – gardening – in her 1984 book *In Search of our Mother's Gardens*: 'I notice that it is only when my mother is working in her flowers that she is radiant, almost to the point of being invisible – except as Creator: hand and eye. She is involved in work her soul must have.'[47] Walker's example of her mother helps describe an alternative temporal modality of making with very limited self-reflection that must be key in any analysis of amateur time, 'a revolution staged in the least conscious domain of culture',[48] as Glenn Adamson has written. At this moment Walker's mother is not engaging in any act of rebellion or any overt statement of individual self-expression, neither is it flow – directed towards a goal-orientated end.

We could argue that this everydayness or compliance is emptied of any sense of subjectivity, but Walker's mother is still engaged in processes that involve skill and making. Her crafting can be described as the wilful subjugation to a structure of work. Georges Perec's metaphor of the puzzle-solver, in the introduction of his book *Life: A User's Manual*, is useful here. Completing a puzzle does represent some kind of subjugation to the puzzle's designer: like a paint-by-number or embroidery kit, every step has been planned in advance. Each act that joins one piece of the puzzle to another involves a degree of skill, yet becomes invisible in relation to its ongoing completion.[49] This metaphor is helpful in describing how a proactive craft practice can be channelled into a completely determined and invisible activity. The completion of a kit can communicate personal narratives, psychologies and subtle political messages or signs, and going over the lines is always seen as a marker of subjective expression. Yet there can be other experiences of amateur making that fall outside these characteristics where self-critical thought diminishes and subjective agency becomes increasingly thin.

Perhaps the idea of repetition best characterizes this space of amateur craft that is bereft of agency: exactly copying a kit and keeping within its lines merely repeats someone else's design. Again, Henri Lefebvre proves useful in providing the critical tools to approach this subject with empathy. In *Rhythmanalysis* Lefebvre presents the truism that A = A, but does not see this as plain equivalence as we might expect, but a demonstration of difference in repetition: the second 'A' is different for being second in the order of As. He concludes: 'Not only does repetition *not* exclude differences, it also gives birth to them; it produces them.'[50] Lefebvre's conclusion that difference happens within a model of repetition helps further our understanding of amateur time and chimes with Felski's proposition that 'repetition can signal resistance as well as enslavement.'[51] Amateur experience is often far more imitative, reliant and devoid of subversive political content than many of its advocates care to admit. However, this repetition involved in following a pattern still 'gives birth' to difference but it is a difference that only makes the weakest incursions into the discursive realm.

The example of Walker's mother highlights the quiet, invisible and politically muted temporal experience of amateur craft that is often not reflected in contemporary understanding of amateur craft due to the tendency to attribute agency to this act of making. In a recent article for *Design and Culture*, Fiona Hackney coins the phrase 'quiet activism' to describe amateur craft practices, but her emphasis is on the potential of amateur craft as a site of individualistic expression and as a direct alternative to existing forms of association and making.[52] Although Hackney frames amateur craft as 'quiet activism' it is clear that she perceives craft activities as containing an activism of sorts as shown by her reference to Craftivism, de Certeau's *la perruque* and Matthew Crawford. This is another example of how critical attention ignores the much broader range of experience within amateur craft that departs from the idea that it is a conduit for powerfully subjective individual expression.

As noted above, Ian Carter states that the amateur railway modelling world 'looks remarkably like' Marx's dream of communist utopia, suggesting similarity between amateur craft and utopia, not equivalence. Key differences do remain. Amateur time can, of course, include both the competitive temporal modality suggested by Csikszentmihalyi, and the political purposefulness often invested in it, but the plurality of amateur experience cannot be reduced to these two theoretical trajectories alone. Amateur time often lacks discursive power, is more discrete, compliant, weak, temporary and dependent, closer to Jameson's understanding of utopian constructions: 'an aberrant by-product . . . its possibility dependent on the momentary formation of a kind of eddy or self-contained backwater'.[53] Amateur time has an elusive quality and does not fully satiate the dream of non-alienated labour but instead offers the possibility for temporary control of one's own labour alienation. Utopianism in amateur time is constrained and it is these limitations that ensure its differential status.

This slippage between utopian possibility and actuality will be kept in mind as I analyse the craft of railway modelling. For the moment, however, the status of amateur time can be described only as partially utopian. It is not the time in which a complete escape from a disenchanted capitalist world is possible, but the chance to temporarily control the means of one's own labour alienation. Like play, amateur time is temporary, constrained and reliant; it is an impermanent temporal displacement.

Amateur time as displacement: 'the busman's holiday'

In conceptualizing amateur time, the idea of displacement proves more useful than any of the options above: whether Adorno's demand for critical self-reflexivity, Arendt's valorization of the *homo faber*, Csikszentmihalyi's emphasis on 'sportization', or contemporary commentators who place amateur craft as some form of subversive opposition. The sole thing that unites the plurality of amateur craft practice is the temporal mode of displacement: that it takes place during 'time left over' from other activities. This framing of amateur time encapsulates its inherently strong relationship to the structures that define and pace everyday life, as well as the particular quality of its departure from these same structures. This limited temporal freedom arises from the fact that amateurs control the conditions of their own alienation for a while – the individual choosing to engage in work of his or her own devising. Amateur time is still the freest temporality available in modern capitalism – it might appear to signal the continuation of work during free time, but it allows some form of suspension of normative temporal conditions.

The displaced condition of amateur time is aptly described by the phrase 'busman's holiday', which describes the situation when an individual spends holiday or 'free' time engaged in a similar activity to his or her work.[54] The phrase originates from the idea of a bus driver spending his holiday on a bus or coach, but it is pertinent to all professions: concert musicians who compose independently or play a different instrument in their free time, businessmen making deals on the golf course, politicians extending their influence by accepting holiday invitations from foreign statesmen,[55] a whole range of ways of spending time that has a tie to one's everyday vocation. Although individuals might replicate skills, abilities, and behaviours inherent to their everyday vocation, the busman's holiday represents some kind of temporal suspension and occupies a differential realm of culture.

Analysis of a hypothetical busman on a holiday might reveal a number of different experiences outside a mere continuation of sensations experienced whilst working to the normal timetable. For example, a busman riding a tour bus might derive great pleasure by seeing someone else do his job and delight in the passivity of being a passenger with someone else in control, or he might criticize and bemoan the driver's lack of skill. Another scenario might situate the driver as driving the bus himself as he would whilst at work but with the difference that he is free from having to observe a timetable, a set route, health and safety standards, perhaps driving his own heritage bus or transporting friends to a holiday destination.

The busman's holiday describes the state of displacement inherent to amateur time while maintaining a link to one's other everyday experiences. An individual does not completely 'switch off' in free time, as we might presume, but continues to engage with the skills, tools and mentalities that are familiar to vocational practice. Once again the comparison to Jameson's description of the science-fiction novel is useful; amateur time is similarly 'momentarily beyond the reach of the social', politically powerless, but nevertheless a zone 'in which new wish images of the social can be elaborated and experimented on'.[56] The displaced condition of amateur time facilitates multiple alternative temporalities that constitute an elaboration, exaggeration and extension of normative experience, which subsequently feeds back into social reality. I aim to account for some of these differential time-states in the course of the case study that follows on amateur railway modelling.

Amateur railway modelling

[The train] is the embodiment of the age, an instrument of power, speed, noise, fire, iron, smoke – at once testament to the will of man rising over natural obstacles, and, yet, confined by its iron rails to a pre-determined path, it suggests a new sort of fate.

LEO MARX, *Machine in the Garden* (1964), p. 191

In no other product of industrialization is humankind's relationship with technology so ambiguous. As Leo Marx demonstrates in *Machine in the Garden*, the steam locomotive has been the subject of literary scepticism with writers both wary of its Promethean power in setting and regulating the pace of modern life, while welcoming its ability to be part of the 'middle landscape', the idealistic balance between technology and nature. Henri Thoreau, during his self-sufficient isolation in the woods at Walden in the mid nineteenth century, clearly seeks the distance from all forms of industrialization but concedes his dependence on the railway track as a pathway to the nearby village, unavoidably linking him to the society he attempts to turn away from.[57]

Like Thoreau, countless amateurs attempt to cut all ties to social and economic reality in an effort to exercise their own autonomy, and experience the 'hard touch of things',[58] but they similarly cannot sever the direct links that connect them back to the structures of capitalism that they have sought to efface. In no hobby is this clearer than in amateur railway modelling, where the very subject of the amateur's attention is the prime symbol of virile modernity, the machine that introduced regularized notions of time and contributed to worldwide economic expansion. The attraction of setting model locomotives within a miniature landscape might initially seem purely sentimental, nostalgic and pastoral, yet the motivations for pursuing the activity are more complex. As I will show, railway modelling is the epitome of a constrained utopia, a vehicle through which subjective desire and technical skill are manifest, which is nonetheless beset on all sides by various structuring mechanisms. These structures are self-imposed and also reflect a very particular relationship to time. For example, modellers often set ambitious targets where accuracy and detail are paramount, more important than finishing a piece within a particular timespan. It is the experience of time while making rather than the end product that is prioritized. This temporal structure generates differential, rather than alternative, experiences: railway modelling exemplifies how amateur time represents an extension, distortion or stretching of everyday reality, rather than a rejection of such structures outright. In this case study I aim to describe the differential time-states that arise from crafting one's own universe. However, I first account for the history of railway modelling – rooted in the acquisition and demonstration of mechanical skill – and the dialectics of superfluity and functionality that are essential to understanding this hobby.

Neither prototypes nor toys: the origins of railway modelling

The history of railway modelling has its roots in the more tangibly productive activity of using locomotive models as prototypes. Miniaturized scale engines provided engineers, like the famous James Watt, an inexpensive means of experimenting with mechanisms intended for their prospective, real-sized equivalents. In one of the earliest manuals on building model locomotives, the 1888 book *Model Engine-making*, John Pocock speculated: 'Who can say but that the model-maker of to-day may be a second James Watt to-morrow?'[59]

When modelling steam engines emerged as a late-nineteenth-century pastime it was often described as 'instructive amusement',[60] echoing the purposive Victorian work ethos that I described in Chapter 2. *The Model Engineer and Electrician* (1903–24) was one journal that encouraged its readers to build working models of steam engines, but *Amateur Work* and *Design and Work* also ran instructive articles on this subject. Building a model locomotive demanded high levels of competence and typically involved the construction of working steam engines, complete with boiler, piston, cylinders and wheels and axles. Often these were 'scratch-built', which meant that they were entirely constructed by hand, but by the late nineteenth century a number of firms, such as Britannia Company, A.A. Dorrington, John Bateman and Lucas & Davies, produced kits and readymade parts that made the task a little bit easier.[61]

Another arm of model railway enthusiasm at this time moved the activity slightly further from these technical and mechanical roots: the production of readymade and complete train kits, in a similar vein to well-known contemporary Hornby products. Firms in Europe started to produce a variety of live steam and clockwork models, most notably Radiguet in France; Stevens Model Dockyard and former official modeller for the British admiralty, Clyde Model Dockyard, in Britain; and Althof Bergmann, Schoenner, Bing and Märklin in Germany.[62] From the early twentieth century this market expanded to appeal to children with pre-made models and all-in-one starter kits. This brought the technical sophistication of railway models to an increasingly broad audience that in turn compelled amateur modellers to distinguish their practice. A scratch-builder using hand-made rivets to build scale model steam engines was quite different from the family who bought a clockwork railway kit. It demanded high levels of skill.

The comparison between modelling as an adult activity and 'playing with toys' has long caused consternation among practitioners. Arthur C. Hide, in an 1885 step-by-step instruction for *Amateur Work* about how to build model yachts, insisted that making a model steam engine is 'as scientific and amusing a hobby, combining both in and out-door pleasure, as can be found. "So there" as the tender sex has it'.[63] Hide's querulous defence suggests that modelling was considered a superfluous, unimportant activity, despite its technical difficulty. Claims of the pointlessness of railway modelling and its association with juvenile play have been hard to shake. In December 2010, John Humphreys on Radio Four's *Today* programme reiterated this common pejorative assumption in an interview with enthusiast Peter Snow, exclaiming 'this is a child's paradise but you are a grown man'.[64] Current enthusiasts, it seems, have a difficult time convincing others that they do not just watch Thomas the Tank Engine go round and round a track, despite the incredible complexity of producing models: the scratch-built 'S' gauge Metropolitan Railway electric engine shown in Figures 3.1 and 3.2 is just one example of the bewildering skill and patience needed to make an accurate scale model.

Railway modelling provides another example of the oscillation of amateur craft between the trajectories of ornament and function, superfluity and need, explored in the previous chapter and brilliantly evoked in the Charles and Ray Eames film *Toccata for Toy Trains* (1957). The model train is neither a toy nor an explicitly useful prototype, but is a material metaphor for the entanglement of the *homo ludens* and the *homo faber*. This unclear status of the object reflects the complexity of the temporal conditions in which it was produced: the technical difficulties

FIGURE 3.1 *'S' Gauge (1:64) scratch-built model of the first type of electric engine built for the Metropolitan Railway by the late Alan Cruickshank. Photograph by author.*

FIGURE 3.2 'S' Gauge (1:64) scratch-built model of the first type of electric engine built for the
Metropolitan Railway by the late Alan Cruickshank. Photograph by author.

that modellers willingly pursue demonstrate how they do more than just play around, but they
are equally not infusing time with pure productivity. Such tensions played a key role in the
development of the sister disciplines of railway modelling and model engineering.

Model engineering or railway modelling?

The late-nineteenth-century amateur model rail enthusiast ensured distinction from the mere
production of toys in two main ways: deriving satisfaction from building a steam engine that
worked – model engineering – or paying attention to accurate scale modelling – railway
modelling. John Pocock, in 1888, was an advocate of building models that worked, stating: 'the
most simple form of steam locomotive must not be despised by the amateur worker; for although
it is not like the slide valve locomotive, an actual model of a full sized engine, its construction
will give some good practice in fitting, while it may be finished in far shorter time than the more
complicated slide-valve locomotive.'[65]

For Pocock, building a simple model steam locomotive (shown in Figure 3.3) allowed the
maker to gain basic (and useful) technical skills. Not all agreed with Pocock's approach. A

Fɪɢ. 24.

FIGURE 3.3 *A simple single cylinder oscillating model steam engine in John Pocock*, Model Engine-Making *(London: Swan Sonnenschein and Co, 1888)*.

reader of Pocock's serial in *Amateur Work* with the location sign-off 'Stadt Dresden', wrote a letter to the publication in 1886 exclaiming that it was an 'extraordinary statement' that miniatures need not be to scale: 'Here [in Germany] unless an exact and precise miniature is made, one would be only throwing away time and material.'[66] This debate between precision scale modelling and operability was repeated with renewed vigour in the summer of 1903 in *The Model Engineer and Amateur Electrician*, a publication set up in 1898 by Percival Marshall, an avid writer of early twentieth-century amateur handbooks on electronics, metalwork and telegraphy.[67] In an editorial of 16 July, it was announced that the Society of Model Engineers was planning to issue a scale-gauge standard that would attempt to coherently define the measurements for accurate scale modelling, both for the convenience of modellers and for the commercial firms that were seeking to supply model rail enthusiasts.[68]

Most readers responded in a pliant manner, echoing Pocock's common sense approach and agreeing that with the equipment available at the time it was very hard to produce any degree of scale accuracy with a gauge below 3½ inches, 'the smallest permissible gauge for a scale *working* model'.[69] This meant that if the distance between the wheels of the model train was less than 3½ inches, all the components that ensure operability (boiler, cylinders, axles and other interior mechanisms) would not be able to fit in the model to scale, a problem exacerbated by the small British loading gauges on the actual railway compared with Continental and American equivalents. Henry Greenly, a frequent contributor and major figure within the modelling world at this time, accepted the difficulty of precision scale detail and incorporated a tolerance for scale error when proposing his scale-gauge standards in December 1903.[70] Greenly wanted to encourage his audience of model locomotive makers to try to be as accurate as possible but he did not allow this concern to take precedence over 'making it work'. To fit in the internal components of a locomotive to ensure it ran well, Greenly suggested that 'a little widening' in the gauge was advantageous, adding that the reader could make the prominent parts of the model locomotive to scale, such as the boiler, 'letting the width between the rails come what will!'[71]

The division between model engineering and railway modelling was concretized in the adoption of Greenly's scale-gauge, with live steam models (gauge 1 and above) becoming the domain of model engineering and smaller gauges (gauge O and below) defining railway modelling, concerned with appearance and setting the scale-modelled train within a wider landscape. These structures served to consolidate these amateur activities, providing parameters of practice. But they also demonstrate how amateur time borrows structures from everyday life in order to distinguish it from pure superfluity – in this case standards of measurement that set a technical challenge that require a high degree of skill to surmount.

Within railway modelling the scale accuracy of engines is a vital structuring mechanism. Modellers had a need to assert the complexity of their production through scale detail, particularly since companies like Märklin, Bing, Bassett Lowke and Hornby started producing sophisticated railway kits in increasing number from the early twentieth century. These companies also adopted erroneous gauges for their engines – the 'O' gauge based on Greenly's 1903 compromise, and the 'OO' gauge adopted by Hornby in 1938, a model size that easily fitted within the confines of domestic space that came to dominate the post-war UK model train market.[72] These gauges became associated with commercially produced models and the juvenile audiences they were mainly targeted at.[73]

The inaccuracy of the 'OO' gauge, with its roots in Greenly's compromise, 'bedevils the hobby to the present day', according to Clive White's history of the Model Railway Club.[74] However, this error has played a major part in defining railway modelling: modellers continue to find ingenious, creative and idiosyncratic ways of distinguishing what they do from what is readily available on the shelf. Idiosyncrasy and plurality of practice is encouraged in Britain in particular because of the geometrically fallible standards that reflect the fact that real British trains run on a narrower gauge than American or European counterparts. There is autonomy in railway modelling, but equally a need for a specific framework that gives the modeller a structure to follow or respond critically to.

One broad framework that has come to define the railway modelling hobby is the insistence on precise scale modelling, known as 'finescale' – making sure that every part of the model (including the width, height and diameter of the wheels) is accurate. The gauges 'EM' and 'P4', introduced by self-constituted special interest societies in 1955 and 1966 respectively, reflect this desire among many modellers to disassociate themselves from erroneous gauges that are too closely allied with mass manufacture. Another way railway modellers used to distinguish their practice was to prioritize the environment within which smaller scale trains were set. Layouts became increasingly complex with impressive pioneering examples, such as John Ahern's 'Madder Valley', dating from the late 1930s.[75] In addition to prioritizing the scenic layout, train modellers started to stress the importance of replicating the temporal context of a train's operation: making sure that there is a structured timetable that your locomotives work to.[76] Timetabling became a marker of a quality layout, something more complex than merely placing a train on a track, pressing the 'on' button and watching a locomotive go round.

The ambivalent attitude railway modellers take towards scale-gauge standards, both depending on its structures yet wilfully departing from it, reflects the mediation that takes place between infinite subjective expression – the individual using amateur time to do what they want – and the drive towards collective and social accreditation that attributes meaning to their making. Complete departure from the rules invites comparisons to infantile play, whereas complete adherence suggests a heightened degree of seriousness not appropriate to the supplemental status of the activity. The brief history of railway modelling not only provides the contextual background for the case study but elucidates the in-between differential temporal experience of amateurs caught between play and making, following scale standards and breaking them, and superfluity and functionality.

Experiences of time in amateur railway modelling

Like all amateur practice, railway modelling offers a qualitative and differential experience of time. Within railway modelling, perhaps we would immediately think that its practitioners are attempting to establish a connection with a lost age – a nostalgic experience of time. Certainly this conclusion can be backed up by the vast amount of literature, festivals and tourism devoted to railway enthusiasm. Yet as I outline, there are other, less expected experiential aspects associated with railway modelling: from the notion of incompletion to accelerating time's pace through miniaturization. The case study elucidates how the permitted, yet limited, freedom of amateur time can stretch everyday reality in unexpected ways.

The never-ending story: the unimportance of finishing in railway modelling

Building model railways consumes vast amounts of time, either in the process of scratch-building scale model locomotives, or designing, planning, constructing and maintaining vast layouts. Dr J. Bradbury's model of a locomotive named COMO is an early example of the meticulousness of building from scratch. By 1899 the model had consumed 13,000 hours of Bradbury's time with nuts, bolts and rivets all hand made, with the tender taking a further 5,000 hours to complete.[77] Similarly, within the field of laying out scenic environments in which model trains run, projects go on for many years. An overview of the Model Railway Club's post-war layouts demonstrates the time required to complete these complex projects: 'The Longbridge, Brampton Sands and Calshot Railway' (1962–78), 16 years; 'Thame' (1975–88), 13 years; and two layouts that remain unfinished today – 'Happisburgh' (1985–present) and 'Copenhagen Fields' (1984–present).[78]

The last of these layouts, Copenhagen Fields, is a 2 mm to the foot finescale model of the northern approach to London's King's Cross Station during the inter-war period, an 'area of outstanding unnatural beauty', according to current Model Railway Club Chairman, Tim Watson (Plate 11).[79] The model is meticulously detailed. First, the 2 mm finescale gauge standard is precise, more accurate than 'N' gauge, a similar sized gauge, but one that it less accurate, with a greater commercial infrastructure of readymade parts. Also, because the model is of an urban scene, there are extraordinarily minute details in the layout, such as an accurately positioned Caledonian Road Underground Station line underneath the top layer of the model, retail outlets within which individual products can be seen (everything from bouquets of flowers to lumps of meat – see Plate 12), farmers leading their livestock to the local meat market that existed in 'real life' during the inter-war period, churches, pubs, tiny models of people involved in their own static drama, not to mention the several streets of terraced housing, all hand-made. Even the cast of the Ealing comedy *The Ladykillers* (1950) are depicted, as this area was where much of the shooting for the film took place. Despite a large team, the model remains unfinished with progress continuing at a 'glacial rate' according to Watson, with something new added every time the model is exhibited.[80] There is no concern among the modellers of Copenhagen Fields to finish the project: when asked when the model will be complete Watson is vague, merely stating 'sometime'.[81]

Similarly, modellers often have a variety of different projects that are left half-finished or are completed at different speeds: it is not always a case of finishing one thing and going on to the next. In the Model Engineering Exhibition 2010 held in Sandown Park, Chairman of the Society of Model and Experimental Engineers, Mike Chrisp, had three of his models on show. The oldest was a half-completed model of the *Lion*, the locomotive star of the film *The Titfield Thunderbolt* (1953) that Chrisp built in his youth. Later on in life, and without finishing the first *Lion*, Chrisp wanted to make a more accurate scale model and tracked down the original *Lion* that he found at the Mersey Docks. Chrisp took many photos with the intention of designing a model of this find, but then another project distracted him. He recalls the shift of direction:

> I thought I better knock up something in the meantime, so there was a designer who was writing for *The Model Engineer*, a designer called Martin Evans and he produced a design for a loco, a simple tank engine, a five inch gauge tank engine, and I thought 'I'll make one of those'. Well that's not finished either. So . . . yeah, we've all got unfinished projects.[82]

As a consequence of the freedom from deadlines, the railway modeller can spend many years on projects. Sometimes only retirement furnishes the modeller with enough time: 'at long last' stated Norman Simmons, a modeller in the 1980s, 'I can use the time between nine to five to do some *actual* modelling'.[83] The nonchalant attitude to the notion of completion, the irreproducibility of most things that are created due to incredible scale detail, and the communal nature of producing model railway layouts are completely at odds with the norms of capitalist production, which demands an endpoint, a temporal moment that signals the object's introduction to commodity exchange. The market's means of attributing value cannot possibly remunerate the labour that goes into models like Copenhagen Fields, as the maker was not concerned to be productive in each hour of work. Moreover, the works are incredibly difficult to store,[84] there is dispersed authorship, willingly acknowledged, and then there is still the pejorative assumption that links railway modelling with 'playing with trains', which prejudices audience reception. The amateur maker's adoption of idiosyncratic and slow production procedures, particularly exaggerated in the case of constructing Copenhagen Fields, creates a situation that the market cannot bear.

The resistance to market conditions might seem to align railway modelling with Helen Carnac's account of 'slowing down life's pace'[85] through a slow revolution. Indeed, a common complaint among craftspeople is that the market fails to recognize the value of slow, idiosyncratic and risky production procedures. Yet there is a difference: the advocates of the slow revolution are attempting to locate a niche demand for their products – they ultimately want to engage with the market – whereas railway modellers are much less concerned with explicitly ethical economic positions. With the railway modeller there is too much labour taking place for the market to manage, stretching the link between labour and value in capitalist production to the limits. The incredibly detailed models are vacuums for labour, like a black hole consuming hours of making in endless digression, endless play with materials, endless experimentation and endless execution.

The partial utopia of the railway model

The small scale of model train layouts situates the maker, or the operator of the model, as a God-like figure looking over all activities within view. As the pioneer of scenic railway modelling, John Ahern, stated in 1947: 'increasing numbers of people are discovering an outlet for their creative powers in constructing not just a model railway, as the term was usually understood 20 years ago, but something approaching a miniature make-believe world of their own.'[86] The image of a railway modeller looking over his layout like an omnipresent figure can be seen at any weekend model railway exhibition throughout the UK. There is a strong contrast in scale, as shown in Figure 3.4, between the modellers and the immaculately detailed railway layout (in this case the layout Copenhagen Fields). This places the modeller/operator in a position of control over the miniature universe and constitutes one of the chief pleasures to be

FIGURE 3.4 *Modellers (Tim Watson and Mike Randall) working on Copenhagen Fields. Photograph courtesy of The Model Railway Club collection.*

FIGURE 3.5 *Le Corbusier*, La Ville Radieuse, *Paris: Editions Vincent, Fréal & Cie, 2nd edn, 1964, p. 135. © FLC/ADAGP, Paris and DACS, London 2014.*

derived from railway modelling. As Peter Snow explained in response to John Humphreys's question as to why he engages with railway modelling: 'Because I can sit there like the fat controller on my little control panel and I can send hundreds of people around the world on my trains.'[87]

An obvious comparison is with architects making, and then looking over, detailed models of city plans, as immortalized in the *New York Times* photograph of Le Corbusier overlooking his *Ville Radieuse* (Figure 3.5). Adnan Morshed's essay sheds light on this aestheticization of aerial vision in modernity through his study of American architect Norman Bel Geddes's 1939 Futurama spectacle at New York's World Fair. Morshed's essay focuses on the aestheticization of the aerial view that allowed modern city planners, like Bel Geddes and Le Corbusier, to filter 'the messy world below into a utopian simplicity, affording him the illusion that he could first impose a neat physical order'.[88] The aerial view was laden with the enlightenment desire for visual clarity and hopes of bringing reason to the chaos of cities and was popularized among a wide public through spectacles like Bel Geddes's Futurama, science-fiction novels and superhero comics that became increasingly popular in the 1930s. Morshed explains how the spectator of the Futurama show temporarily became Superman himself, a point made by Umberto Eco in his essay on the superhero ethos in modernity:

In an industrial society, however, where man becomes a number in the realm of organisation which has usurped his decision-making role, he has no means of production and is thus deprived power to describe. Individual strength, if it is not exerted in sports activities is left abased when confronted with the strength of the machines which determines man's very movements. In such a society the positive hero must embody to an unthinkable degree the power demands that the average citizen can nurture but cannot satisfy.[89]

Eco outlines the superhero's power of attraction: his abilities can easily be imagined, both conceptually with the inherent desirability of the all-seeing eye, and in its partial realization in the spectator experience of ascension within the Futurama exhibition, other spectacles like the Eiffel Tower,[90] or air travel. Similar to Superman and the city planner, the railway modeller is also granted the temporal and spatial suspension that aerial mastery offers, but how does the deployment of this power differ?

First of all, the architect's relationship to the model is more demanding than that of the railway modeller: the architect's model works to visualize the probable appearance of the 'real thing' either to satisfy the clients' need for a visual representation or to illuminate technical properties that might require alteration. Of course, as Morshed explains, there is an ideological drive to this visualization in the context of aggressive positivism, but there clearly is a prosaic functionality to this type of model as well. The weight of responsibility on the model is at its height when planning cities, like the developments in Manhattan in the 1930s.[91] Models remain an inexpensive way of visualizing and resolving problems that might occur in building units that will exist in the real world, from architecture to design of major exhibitions.[92]

The God-like status of the amateur railway modeller is utterly different. The railway layout can be a model 'in-and-of-itself' rather than a model for application, situating it closer to the dynamics of a painting than the prototypical qualities of architectural models to which it bears a closer material resemblance. The lack of economic demand placed on the model railway layout in contrast to the architectural model or engineering prototype, means that the maker can play with the narrative, subvert and invent it, exercising the creative freedom granted by amateur time. The modeller has no need to put forward a solution or solve urban problems as Le Corbusier or Bel Geddes did. Freed from the pressure that comes with the prospect of one's model being built, the railway modeller follows his own will and imagination. In a peculiar twist the railway modeller is, in theory, the freest of those with the God-like view, the anarchist of the cast that includes the aviator, the architect and Superman. Could we go so far as to say that the railway modeller is the closest realization of Nietzsche's *übermensch*, reaching the goal of 'self-overcoming'?

> That is your entire will, you wisest men, it is a will to power; and that is so even when you talk of good and evil and of the assessment of values.
>
> You want to create the world before which you can kneel: this is your ultimate hope and intoxication.[93]

Clearly not. The modeller's God-like control is only a temporary affair that sits alongside a variety of less Nietzschean activities and, like Superman who changes back into the journalist Clark Kent, the modeller returns to an everyday persona. Even though the modeller is theoretically free from responsibility, he is subject to multiple self-imposed constraints in practice. Models are copies of real-life railway geographies that typically are drawn from the past and do not represent the expression of either infantile liberated expression or a self-overcoming. On the contrary, the amateur modeller seeks to impose a structure that gives the parallel world a meaningful narrative that typically relies on the persistence of lived experience, memory or history – for example, the narrative of the golden age of steam in Britain. Presented with the spatial-temporal flux, the modeller seeks structure, and often this regulatory mechanism is drawn from the past.

Nostalgia

> Why shouldn't the person – if he wants to – let it pander to his old-fashioned outdated ideas and let him enjoy his backward looking sentiment?

> NORMAN SIMMONS, *How To Go Railway Modelling* (1979), p. 37

The reason often given for the popularity of railway modelling is that it is a nostalgic act, an attempt by the modeller to relive a previous joyous encounter with railways: perhaps a childhood encounter with a Hornby train set or a visit to a heritage steam route.[94] David Crossley, Exhibition Manager for the Chiltern Model Rail Association, stated that modellers tend to recreate the landscape of their childhood, suggesting that trends adhere to the age of the modellers: the pre-war layouts depicted the 'big four' railway companies formed by the 1922 Groupings Act,[95] shifting to modelling the last days of steam in the late 1950s, finally progressing on to diesels today 'because that is all they [the new generation of modellers] can remember'.[96] This argument of a generational shift in model railway layouts is not concrete; many modellers work on layouts that do not correspond to the time of their first interaction with steam, but it is a fair observation that hints at the impetus to evoke childhood encounters.

Miniaturization is a means by which to evoke this nostalgic sentiment, according to Susan Stewart, who explains through her example of the doll's house how the miniature serves to bring former times to life while simultaneously blocking historicity, or the passing of time. Yet, as Stewart reminds us, this attempt to monumentalize and compartmentalize history and subject it to one's own conception or ordering procedure seeks to make static a temporal moment that 'never existed except as narrative' which 'constantly threatens to reproduce itself as a felt lack'.[97] In line with Stewart's analysis, even with a perfect representation of a former image, immortalization through the model will only temporarily abate the unceasing longing for that which is lost.

Suppositional histories and geographies

While it is true that most modellers do venerate the past, to inhabit a nostalgic vision is not always the strongest motivation for practice. For example, historical accuracy offers a particularly demanding technical brief that is appealing to the modeller looking for a challenge. Making a railway layout is usually preceded by in-depth historical research to ascertain the models that were running on a line, the buildings that existed in the time depicted, as well as road and rail plans, so much so that Chairman of the Model Railway Club, Leslie Bevis-Smith, described model railway layouts as 'historical documents'.[98] This is certainly apparent when viewing most layouts at model railway exhibitions, but the clock is not always set to the bygone age of steam. Farkham, made and run by the Mickelover Model Railway Group, is set to the summer

FIGURE 3.6 *Farkham, owned by Mickelover Model Railway Group (2011). Photograph by author.*

of 1990 when England lost to West Germany in the World Cup, depicting how despite this great national event 'life goes on as normal' (Figure 3.6).[99] Railway modellers often become specialists in specific slices of local history in order to provide an historical framework for their modelling activities.

Railway modelling is structured by a temporal rigidity, an historical narrative that gives the layout more depth than a readymade toy. Yet the method by which this is done and the reasons that govern such decisions are loose, flexible and idiosyncratic. Historical research is not a straitjacket that constricts modellers, but rather provides source material for inspiration and a creative re-animation of the past, with modellers constructing their own suppositional geographies and narratives. There is room for blatant inaccuracy: station names are made up, towns are granted stations in the model world that were never afforded them in real life and there are multiple subversions and digressions. For example, Graham Hedges's Stoney Lane Depot is recognizable to Londoners as the area where an elevated train line bisects London's South Bank, with Southwark Junction (a fictitious name) looking remarkably similar to Waterloo

FIGURE 3.7 *Replica of Stonegate station building in Whatlington railway layout, by Peter Bossom (2011). Photograph by author.*

East or Blackfriars station (as they existed in the 1990s) (Plate 13). The area looks familiar, the buildings seem accurate, the station design is spot on and there is even a scale version of a famous 1979 Saatchi & Saatchi Conservative Party election poster; yet it is an interpretation.

In his description of his model, Whatlington (Figure 3.7), Peter Bossom describes how the creation of his own supposition geography is a common practice within the hobby:

> When it suits them, modellers rewrite history and/or geography to create plausible settings and this model is no different. Whatlington – with an 'h' – does exist, near Battle in East Sussex, but in order to create a station and make it a plausible 'might have been' the village has become a small country town and distances to the surrounding villages etc. have been increased by just a few miles.[100]

Bossom's Whatlington is a creative, yet informative, fiction. He changes Whatlington, a hamlet, into a small town that is connected to the mainline passenger line from London to Hastings, in East Sussex. The station's ticket office is a scale replica of the one that exists (in real life) at Stonegate station, two stops closer to London (Figure 3.7). In addition, Bossom has made a sister layout called Hoath Hill with a narrative that connects it to Whatlington. Hoath Hill exists, but as a road junction, and in the model it is transformed into a goods station. This is a deliberate reference to the real-life operation of a gypsum mine in the area operated by the Sub Wealden Gypsum Company since 1876.[101] There is a curious blend of fact and fiction on show here.

The phrase Bossom uses, 'a plausible might have been', encapsulates the elastic relationship of the railway modeller to historical and geographical parameters, stretching normative temporal and spatial restrictions without collapsing into unordered chaos. Representation is still tied to recognizable histories and geographies and, despite the twisting of reality, railway layouts still effectively visualize a general picture of the past: in the Copenhagen Fields layout models of farmers cajoling livestock across the streets of London inform the audience of a former meat market in the area and the Whatlington model raises awareness of local mineralogy. But within the guiding principles of geographic and historic contextualization, the modeller is granted freedom to personalize the layout.

These subversions of historical narrative often reflect a light humour that pervades the craft. For example, there are whimsical televisual references in many layouts including Ian Allington's depiction of a rail yard that features in the American television serial *Starsky and Hutch*; the graffiti on the railway bridge in Hedges's 'Stoney Lane Depot' (Figure 2.9);[102] the insertion of modellers' names in the layout as seen in the Model Railway Club's 'Copenhagen Fields' (lead modeller Tim Watson has a 'Modern Dentistry' named after him – Plate 12); as well as the more frivolous and bawdy scenes on show at Hamburg's Miniatur Wunderland.[103] Reality is putty in the modellers' hands and this humour and twisting of historical narrative shows a departure from pure imitation. Ahern recognized this, explaining how the freedom to shape the temporal and spatial register of a model railway allows a practitioner to conceive of a 'countryside' in a similar vein to a painter, producing 'imaginative work to so high a level as to be worthy to rank as a work of creative art'.[104]

Right on time

Out of the many structures that are imposed in the realization of a model layout perhaps the most rigorous is setting a specific timetable. Made easier by increasing availability of commercially produced track from the 1920s, and encouraged by Greenly in the 1930s, by mid-century setting a timetable was a barometer by which to judge accomplished model layouts. As Greenly stated: 'A model railway which does not work in the way that it is intended to lacks 9/10ths of its fascination and if, on the other hand, it is operated in an aimless, unrailwaylike manner, it also entirely fails in its object.'[105] Greenly's urge to avoid operating model layouts in an 'unrailwaylike manner' reflected the author's continuing prioritization of ensuring effective operation of model railways in the context of increasing provision of readymade parts. For Greenly, 'fascination' depended on running trains in close approximation to their real-life equivalents. By closely aligning the operation of a model railway to the labour of a signalman, the amateur is able to manipulate time's organization, an ordering of the temporal conditions of the layout that is neither purely nostalgic nor haphazard, but highly structured.

In no case study in the history of twentieth-century railway modelling is this punctilious attention to timetabling more apparent than in the case of Norman Eagles's track layout 'The Sherwood Section of the L.M.S.'[106] By 1928, when Eagles was a teenager, he had tired of ready-to-run circle layouts and first indulged in his passion for planning timetables. Throughout the late 1920s and 1930s he developed a clockwork-operated 'O' gauge model railway with multiple stations loosely based on the landscape and towns of 'Robin Hood' country near Nottingham.

For Eagles it was not accurate landscaping or scratch-building that was the priority but timetabling, echoing his professional life as an employee of London's bus system. Eagles set the date of his model at 1947, writing separate timetables for each station in his fictitious slice of the English countryside, even running a 24-hour timetable during his later life when the layout occupied an entire shed in the garden of his family home at Saunderton, Buckinghamshire. The scale model needed 'scaled-down' time and a clock on the wall sped up by four times set the pace, ensuring a difficult task for the operators. As one visitor recalled, 'Heaven help you if were even a little bit late or hadn't wound the clockwork motor up enough!'[107] Eagles's interest in time management was so acute that he would deliberately introduce chaos into his system, such as closing a line for essential maintenance works on a collapsing bridge or running a special excursions train, so that he could effect a prepared emergency timetable and test 'single track' operation.

Eagles's strict timetable required a team of nine operators. Visitors who were invited to operate signal boxes at one of the smaller, quieter stations described even one morning of participation as exhausting: 'it was not like operating a model railway but it was like operating a small railway.'[108] The focus on time within Eagles's Sherwood layout would require levels of attentiveness that would have matched or even exceeded the temporal exigencies of professional labour. This was far from an exercise in nostalgia, and the experience of time was more like a thoroughly efficient parallel universe where trains operate efficiently according to a pre-arranged timetable, as they should. Humphreys wryly made this point in his interview with Peter Snow, when he joked that only Snow's trains in his attic were running to schedule, on an early December day when the UK railway infrastructure had been crippled by heavy snowfall.[109] As the world is subject to the chaotic forces of natural environment, social activity and multiple contingent factors, the railway modeller creates an alternative time-space where things can work properly.

Granted the power of being master of one's own universe, the railway modeller imposes certain self-imposed structures. The overpowering nostalgia that pervades much railway enthusiasm should not blind us to the dynamism of the other experiences that result from building and maintaining a layout, manifest in the traces of personal humour, mild subversions of geographical and historical contexts and visions of perfect operability. The examples given above show the ways in which modellers control and determine the miniature world they created, but as hinted at by the story of Norman Eagles's layout, the pursuit of such exacting goals can be incredibly demanding, often requiring levels of devotion that threaten to destabilize this control.

Obsession

. . . how far could one go in the pursuit of the true detail?

JEAN-PIERRE GORIN in *Routine Pleasures* (1986),
quoted by Neil Young in a review of the film available at jigsawlounge.co.uk

Jean-Pierre Gorin asks this question in the course of making *Routine Pleasures* (1986), a film in which the French director pays homage to a railway modelling group in San Diego, USA. Like Gorin, any outsider to railway modelling can be overwhelmed by the extent of detail. Precision goes beyond merely ensuring the correct scale-gauge standard; finescale replication of locomotive wheels and the curves on the track, precise historical accuracy and constructing detailed models without the help of pre-made parts are other ways of achieving greater accuracy (Figures 3.1 and 3.2). Such demands require a level of single focus that can be akin to obsession.

The desire to be accurate is, of course, understandable: enthusiasts want models to demonstrate their advanced technical and artistic skills. On becoming aware of the scale inaccuracy of 'OO' models[110] when returning to the hobby in his thirties, David Crossley said to himself: 'Hang on, "OO", 16 and a half mm gauge, but it should be 18.83. It's at least an eighth out. Is that sensible? Does that make sense? Can I actually, with my own feeling about the whole thing, do that?'[111] A level of inaccuracy is no problem for a child who simply wants to set up his or her own layout but the modeller wants to do more than fritter away time and money in the production of an inaccurate scale model. This explains Crossley's crisis of conscience above.

However, the pursuit of utter precision can be a difficult affair. During a visit to the Model Railway Club I saw someone converting 'OO' gauge track to the more accurate 'EM' gauge, which prompted a discussion on scale-gauge standards. One member joked about the 'P4' standard (which is more precise than 'EM') as being the 'S&M wing of the hobby', adding 'if they can't be modelling in "P4", they are usually standing under a cold shower beating themselves with sticks'.[112] This quip hints at the wilful suffering undertaken by railway modellers who deliberately pursue difficulty. When under no specific obligation to work, they set themselves tasks that are more challenging and more time consuming than any regular activity of paid work, stretching the extent of their competence and patience. Being master of one's model universe is not plain sailing.

Lennard Davis's social and cultural history of obsession is useful in this context. He resists classing obsession as a clinical condition strictly apart from 'normal' behaviour, a scientific division that would unfairly characterize certain types of amateur devotion as akin to some form of medical disorder. Davis considers other analytical methodologies outside clinical assignation and Freudian psychotherapy, directing attention to the longevity of the monomaniacal tendency within Western culture. He demonstrates how focusing too much on one thing is a human affliction shown in medical treatises, early scientific inquiries and literature, from William Godwin's *Caleb Williams* to Gustave Flaubert's *Bouvard et Pécuchet*. Critical is Davis's qualification that the state of obsession demonstrates 'both an awareness of obsessive symptoms and an inability to stop the symptoms',[113] capturing this fluid dialectic between control over one's behaviour and its temporary abandonment once transfixed by the object of one's obsession. This is a definition of obsession that is applicable to the amateur railway modeller (and other amateur practitioners). Modellers are aware of the relative superfluity of their arduous attempt to achieve perfect accuracy, but when pursuing their hobby it is the goal that obfuscates all others. As Davis suggests: 'Could we perhaps see obsession at the visible end of a regulatory mechanism gone wrong?'[114]

Extreme attention to detail can be a consequence of this internally generated competition to achieve a certain standard. Steven Gelber, in his monograph on American hobbies, recalls the story of an obsessed San Antonio railroader in the 1940s who allegedly spent $80,000 on a massive model layout, filling his house with spare track and spending his family's food budget on supplies.[115] When the man refused to give up his hobby, his wife unsurprisingly left him. Here is a clear example of how obsession can be to the detriment of other everyday tasks and an individual's relationships with others.

The obsessive degrees of focus that can be witnessed in railway modelling share parallels with the work of some artists who have been consumed by their output to the detriment of their own sanity. This image of the obsessed artist was extensively depicted in Émile Zola's novel *L'oeuvre*[116] and is also exemplified by the beat artist Jay Defeo, whose monumental work *The Rose* (1958–65) eventually reached a weight of 2,000 lb, after continued painting, scratching and re-painting over the course of eight years.[117] Obsession is also the key theme of Polish director Krzysztof Kieslowski's 1979 film, *Amator*, about a factory worker who is pushed to the brink after taking up amateur film. All these cases of monomania clearly differ in extent – Defeo's gargantuan painting is an extreme example – but they do serve to contest Richard Sennett's claim that negative obsession does not afflict the craftsperson. Sennett explains how 'craft routines relieve stress by providing a steady rhythm of work', conforming to the expectation that making with one's hands leads to an atemporal experience; similar to Csikszentmihalyi's notion of 'flow'. Sennett does distinguish between negative and positive obsession, defining the latter as an awareness of the need to adapt, the need to avoid pursuing one problem relentlessly, resistance to showing off skill for its own sake, and the knowledge of when to stop.[118] If judged according to these parameters of 'good' craftsmanship, railway modelling falls short, particularly because the practice is often so committed to the single goal of accurate scale detail and does not know when to stop, as shown in the case of Copenhagen Fields. This does not necessarily mean such practice is obsessive.

Negative obsession does not derive from a particular attitude to materials as Sennett expects but an attitude to time. The figure of the railway modeller working away in the isolation of the workshop is akin to Mary Shelley's construction of the mad doctor in *Frankenstein* and can come close to forms of highly exploited labour apparent in more conventional work environments, perhaps developing into something that is even more destructive due to the absences of socialized, regulatory frameworks. There is a danger of having temporary control over one's own labour-power but it is offset by the sociability of amateur craft – the many forms of social organization that develop around a particular activity – and the fact that amateur time is supplementary. These are regulatory mechanisms that monomaniacal trajectories can disrupt. Obsessive amateur practice is a natural consequence of amateur time's differential status, another example of how regulatory mechanisms that normally structure labour are stretched to the nth degree.

Sociability

Social association lessens problems associated with obsession. Throughout the history of railway modelling self-constituted clubs have encouraged knowledge sharing and the meeting of like-minded people; providing facilities that allow members to run and test models, attend lectures and engage in large-scale projects that cannot easily fit within the confines of the home. There is also a degree of devolved localism within the organization of railway modelling groups, with informal ties between larger clubs like the Model Railway Club and associations like the Chiltern Model Rail Association and smaller groups. Clubs are often made up of various individuals attracted by different aspects of the hobby, from those who enjoy modelling landscapes, those who prefer to operate the layouts, to those who are more interested in the history of railways.[119] Not enough research has been undertaken to attempt a thorough anthropology of railway modelling societies, but the existence of clubs shows that time spent railway modelling is rarely just an isolated or solitary affair. The description of railway modelling as a 'model collective',[120] in the words of one observer, is quite justified.

In addition to these broader structures of support for the railway modeller there is also an inherent sociability that derives from communicating these visions of a parallel universe to an audience. The railway modeller, like many painters, is an illusion maker, with scenery at the centre of the discipline. Ahern's book, *Miniature Landscape Modelling*, underlines this approach: 'Now scenic modelling should be a comparatively light-hearted business and a bolder and broader approach is indicated; it is the general effect of the whole which matters and not the accuracy and precision of any detail.'[121] This focus on how the detail fits within the context of the overall picture saves the craft from being reduced to the obsessive pursuit of scale detail alone and closer to a holistic art, poetically expressed by Michael Longridge, editor of the *Model Railway Club Bulletin*, in the 1950s: 'In the same way that every painter has his own methods and style when reproducing a tree on canvas, so modellers are able to exercise their judgement, not only on individual items but on the "picture" as a whole.'[122]

For Longridge, the presence or absence of detail is not the priority, rather a sense of balance should be achieved in the attempt to create a 'general picture', or in other words to communicate a narrative of some sort. The processes that are used to achieve this might include proportionally reducing the scale of a model at the back of a layout to create the illusion of depth, as is the case with Copenhagen Fields;[123] replicating the experience of viewing a train in the city by placing trees and buildings at the front of a layout 'to break up direct lines of sight between the viewer and the trains' as seen in the layout 'Farkham';[124] weathering buildings to give the illusion of age; and the additional framing given by appending historical information gathered during the course of researching for a layout.

The reason for stressing these links to the painter and the notion of 'illusion making' is to emphasize the importance of communication: railway modelling is not exclusively about detail, despite the prevalence of discussions about scale-gauge standards seen in the model railway press, but is concerned with creating narratives of alternative model universes. This reflects the collective impulse at the core of illusion making. As Jameson explains, in the attempt to materialize the utopian impulse individuals rely upon aesthetic parerga, common rhetoric and established symbolic forms, which render the dream image communicable to others. The expression of the individual ego, primal wish fulfilment, threatens to sink 'to a rather private activity that needs to be disguised at all costs' and instead must depend on the supplemental to lend the expression coherence.[125] Jameson's explanation of the collective will at the source of utopian expression reflects the interconnected nature of attempts to build a differential temporality, a constraint that amateur railway modellers accept through their wilful subjugation to frameworks that structure their practice. In the course of constructing an illusion, the aesthetic is no longer a 'secondary hobby but rather goes around behind creation to identify the very sources of reality'.[126] The time-states that abound in the practice of amateur railway modelling bend, twist and quietly feed back into social reality.

These diversionary experiences of time are to be found in all examples of individually, autonomously chosen craft. They provide opportunities to fashion a utopian world that remains an inherently social form of expression: time-states instilled with the desire for control, nostalgic reflection, humour, the productive ethos, skill development and obsession. Given this mélange of different motivations it would seem presumptuous to settle on any broader definition of the experience of amateur time. However, French sociologist Georges Friedmann, in his book *Anatomy of Work* (1964), furnishes us with appropriate terminology. In opposition to work, which Friedmann (perhaps rather simply) characterizes as some form of oppression, leisure is described as a 'reply', a compensatory response to what is lacking during the working hours.[127] The relativism of this approach is helpful when considering the vast spectrum of amateur craft practice. Amateur time often provides the experiences that are lacking in other parts of life, whatever that might be, but is also linked to them as shown, for example, by the vast number of railway modellers who work or have worked on the railways and associated industries.[128]

Friedmann follows other Frankfurt School thinkers in his belief that leisure is more likely to lead to debasement rather than enrichment.[129] Nevertheless, free time facilitates a reply to conditions of work. This is not loaded with the discursive and political power of rejection, and is instead muted. Utopia is only realized through some part-time, miniaturized form, within the confines of an infrastructure that ceaselessly commodifies leisure. The concept of the busman's holiday explored in the introduction is again helpful: on a coach holiday the bus driver can sit back and enjoy someone else doing his work, deriving pleasure from his passive position. Yet after my examination of railway modelling perhaps we can suggest that, given the freedom of choice, the metaphorical bus driver might still want to drive. It is just that in his own time he might want to drive a different route, order others around or, in other words, be the master of his own exploitation.

From bodge to botch

The constrained freedom of amateur practice that I have described above has proven an attraction to contemporary artists and designers who want to grasp something of the autonomy or diversion that is associated with voluntary making. The prospect of making under non-alienated conditions is attractive to artists, especially in the contexts of specialization in artistic education where mastery over a limited set of tools and materials continues to play a vital role in structuring practice. In my final case studies of the chapter I do not want to look at projects where amateur time is seen as some kind of clear rejection of capitalist, professional time (as I have done above with reference to Premsela and Craftivism), but instead see how two groups of artists and designers have occupied a temporal mode analogous to the amateur as a way of rejuvenating or enlivening their practice.

Being a 'beginner' in a craft is something that is common to amateur practice – an experience of time full of trepidation and anticipation. There is a palpable naivety to the amateur craftsperson, limited by skill alone, that is clearly absent in professional or specialized practice where a maker is expected to reach or demonstrate certain standards or has to work to deadlines. This reverie of the freedom of non-professional practice is central to former England cricketer Ed Smith's intention to preserve traces of that first 'amateur' interaction in any given sport, to counter the 'professional orthodoxy' defined by gym programmes, dieting schedules and extensive analysis of performance.[130] In the realm of acquiring craft skills it is similarly tempting to romanticize the innocence of former stages of learning.

The contemporary artist, like the professional sportsperson, cannot genuinely return to a former stage of learning; skills cannot be unlearnt. However, the experience of the naive amateur at the first stage of learning can be partially appropriated by artists and designers through the process of temporary abandonment of the set of tools that defines their specialism, in preference for those of another with which the artist is not familiar. This can be described as adopting a different tool order. This intentional diversion of practice could be described as containing the qualities of Michel Foucault's heterotopia of the mirror, cementing the reality of a person looking into the mirror through the unreal virtual non-place of the reflection.[131] For the artist, learning new skills might provide this mirror: the occupation of an alternative spatial-temporal zone from which the constraints of disciplinary specialism can be viewed, understood, challenged and renewed, even providing a time and space for experimentation.

A recent example of this assumption of a different tool order was the *Bodging Milano* project (2010–ongoing). The project involved a collaboration between nine metropolitan designers[132] and Gudrun Leitz's green-woodworking chair-making course that she runs in Clissett Wood, Herefordshire, primarily for amateurs looking to spend a holiday learning how to shape

FIGURE 3.8 Bodging Milano *group shot (2010). Photograph by Gudrun Leitz.*

greenwood into chairs and stools (Figure 3.8). *Bodging Milano* originated in 2009 when one of the participants, Chris Eckersley, attended the week-long course, after being invited to add a modern twist to the traditional Windsor chair by Dave Green, founder of the furniture company Sitting Firm. A year later Eckersley returned with eight other designers from London all ready to abandon the digital interfaces, smooth surfaces and geometric exactitude of their studios in exchange for hand tools and manually powered pole lathes made from locally gathered wood, all collated underneath a large canvas-roofed workshop (Figure 3.9). One of the participants, Rory Dodd of design agency Designerblock, provided the participants with a specific goal: the chairs that resulted from the workshop would be immediately shipped to Italy after the week and displayed as a part of the Milan furniture fair.

Since 1994, Leitz has offered a range of greenwood craft courses of varying complexity, pitching them as holidays suitable for 'novices, amateurs and experienced craftspeople'.[133] Leitz's courses appeal to a wide demand for a therapeutic, pastoral ideal, unplugged from the complexity, noise and pressures of urban life and join a long list of craft retreats from William Morris's Kelmscott Manor in the nineteenth century to summer courses held every year at West Dean in Sussex. Like Leitz's normal clientele, the designers and artists start from a position of inexpertise, for although they are established practitioners, the conditions of practice were entirely new (with the exception of Chris Eckersley, who in 2009 returned to the woods for a second time). They had to learn the craft of bodging: riving the locally sourced wood; using

FIGURE 3.9 *Gareth Neal in open-air workshop*, Bodging Milano *(2010). Photograph by Chris Eckersley.*

drawknives and shaving horses; and enduring the difficulty of manually powering a pole lathe to make chair supports and legs. These were the practices adopted by itinerant bodgers in the nineteenth century and before; craftsmen like Phillip Clissett, who Leitz's wood is named after, who produced simple, vernacular chairs in rural Herefordshire in the nineteenth century and subsequently became an inspiration for supporters of the Arts and Crafts Movement when discovered in the late 1880s, and in particular the furniture maker Ernest Gimson who learnt from the maker in 1890.[134]

The modern-day bodgers had the added pressure of producing a chair for exhibition at the end of the week, distinguishing them from Leitz's normal students. This was a skills holiday with a defined output. The designers' ambition to reach a standard had to be negotiated with the difficulty of confronting the material by hand and using manually powered tools like the pole lathe (Figure 3.10). Amos Merchant, talking to *Crafts* magazine editor, Grant Gibson, explained how the bowed wood that was going to form the back of his chair needed to be changed to the rocker and vice versa: 'It's really about being flexible. . . . You're using live materials and it's got its own ideas.'[135] The idea of the material breaking free from the subjugation normally imposed on it by the conventional certainty of workshop production conforms to David Pye's qualification of craft as closer to the workmanship of risk, something Gibson mentions.[136] And here, one could argue, is the central regenerative trajectory of the *Bodging Milano* project: greater sympathy for the hand-made, imperfect, and on-the-spot design that directly responds to the material being shaped. This experience has the potential, as Gareth Neal and Merchant mentioned,[137] to transform practice when the designers return to their workshops and once again have full mastery over their materials.

For the bodgers there was delight, surprise and real interest in using a different set of tools and working out in the open, an example of how the enthusiasm to acquire new skills, a prominent dimension of amateur experience, can be used as a strategy to advance creative practice. However, the pre-determined output of exhibiting in Milan and the level of expertise and pre-knowledge in furniture design each designer brought to the course distinguishes the *Bodging Milano* project from Leitz's normal students: Leitz's expertise was constantly in demand as her students wanted to bring their skills as furniture designers and ambition to the work. Among the designers there was limited tolerance for error as they worked towards perfection and indeed a hint of competition, at least with themselves. The reconvening of *Bodging Milano* after the Milan fair in Dave Green's furniture-making factory to make production models of their 'one-off' asymmetrical, roughly hewn designs from Clissett wood, reflects the re-absorption of the amateur-like experience of learning new skills back into professional practice.[138]

There was seriousness to this tool holiday: a clear, defined output that is less similar to amateur craft practice. As I have argued in the railway modelling case study above, the amateur is notionally free of pressures of this kind. However, the reinvigoration, experimentation and skill development in the *Bodging Milano* project derive from the temporary occupation of the 'first stage' of learning, the partial appropriation of the state of amateur-as-beginner. For the designers this resulted in a palpable reminder of the true extent of the 'workmanship of risk' evident in using hand tools. The project has subsequently promoted the ideals of learning these anachronistic skills and, by association, the delight and difficulty of working in greenwood and wood in general, as demonstrated by *Bodging Milano*'s 'V&A Broomstick Bodge' where William Warren and Gareth Neal helped inexpert gallery goers at one of the museum's Friday Lates make furniture from broom handles and plywood.[139]

The work of the Swedish collaborative group We Work In A Fragile Material similarly explores the dynamics of temporarily working with unfamiliar tools, materials and procedures

FIGURE 3.10 *Rory Dodd on a pole lathe,* Bodging Milano *(2010). Photograph by Chris Eckersley.*

in a holiday-like manner. The collective, founded in 2003, is formed of nine individual practitioners who attended Konstfack, a College of Art and Design in Stockholm. There is no grand manifesto that unites the broad scope of projects undertaken by the collective – from exhibitions that encourage public participation, the construction of a giant troll in New York, parodying Kylie Minogue's music video 'Slow', to playing a giant game of paintball in a three-dimensional grid in Gustavsbergs Kontshall[140] – simply a desire to 'be seen as a complement to the traditional arts and craft scene', 'expanding' aesthetic norms, and providing a reprieve from each individual's own practice. Glenn Adamson cites Pontus Lindvall, who describes the group as 'nine very smart people on vacation from their own cleverness'.[141]

Unlike the Bodgers, the collective's use of new tools, materials and techniques is not intended to hone each member's craft skills but instead provide a form of release from individual practice. There is a degree of freedom offered by the collective nature of the enterprise: each individual is not required to author any work and thus can pursue a form of skill acquisition that contrasts remarkably with valorised methods of learning craft. The approach is less about returning to school, more like playing the fool.

This was particularly obvious in the 2009 show in London entitled *We Built This City* in which the collective worked with papier mâché to create a temporary bulbous, webbed structure, with mess strewn across the gallery floor (Plate 14). The Bodgers went to Clissett Wood to learn new processes in traditional woodworking to create individual, permanent objects; We Work In A Fragile Material took time out to be silly, child-like and crafted as a collective. They countered essentialist notions of rarefied craft procedures and challenged traditional perceptions of the position of craft in 'larger, more market-orientated scenes' of America and Britain that are liable to defend craft as a 'serious business' saturated with the nostalgic, anti-industrial legacy of the Arts and Crafts movement.[142]

Both projects attempt to reinvigorate professional practice through a tool holiday, to release the pressures that build up from over-familiarity. Yet, the Swedish collective let off steam within the context of collaborative authorship, resulting in the adoption of playful and farcical attitudes to making. Consequently the final output does not matter to We Work In A Fragile Material. The fragmented sculpture they built in London was thrown away within a week, like the ragdoll troll made in New York that was left in an alleyway next to rubbish bins.[143] With the lack of pressure to produce a defined output the artists are free to play around, at liberty to test their understanding with tools, invite failure and make without having the necessity of demonstrating learning.[144] This approach contrasts with the Bodgers' escapade in the woods that was structured according to a specific end to attain certain skills.

The comparison between the Bodgers group and We Work In A Fragile Material elucidates two approaches to adopting a different tool order, both of which draw from contrasting trajectories of learning, familiar to amateurs. The first places a premium on the acquisition of certain skills, using specific tools and historically validated procedures to create permanent, durable objects. This form is closer to what we might expect from craft education, chiming with craft theorist Peter Dormer's project to understand and write about the process of learning calligraphy and cabinet making in *The Art of the Maker*.[145] It is also similar to the way craft is taught, on the whole, in evening classes, how-to books and through the media. An amateur might not to be impressed with the whimsical and absurd trajectories of We Work In A Fragile Material, many would question the craftsmanship in their projects. But the Swedish group express a more anarchic relationship between amateurs and tools, where the individual is free to experiment with tools and play the fool, which has the potential to result in invention, discovery, error and joy. They are deliberately 'adhocist', using whatever is to hand. Neither is more or less amateur than the other: from the specific, structured instruction needed to bodge, to the improvised, slipshod characteristic of the botch, both these relationships to tooling are evident in amateur time.

The idea that the participants of We Work In A Fragile Material are taking a break from 'their own cleverness' might strike us as luxurious, predicated on their status as artists. However, the strategy of temporarily diverting practice has proved regenerative for many artists as both case studies above demonstrate; a tactic that mitigates the exhaustion and disillusionment that could potentially derive from over-specialization. The away day mentality mirrors the social reality of amateur time: a temporary displacement that results in experiences that feed back into everyday life.

The busman's holiday manifesto

For there is no prison that does not have its chinks. So even in a system that tries to exploit every last fraction of your time, you discover that with proper organisation the moment will come when the marvellous holiday of a few seconds opens up before you and you can even take three steps backward and forward, or scratch your stomach or hum something: 'Pompety pom . . .' and assuming the foreman isn't around to bother you, there'll be time, between one operation and the next, to say a couple of words to a workmate.

ITALO CALVINO, *The Workshop Hen* (2009), p. 45

In his short story about a security guard who decides to keep a hen in the disused courtyards of the factory in which he works, the Italian writer Italo Calvino succinctly explains the potential for individual autonomy even within the most regimented structures of everyday life. His words echo Adorno's presumption that capitalist regulation of time and space severely restricts individual autonomy, but highlights how everyday activities usually considered unimportant – humming, taking strides backward and forward and chatting with a co-worker – offer a degree of individual empowerment. This diversionary gesture, existing within the system, is analogous to amateur craft. Once equipped with the necessary tools and materials, amateurs can occupy the time and space of these constrained freedoms within capitalism and produce some kind of expression.

In this chapter, and in the book as a whole, I have attempted to highlight the differential characteristic of amateur craft: how its practice operates within structures of everyday life in ways that are unexpected and unique. Despite the constraints inherent to amateur time, self-imposed and otherwise, there is still potential for utopian impulses to bubble through to the surface. This motivates the appropriation of features of amateur craft among curious artists, designers and craftspeople who have been drawn to its unpredictable, roguish, anarchic, weak, quiet, idiosyncratic, playful, regenerative, socially orientated and politically ambiguous qualities.

What unites and underpins the plurality, complexity and richness of amateur experience is its relational status, the fact that it is a reply to other temporal experiences of everyday life, as Friedmann stated, not an escape: the potential to temporarily control one's own alienation. This is true of contemporary artists 'taking a break from their own cleverness' and nineteenth-century housebound wives creating patchwork quilts from offcuts and scraps. Both activities relate to a form of more overt labour alienation yet at the same time constitute a temporary release.

The phenomenon of amateur craft in modernity is more effectively grasped when it is understood as an *alternating* feature of everyday life (occur in turn repeatedly), rather than the *alternative* (available as another opportunity). This is the busman's holiday manifesto, a call for permanent part-timeism. Nineteenth-century French philosopher Charles Fourier provides the intellectual backbone for this manifesto as he argued that the human condition was better suited to variety rather than specialization, stating that 'the liveliest pleasures become insipid if others do not promptly succeed them'.[146] He named this characteristic the butterfly passion. Even something as pleasurable as fine dining depends on its temporary appearance within the routines of the everyday, as Fourier observed. He even went so far as to suggest that any activity could not be pursued profitability if it lasts longer than two hours without a break.[147]

Fourier's radical suggestions, cited by fellow theorist of utopia, Jameson,[148] contrast with the specialization and pursuit of a single vocation that had come to define the organization of labour in Western capitalism at least, and the attendant notion that mastery of a particular skill should be socially valued in and of itself. What Fourier and Jameson realized is that commitment to a single task, even if you love doing it, needs to be offset by frequent, temporary releases, through idleness, play, or deploying one's labour in a different context. Amateur craft principally concerns this re-deployment of labour, which, as I have shown, provides differential experiences of working, making, organizing, and thinking. To continue the musical metaphor that I introduced in the opening of this chapter, the melodies of amateur time have to be laid on top of the dominant harmonies of everyday life and they only make music when joined.

Amateur craft cannot exist in isolation. The optimism of Aram Sinnreich, who wishes that the whole world be 'composed of amateurs' pursuing activities out of love alone,[149] needs to be qualified. This is because amateur time only gains content through its mutual relationship with other temporal experiences and is only possible if structures of capitalist infrastructure survive – whether it be legal frameworks that limit the hours of the working week, or global networks of artistic supply, that would allow me, if I wanted, to take up rosewood carving.

This manifesto of labour diversification is not an attack on specialization and the social value placed on the mastery of a skill. There have been many examples of artists, highly specialized within their field of practice, who excelled in areas outside their primary vocation. French artist Jean Auguste Dominique Ingres (1780–1867) was a concert violinist, and the phrase 'Violon d'Ingres' – deriving from the title of a Man Ray painting influenced by Ingres (*Le Violon d'Ingres*, 1924), in which Man Ray transformed a photograph of a nude woman's back through the addition of painted 'f' holes – has become a term to describe a supplemental activity in which one excels, blurring the boundary between primary and secondary occupation. Another example where the dynamics of the 'Violon d'Ingres' were to the fore was when the small watercolour paintings and sketches of the nineteenth-century French romantic novelist, Victor Hugo, attracted critical attention in the 1910s. Art historian Henri Focillon claimed that Hugo's painted art was more unique than his well-known literary oeuvre.[150] Regardless of this critical reception, for Hugo painting offered him frequent and miniature distractions. In a letter to Charles Baudelaire in 1860 he stated of his painted art: 'It keeps me amused between two verses'.[151]

Amateur craft, the distraction, the aside, the supplemental is an expression of Fourier's butterfly passion: the pursuit of transferring between different tasks each replete with their own skills and structures, with each benefiting from their mutual undertaking. This busman's holiday manifesto for many merely reveals what is hiding in plain site. Diversification of labour is the default for many artists, designers, and craftspeople, as both Lippard and David Pye observed in the 1970s,[152] their income usually supplemented by teaching, writing, lecturing, private tuition and a variety of voluntary and social activities. The result is that the artist's primary labour is confined to the day off, weekend or spare time: the alternate temporal modality known as amateur time.

The 'Violon d'Ingres' is an intensified version of the busman's holiday whereby the individual excels in activities taking place both in and outside amateur time. However, both phrases accentuate the importance of harnessing labour-power to multiple ends and the need to withdraw from one structure of labour deployment to another. To learn from amateur craft practice, the artist and any other individual should recognize the differential qualities of this reprieve and how it both departs from and is linked to everyday experiences of life. Winston Churchill, voted the greatest Briton in a 2002 BBC poll, inhabited the *alternating* state offered by amateur craft when he painted landscapes in oils in order to exercise a different set of 'mental muscles' from those required for the affairs of state.[153] Do you?

NOTES

Introduction

1 David Pye, *The Nature and Art of Workmanship* (London: Herbert, 1995), pp. 134–5. See also Tanya Harrod, 'Paradise Postponed: William Morris in the twentieth century' in Jennifer Harris (ed.) *William Morris Revisited: Questioning the Legacy* (London: Crafts Council, 1996), p. 20.

2 Claude Lévi-Strauss, *The Savage Mind* (London: Weidenfeld and Nicolson, 1974), p. 17.

3 Lefebvre's concept of difference does not depend on the idea of novelty that so dominates our perception of artistic or poetic production but on the body's and nature's inherent ability to produce difference unconsciously within limiting structures: for example the difference of every leaf 'produced *within* the realms of the tree form, which is of course circumscribed by its own limiting conditions'. Henri Lefebvre, *The Production of Space* trans. by Donald Nicholson-Smith (Oxford: Blackwell, 2009), pp. 395–7.

4 The term 'amateurish' is widely used today pejoratively as a byword for incompetence or poor skill. For example see Peter Conrad's use of the term to describe Damian Hirst's painterly skill. Peter Conrad, 'Damian Hirst: No Love Lost, Blue Paintings' *Guardian* (18 October 2009).

5 See Albert Roland, 'Do-It-Yourself: A Walden for the Millions?' *American Quarterly* 10:2 (1958), p. 155.

6 Glenn Adamson, *The Invention of Craft* (London: Bloomsbury, 2013), xviii and xv. In this book Adamson explores the conditions of craft's self-definition in opposition to the factory, alienation and the mechanistic between 1750 and 1850 – the period associated with industrial progress – and uses this revised understanding of craft established through historical research to understand its ambiguous position in art and design practice today.

7 Betsy Greer, 'Craftivist History' in Maria Elena Buszek (ed.) *Extra/Ordinary: Craft and Contemporary Art* (Durham: Duke University Press, 2011), pp. 175–83.

8 Andy Warhol, *The Philosophy of Andy Warhol: From A to B and Back Again* (London: Penguin, 2007), p. 82.

9 Ann Bermingham, *Learning to Draw: Studies in the Cultural History of a Polite and Useful Art* (New Haven and London: Yale University Press, 2000); Kim Sloan, *A Noble Art: Amateur Artists and Drawing Masters c.1600–1800* (London: British Museum Press, 2000).

10 Paul Langford, *A Polite and Commercial People* (Oxford: Clarendon Press, 1998), p. 111; Thorstein Veblen, *Conspicuous Consumption* (London: Penguin, 2005), p. 26; Ann Bermingham, 'Aesthetics of Ignorance: The Accomplished Woman in the Culture of Connoisseurship' *The Oxford Art Journal* 16:2 (1993).

11 Arthur Schopenhauer, 'On Learning and the Learned' *Parerga and Paralipomena: volume 2* trans. by E. F. J. Payne (Oxford: Clarendon, 2000), p. 481.

12 Sloan, *A Noble Art*, p. 7.

13 Karl Marx, *Economic and Philosophical Manuscripts* in Erich Fromm (ed.) *Marx's Concept of Man* trans. by T. B. Bottomore (New York: Ungar Pub. Co., 1961), p. 151.

14 German sociologist Max Weber in his seminal work *The Spirit of Capitalism*, described capitalism as the 'vast cosmos into which a person is born. It simply exists, to each person, as a factually unalterable casing in which he or she must live'. Weber argues that capitalism in the modern world is transformed into a spirit (one to which he argued Protestantism was particularly attuned) and is not reduced to the description of economic forces but spreads into all aspects of life in which 'competence and proficiency in a vocational calling' is key. Max Weber, *The Protestant Ethic and the Spirit of Capitalism with Other Writings on the Rise of the West* trans. by Stephen Kalberg (Oxford: Oxford University Press, 2009), p. 73.

15 Karl Marx and Frederick Engels, *The Communist Manifesto* trans. by S. Moore (London: Penguin, 1967), p. 83.

16 The last chapter of Glenn Adamson's *Thinking Through Craft* – a book that re-assesses the basis of craft's inferiority in the context of modern art – entitled 'Amateur', is one of the few exceptions within material culture studies, art criticism and design history to explore this term. Adamson's focus is primarily on how various artists, including Tracey Emin, Judy Chicago and Mike Kelley, respond to the presumed abject status of amateur craft and its place in the discourse of feminism in the 1970s. I cover this subject in detail within Chapter 3. Glenn Adamson, *Thinking Through Craft* (Oxford: Berg, 2007), pp. 139–63.

17 Robert Stebbins, *Amateurs, Professionals and Serious Leisure* (Montreal and London: McGill Queen's University Press, 1992), p. 5.

18 Paul Atkinson classifies amateur do-it-yourself phenomena into four categories (pro-active, reactive, essential and lifestyle DIY). Paul Atkinson, 'Do It Youself: Democracy and Design' special issue of *Journal of Design History* 19:1 (2006), pp. 1–4.

19 Robert Hutchinson and Andrew Feist, *Amateur Arts in the UK: The PSI Survey of Amateurs Arts and Crafts in the UK* (London: Policy Study Institute, 1991), pp. x, xiii, xv and 9. For a survey of evening classes in craft education see Cherry Ann Knott, *I Can't Wait For Wednesday: The Crafts in Adult Education: A Study of Courses, Students and Tutors in Selected Geographic Areas in England and Wales* (London: Crafts Council, 1987).

20 Siegfred Kracauer, 'The Mass Ornament' in *The Mass Ornament: Weimar Essays* trans. by Thomas Y. Levin (London and Cambridge, Massachusetts: Harvard University Press, 1995), p. 75; Adamson, *Thinking Through Craft*, pp. 1–7.

21 Lefebvre, *The Production of Space*, p. 52.

22 Henri Lefebvre, *Critique of Everyday Life* vol. 2 trans. by John Moore (London: Verso, 2008), p. 131.

23 Colin Campbell, 'The Craft Consumer: Culture, Craft and Consumption in the Postmodern Era' *Journal of Consumer Culture* 5:1 (March 2005).

24 Judith Attfield, *Wild Things: The Material Culture of Everyday Life* (Oxford: Berg, 2000), p. 48; Arjun Appadurai (ed.) *The Social Life of Things: Commodities in a Cultural Perspective* (Cambridge: Cambridge University Press, 1986); Danny Miller, *Home Possessions: Material Culture Behind Closed Doors* (Oxford: Berg, 2001); Nicky Gregson and Louise Crewe, *Second-Hand Cultures* (Oxford and New York: Berg, 2003); Laura Tiersten, *Marianne in the Market: Envisioning Consumer Society in Fin-de-Siècle France* (New Haven: Yale University Press, 1991).

25 Stephen Knott, 'Design in the Age of Prosumption: The Craft of Design After the Object' *Design and Culture* 5:1 (March 2013).

26 For example Charles Leadbeater, *We Think* (London: Profile Books, 2009); Clay Shirky, *Cognitive Surplus: Creativity and Generosity in a Connected Age* (London: Penguin, 2010); David Gauntlett, *Making is Connecting: The Social Meaning of Creativity from DIY and Knitting to Youtube and Web 2.0* (Cambridge: Polity Press, 2011).

27 Andrew Keen, *The Cult of the Amateur: How Today's Internet is Killing Our Culture* (London: Nicholas Brealey Publishing, 2008).

28 See Bernhard Rieger, 'Fantasy as Social Practice: The Rise of Amateur Film', in Bernhard Rieger, *Technology and the Culture of Modernity* (Cambridge: Cambridge University Press, 2005), pp. 194–222; Patricia Zimmerman, *Reel Families: A Social History of Amateur Film* (Bloomington: Indiana University Press, 1995).

29 Charles Tepperman introduced this phrase in his paper '"We are all artists": Amateur Film and Fashion and the Art of the Everyday' at the Courtauld Institute of Art, 14 January 2014. See also Charles Tepperman, *Amateur Cinema, 1923–1960: The Rise of North American Moviemaking* (Oakland: University of California Press, 2014).

30 Karen Cross, 'The Relational Amateur' and Graham Rawle, 'Photographic "artistry" in 1950s men's magazines' in 'Reconsidering Amateur Photography' http://eitherand.org (accessed 11 June 2014). See also Karen Cross, *Amateur Photography: Work, Materiality and the Everyday* (Bristol: Intellect Books, forthcoming).

31 Steven Gelber, *Hobbies: Leisure and the Culture of Work in America* (New York: Columbia University Press, 1999), p. 20.

32 For example Andrew Jackson, 'Constructing at Home: The Experience of the Amateur Maker' *Design and Culture* 2:1 (March 2010), pp. 5–26; Fiona Hackney, 'Quiet Activism and the New Amateur: The Power of Home and Hobby Crafts' *Design and Culture* 5:2 (July 2013), pp. 179–83.

33 Grace Lees-Maffei, 'Introduction. Studying Advice: Historiography, Methodology, Commentary, Bibliography' *Journal of Design History* 16:1 (2003), pp. 1–14.

34 Elizabeth Shove, Matthew Watson, Martin Hand, and Jack Ingram, *The Design of Everyday Life* (Oxford: Berg, 2007), p. 59.

35 This idea of the overlap of function and ornament can be attributed to Seigfred Kracauer, in particular his essay 'The Mass Ornament'. See Chapter 2 for further discussion.

Chapter 1

1 George and Weedon Grossmith, *Diary of a Nobody* (London: Penguin, 1965), p. 19.

2 Ibid., pp. 42–5.

3 Describing these objects as 'things' is deliberate as it refers to work done within anthropological theory and material culture that builds on Bruno Latour's thinking to describe entities that exist between the subject–object, human-non-human dichotomy. As summarized by Bill Brown, things 'lurk in the shadows of the ballroom and continue to lurk there after the subject and object have done their thing'. Bill Brown (ed.) *Things* (Chicago: University of Chicago Press, 2004), p. 3.

4 Elizabeth Shove, Matthew Watson, Martin Hand and Jack Ingram, *The Design of Everyday Life* (Oxford: Berg, 2007), p. 16.

5 Harriet A. L. Standeven, 'Oil-Based House Paints from 1900 to 1960: An Examination of Their History and Development, with Particular Reference to Ripolin Enamels' *Journal of the American Institute for Conservation* 52:3 (2013), p. 131.

6 F. Wiltshire, 'Enamelling Bath' *Illustrated Carpenter and Builder* (26 February 1886). For an explanation of the firing process as understood by a contemporaneous source see W. N. Brown, *A Handbook on Japanning and Enamelling* (London: Scott Greenwood & Co, 1901), p. 17.

7 Editor (Francis Chilton-Young), 'Notes and Novelties' *Amateur Work* 4 (May 1886), pp. 329–30.

8 Standeven, 'Oil-based House Paints', p. 132. For a broader overview of the late-nineteenth- and early twentieth-century development of hygiene see Bruno Latour, *Pasteurization of France* trans. by Alan Sheridan and John Law (Cambridge, Massachusetts and London: Harvard University Press, 1988).

9 H. Hartnell (12 March 1886), 'An Amateur' (11 November 1887) and S. Smith (10 August 1888) are among the readers of *Illustrated Carpenter and Builder* who recommend Chez Lui and Aspinall's Enamel.

10 Gavin Stamp, 'Probably the Best Corporate Slogan' *BBC News* (2006), http://news.bbc.co.uk/1/hi/business/5036084.stm (accessed 15 June 2014).

11 As new enamel paint products became more accessible and popular between the years 1885 and 1892, the chief voice of criticism of these new products in the *Illustrated Carpenter and Builder* was Ernest W. Lethaly. Lethaly claimed that stoving was still the 'proper' way of proceeding with enamelling (particularly baths). Ernest W. Lethaly, 'Notes and Queries' *Illustrated Carpenter and Builder* (30 September 1892).

12 Harry A. Spurr, *Mel B. Spurr: His Life, Work, Writings and Recitations* (London: Brown and Sons, 1920).

13 'Aspinall's Enamel', written by W. M. Mayne, composed by Leslie Harris, sung by Mel B. Spurr (London: Reynolds & Co, Berners Street).

14 Shove, *The Design of Everyday Life*, pp. 54–6.

15 Thierry de Duve, 'The Readymade and the Tube of Paint' *Artforum* 24:8 (April 1986), pp. 113–14.

16 James Ayres, *The Artist's Craft: A History of Tools, Techniques and Materials* (Oxford: Phaidon, 1985) p. 87.

17 John Roberts, *The Intangibilities of Form: Skill and Deskilling in Art After the Readymade* (London: Verso, 2007), p. 159.

18 *Twentieth Century Painting and Sculpture in the Philadelphia Museum of Art* (2000), p. 48.

19 De Duve, 'The Readymade', p. 116.

20 Marcel Duchamp, 'A propos the ready made' *Art and Artistry* 1:4 (July 1966) in Gloria Moure, *Marcel Duchamp: Work, Writings and Interviews* (Barcelona: Ediciones Polígrafa, c2009), p. 123.

21 Editor, 'Notes and Novelties', pp. 329–30.

22 This is exemplified by two essays in a recent issue of *The Journal of Modern Craft* where Duchamp's *Fountain* is discussed from the perspective of its material constitution as a ceramic vessel. John Roberts and Ezra Shales's essays in *The Journal of Modern Craft* 6:3 (November 2013).

23 Anthea Callen, *The Art of Impressionism* (New Haven and London: Yale University Press, 2000), p. 3; Kimberly Schenck, 'Crayon, Paper and Print' in Jay Fisher and David Becker (eds) *Essence of Line: French Drawings from Ingres to Degas* (London: Pennsylvania State University Press, 2005), p. 58; David Bomford, *Impressionism* (London: National Gallery in association with Yale University Press, 1990), p. 40.

24 In *Ornament and Crime*, Loos equates decoration with a pre-modern Papuan or childish degeneracy and states that he would always prefer a plain gingerbread man rather than one shaped like a heart. Adolf Loos, 'Ornament and Crime' [1908] in Adolf Loos, *Ornament and Crime: Selected Essays* trans. by Michael Mitchell (California: Ariadne Press, 1998), pp. 167–9.

25 Clement Greenberg, 'Avant-garde and Kitsch' [1939], in Clement Greenberg, *The Collected Essays and Criticism* (Chicago and London: Chicago University Press, 1986), p. 12.

26 Elissa Auther explains how Greenberg thought Pollock was able 'to wrench from the decorative the flat, all-over surface and use it in the service of high art'. Elissa Auther, 'Wallpaper, the Decorative, and Contemporary Installation Art' in Maria Elena Buszek (ed.) *Extra/Ordinary: Craft in Contemporary Art* (Durham and London: Duke University Press, 2011), p. 121.

27 Jacques Derrida, *The Truth in Painting* trans. by Geoff Bennington and Ian McLeod (Chicago and London: The University of Chicago Press, 1987), p. 59.

28 Ibid., p. 61.

29 Ibid., p. 81.

30 Carl Knapett, 'Photographs, Skeuomorphs and Marionettes' *Journal of Material Culture* 7:1 (2002), p. 99. Alfred Gell, *Art and Agency: An Anthropological Theory* (Oxford: Clarendon, 1998), pp. 7–12. Bruno Latour, *We Have Never Been Modern* trans. by Catherine Porter (New York and London: Harvester Wheatsheaf, 1993).

31 Gell, *Art and Agency*, pp. 73–95.

32 Grant McCracken, 'Ever Dearer in Our Thoughts' in *Culture and Consumption: New Approaches to the Symbolic Character of Consumer Goods and Activities* (Bloomington: Indiana University Press, 1988), pp. 31–43.

33 Celeste Olalqiaga, *Artificial Kingdom: On the Kitsch Experience* (Minneapolis: University of Minnesota Press, 2002), p. 28 and pp. 90–4.

34 Manuel Charpy, 'Patina and Bourgeoisie: Appearances of the Past in Nineteenth-Century Paris' in Glenn Adamson and Victoria Kelley (eds) *Surface Tensions: Surface, Finish and the Meaning of Objects* (Manchester: Manchester University Press, 2013), pp. 45–59.

35 Adamson and Kelley, *Surface Tensions*, pp. 1–12.

36 Victoria Kelley, 'Housekeeping: Shine, Polish, Gloss and Glaze as Surface Strategies in the Domestic Interior' in Deirdre McMahon and Janet Myers (eds) *Material Possessions: The Objects and Textures of Everyday Life in Imperial Britain* (Athens: University of Ohio Press, forthcoming).

37 J. G. Ballard, *Millennium People* (London: Harper Perennial, 2008), p. 93.

38 For example Martin Kemp, *Science of Art: Optical Themes in Western Art from Brunelleschi to Seurat* (New Haven: Yale University Press, 1990); John Gage, *Colour in Art* (London: Thames and Hudson, 2006); Trevor Lamb and Janine Bourriau (eds) *Colour: Art and Science* (Cambridge: Cambridge University Press, 1995); Vojtěch Jirat-Wasiutynski, *Technique and Meaning in the Paintings of Paul Gauguin* (Cambridge: Cambridge University Press, 2000); Marjorie Wieseman, *A Closer Look: Deceptions and Discoveries* (London: National Gallery, 2010); Rita Jones refutes claims of the sub-discipline's 'ancillary' character in the introduction to Stephen Hackney (ed.) *Paint and Purpose: A Study of Technique in British Art* (London: Tate Gallery, 1999), p. 9.

39 Charles Rosen and Henri Zerner, 'The Ideology of the Licked Surface' in *Romanticism and Realism: The Mythology of Nineteenth Century Art* (London: Faber, 1984), pp. 222–3.

40 Albert Boime, *The Academy and French Painting in the Nineteenth Century* (London: Phaidon, 1971), p. 87.

41 Callen, *The Art of Impressionism*, p. 12.

42 Ulrich Lehmann, 'The Trademark Tracey Emin' in Mandy Merch and Chris Townsend (eds) *The Art of Tracey Emin* (London: Thames & Hudson, 2002), p. 60.

43 Marcel Proust, *Swann's Way: Remembrance of Things Past* trans. by C. K. Scott Moncrieff (London: Chatto & Windus, 1922), pp. 51–2.

44 Pierre Bourdieu, *Distinction: A Social Critique of the Judgment of Taste* trans. by Richard Nice (New York and London: Routledge, 2007), pp. 3–4.

45 Thomas Crow, 'Hand-Made Photographs and Homeless Representation' *October* 62 (Autumn 1992), pp. 123–32.

46 Glenn Adamson, *The Invention of Craft* (London: Bloomsbury, 2013), p. 57.

47 For example Waldemar Januszczak, *The Impressionists: Painting and Revolution. Episode 1: 'Gang of Four'* (BBC 2: first broadcast 16 July 2011).

48 Marshall McLuhan, *The Medium is the Message* (London: Penguin, 2008).

49 R. D. Harley, *Artists Pigments c1600–1835* (London: Butterworth Scientific, 1982), p. 41.

50 Roger Magraw, *A History of the French Working Class Volume 1: The Age of the Artisan Revolution* (Oxford: Blackwell, 1992), p. 14.

51 Adam Smith, *The Wealth of Nations* (London: Penguin, 1970), pp. 109–10.

52 See supplementary catalogue to Henry R. Robertson, *The Art of Etching Explained and Illustrated: With Remarks on the Allied Processes of Drypoint, Mezzotint, and Aquatint* (London: Winsor & Newton, 1883), p. 3. Also Don Pavey, *The Artists' Colourmen's Story: a Guide to the History of Artists' Colourmen of London* (Harrow: Reckitt & Colman Leisure Limited, 1984), pp. 28 and 35.

53 Leslie Carlyle, *The Artist's Assistant: Oil Painting Instruction Manuals and Handbooks in Britain 1800–1900* (London: Archetype Publications, 2001), pp. 185–6. For examples in art supply firms' catalogues see 'Geo Rowney & Co's Catalogue' supplement to Alfred Clint, *A Guide to Oil Painting* (London: Geo Rowney & Co., 1855), pp. 56–7 and Winsor & Newton's supplement to Henry Murray, *The Art of Portrait Painting in Oil Colours, With Observations on Setting and Painting the Figure* (London: Winsor and Newton, 1851), pp. 2–3.

54 Bomford, *Impressionism*, p. 44.

55 Callen, *The Art of Impressionism*, p. 67.

56 Nicola Moorby, 'Water + Colour: Explaining the Medium' in Alison Smith (ed.) *Watercolour* (London: Tate, 2011), pp. 25–6; Ayres, *The Artist's Craft*, pp. 56 and 83.

57 Peter Bower, 'The Evolution and Development of "Drawing Papers" and the Effect of This Development on Watercolour Artists, 1750–1850' in *The Oxford Papers: Proceedings of The British Association of Paper Historians Fourth Annual Conference held at St. Edmund Hall, Oxford*, Peter Bower (ed.) (London: The Association of Paper Historians, 1996), p. 63.

58 Carlyle, *The Artist's Assistant*, p. 147; Pavey, *The Artists' Colourmen's Story*, p. 1.

59 Pavey, *The Artists' Colourmen's Story*, p. 8.

60 Moorby, 'Water + Colour', p. 23.

61 Bomford, *Impressionism*, p. 39.

62 Adverts for collapsible metallic tubes of paint first appeared in trade magazines from the 1850s and as supplementary price lists in the back of art advice manuals published by large firms such as Winsor & Newton and LeFranc et Cie. For example see 'Winsor & Newton's List of Materials for Oil Painting' supplement to Murray *The Art of Portrait Painting*, pp. 4–5; a similar supplement also advertises these oils in Henry Murray, *Artistic Anatomy of the Human Figure* (London: Winsor and Newton, 1853). Moist watercolours in tubes were also sold as shown in Winsor and Newton's catalogue supplement in Charles William Day, *The Art of Miniature Painting, Comprising Instructions Necessary for the Acquirement of that Art* (London: Winsor & Newton, 1852).

63 De Duve, 'The Readymade', p. 115.

64 Ibid., p. 116.

65 Callen, *The Art of Impressionism*, pp. 3–4.

66 Schenck, 'Crayon, Paper and Print', p. 58.

67 Callen, *The Art of Impressionism*, p. 98. Cornelia Peres, *A Closer Look: Technical and Art-Historical Studies on Works by Van Gogh and Gauguin* (Waanders: Zwolle, 1991), p. 30.

68 Johan Georges Vibert, *La science de la peinture* (Pairs, 1891), p. 12.

69 Karl Robert, *Traité practique de la pienture à l'huile. Paysage* (Paris, 1891), pp. 34–5. Author's translation.

70 Vibert, *La science*, pp. 100–7.

71 Gabriel Déneux, *Un procédé de peinture inaltérable. La peinture à l'encaustique* (Paris, 1890), p. 9. Author's translation.

72 Henry Seward, *Manual of Colours: Showing the Composition and Properties of Artists' Colours, with Experiments on their Permanence* (London: Rowney, 1889), preface.

73 Cited in W. E. Killik, *A Short History of the House of Winsor & Newton* (Winsor & Newton Library, Turner Room) in Pavey, *The Artists' Colourmen's Story*, p. 19.

74 Winsor & Newton, *The Art of Landscape Painting* (London: Winsor and Newton, 1855), p. 1.

75 Moorby, 'Water + Colour', p. 24.

76 Armand Cassagne, *Traité de l'aquarelle* (Paris, 1886), p. 3. Author's translation.

77 De Duve, 'The Readymade', p. 116.

78 Murray, *The Art of Portrait Painting*, p. 10.

79 Murray, *The Art of Portrait Painting*, pp. 11–12 and 20–6. Cassagne suggests that twenty colours are enough for a masterpiece, Cassagne, *Traité de l'aquarelle*, p. 5.

80 Stewart argues that miniaturization is an 'antithetical mode of production' producing something by the hand, or artisanal labour to stand in for what the original lacks. Susan Stewart, *On Longing: Narratives on the Miniature, the Gigantic, the Souvenir, the Collection* (London and New York: Johns Hopkins University Press, 1984), pp. 57 and 68.

81 Jeremy Aynsley and Kate Forde (eds) *Design and the Modern Magazine* (Manchester: Manchester University Press, 2007), p. 6, and Kelley pp. 79–80 in the same publication.

82 Harry Peacham, *The Art of Drawing with a Pen, and Limming in Watercolours . . . with the True Manner of Painting Upon Glasse, the Order of Making your Furnace, Annealing, etc.* (London: R. Braddock for W. Jones, 1606). See also Harry Peacham, *The Compleat Gentleman: Fashioning Him Absolute in the Most Necessary and Commendable Qualities Concerning Minde or Bodie, etc.* (London: F Constable, 1622).

83 Peacham, *The Art of Drawing*, Introduction.

84 Ibid.

85 Penny Sparke, 'Furnishing the Aesthetic Interior: Manuals and Theories' in Stephen Galloway and Lynn Orr (eds) *The Cult of Beauty: the Aesthetic Movement 1860–1900* (London: V&A Publishing, 2011), pp. 124–33; Emma Ferry, ' ". . . information for the ignorant and aid for the advancing . . .": Macmillan's "Art at Home" series, 1876–83' in Aysley and Forde, *Design and the Modern Magazine*, p. 151. See also Emma Ferry, ' "Decorators May Be Compared To Doctors": An Analysis of Rhoda and Agness Garrett's *Suggestion For House Decoration in Painting, Woodblock and Furniture (1896)'* and Penny Sparke, 'The "Ideal" and the "Real" Interior in Elsie de Wolfe's "The House in Good Taste" of 1873' *Journal of Design History* 16.1 (2003).

86 Grace Lees-Maffei, 'Introduction. Studying Advice: Historiography, Methodology, Commentary, Bibliography' *Journal of Design History* 16:1 (2003), p. 5. The ideological content of advice literature has proved to be of continuing interest as shown by a recent issue of the academic journal *Interiors* where a special issue was devoted to the topic. Patricia Lara-Betancourt and Emma Hardy (guest editors), 'Seductive Discourses: Design Advice for the Home' *Interiors* 5:2 (2014).

87 Bourdieu, *Distinction*, p. 176.

88 Couleru's genre hierarchy elevated landscapes and belittled still life and animal painting. Couleru, *Cours elementaire de coloris et d'aquarelle* (Paris, 1856), pp. 5–6. Francis Nicholson states that talent cannot be fully expressed in subjects such as 'scoured pots and pans' or a 'man eating oysters'. Francis Nicholson, *The Practice of Drawing and Painting Landscape from Nature in Water-colours Exemplified in a Series of Instructions . . . Including Elements of Perspective . . . With Observations on the Study of Nature . . . and Various Other Matters Relative to the Arts* (London, 1823), p. 52.

89 George Brookshaw, *A New Treatise of Flower Painting, Or, Every Lady her Own Drawing Master: Containing Familiar and Easy Instructions for Acquiring a Perfect Knowledge of Drawing Flowers with Accuracy and Taste* (London: Longman, Hurst, Rees, Orme and Brown, 1818), pp. 2–3.

90 Ann Bermingham, *Learning to Draw: Studies in the Cultural History of a Polite and Useful Art* (New Haven and London: Yale University Press, 2000), p. 129.

91 Nicholson, *The Practice of Drawing*, pp. 32–3.

92 Joshua Reynolds in John Clark, *The Amateur's Assistant: Or, a Series of Instructions in Sketching from Nature* (London: printed for Samuel Leigh, 1826), pp. 1–2.

93 Nicholson, *The Practice of Drawing*, p. 45.

94 Graham Rawle, *Woman's World* (London: Atlantic, 2006); Graham Rawle, *Diary of an Amateur Photographer* (London: Picador, 1998).

95 For example, in their pursuit of horticulture and landscaping, Bouvard and Pécuchet notice that different manuals contradict each other. Gustave Flaubert, *Bouvard and Pécuchet* trans. by A. J. Krailsheimer (Harmondsworth: Penguin, 1976), pp. 47 and 205.

96 Thomas Leeson Rowbotham, *The Art of Sketching From Nature* (London: Winsor & Newton, 1851), p. 47.

97 Thomas Colman Dibdin, *A Guide to Water Colour Painting* (London: Reeves and Sons), p. 1.

98 Peter Dormer, *The Art of the Maker* (London: Thames & Hudson, 1994), pp. 41–3.

99 For example see Bernard Leach, *A Potter's Book* (London: Faber and Faber, 1940); Edward Johnston, *Writing, Illuminating and Lettering . . . With Diagrams and Illustrations by the Author and Noel Rooke* (London: The Artistic Crafts Series of Technical Handbooks, 1906); Christopher Whall, *Stained Glass Work: A Text-book for Students and Workers in Glass* (London: John Hogg, 1905); Ethel Mairet, *Vegetable Dyes* (London: Faber and Faber, 1916).

100 David Hockney, *Secret Knowledge: Rediscovering the Lost Techniques of the Old Masters* (London: Thames & Hudson, 2001), p. 14.

101 Leonardo da Vinci quoted in Kemp, *Science of Art*, p. 163.

102 Arnaud Maillet, *The Claude Glass: Use and Meaning of the Black Mirror in Western Art* trans. by Jeff Fort (New York: Zone, 2009), p. 27.

103 On the eighteenth-century amateur audience for the Claude Glass see ibid., p. 20; Sloan, *A Noble Art*, p. 175; Kemp, *The Science of Art*, p. 199.

104 Maillet, *The Claude Glass*, pp. 100–1.

105 Kemp, *The Science of Art*, p. 199.

106 Jonathan Crary, *Suspensions of Perception: Attention, Spectacle and Modern Culture* (Cambridge, Massachusetts and London: MIT Press, 1999), p. 12.

107 Maillet, *The Claude Glass*, p. 147.

108 Armand Cassagne, *Guide de la nature chez toi, suite aux modèles à silhouette* (Paris, 1886), p. 19. Author's translation.

109 Ibid., p. 19.

110 Cassagne's progressive lessons came in a series of twelve volumes and were later translated into English as *Drawing for the Million*. Armand Cassagne, *Dessin pour tous. Méthode Cassagne. Cahiers d'exercices progressifs* (Paris, 1862).

111 Deborah Silvermann, 'Weaving Painting: Religious and Social Origins of Vincent Van Gogh's Pictorial Labour' in Michael Roth (ed.) *Rediscovering History: Culture, Politics and the Psyche* (Stanford, California: Stanford University Press, 1994), p. 155.

112 Among the many examples of books that provide this detailed walkthrough are Dibdin's *Guide*, Cassagne's *Dessin pour tous*, and John Burnet, *Practical Hints on Portrait Painting: Illustrated by Examples from the Works of Van Dyck and Other Masters* (London: J. S. Virtue, 1860).

113 Louis Gelber in 1917 made a simple paint-by-number sketch of a girl with a duck. Lawrence Rinder, 'Paint-by-number' *Nest Magazine: A Quarterly of Interiors* (Spring 2001), p. 169. Dan Robbins, *Whatever Happened to Paint-by-numbers: A Humorous Personal Account of What It Took to Make Anyone an 'Artist'* (Delavan, Wisconsin: Possum Hill Press, 1997), p. 24.

114 Karal Ann Marling, *As Seen on TV: Visual Culture in Everyday Life in the 50s* (Cambridge, Massachusetts and London: Harvard University Press, 1994), p. 59.

115 'Art World Battles' *The Grand Rapids Herald* (13 June 1954).

116 Greenberg, 'Avant-garde and Kitsch', p. 17.

117 William Bird, *Paint by Number: The How-to Craze that Swept the Nation* (New York: Princeton Architectural Press, 2001). See also website for the exhibition: http://americanhistory.si.edu/paint/introduction.html (accessed 4 September 2011).

118 Michael O'Donoghue, 'Paint-by-number' *Nest: A Quarterly of Interiors* (Spring 2001), p. 172.

119 Ibid.

120 Ibid.

121 Marling writes a chapter that situates the paint-by-number medium in the wider context of post-war leisure. Chapter 2, 'Hyphenated culture' in Marling, *As Seen on TV*, pp. 50–85. Albert Roland describes do-it-yourself hobbies as a way of 'freeing people from guilt feelings about their abundant leisure'. Albert Roland, 'Do-It-Yourself: A Walden for the Millions?' *American Quarterly* 10:2 (1958), p. 158.

122 See Chapter 2.

123 Ernest Dichter, *Handbook of Consumer Motivation. The Psychology of the World of Objects* (New York: McGraw Hill Book Co, 1964), p. 449.

124 David Smith explains how for amateurs in the 1950s 'it was far more rewarding to imitate Norman Rockwell then Jackson Pollock'. David Smith, *Money For Art: The Tangled Web of Art and Politics in American Democracy* (Chicago: Ivan R. Dee, 2008), p. 44.

125 O'Donoghue, 'Paint-by-Number', p. 172. Marling, *As Seen on TV*, p. 66.

126 See Chapter 3.

127 Carol Belland, 'Post-a-Reminiscence' (15 May 2001). See other contributors to the Smithsonian's 'Post-a-Reminiscence' blog on the website set up to accompany William Bird's 2001–2 show, *By the Numbers: Accounting for Taste in the 1950s* for more tales of encounters with the kit. Shirley Bumbalough (14 June 2001), Barbara (22 April 2002), Carol W. Elliott (7 April 2001), Loren Blakeslee (23 April 2001), Reatha Wilkins (19 February 2002), and Betsy Holzgraf (24 August 2001).

128 Anonymous, 'Post-a-Reminiscence' (30 April 2001).

129 Marsha Rogers (29 June 2001), Kathryn L. Bergstrom (10 April 2001), Julie Hulvey (5 May 2001), and Reatha Wilkins (19 February 2002) on the Smithsonian's 'Post-a-Reminiscence' website. Reatha Wilkins's work can be seen on Saatchi's online catalogue: http://www.saatchionline.com/art/view/artist/96851/art/1085380 (accessed 28 June 2014).

130 Bird praises the democratic associations of paint-by-number. Sasha Archibald and David Serlin, 'By The Numbers: An Interview with William L. Bird Jr' *Cabinet* 15 (2004).

131 Peter Skolnik, *Fads: America's Crazes, Fevers and Fancies, from the 1890s to the 1970s* (New York: Crowell, 1978), pp. 160–1.

132 Anonymous, Post-a-Reminiscence (16 February 2005).

133 Bird, *Paint by Number*, p. 17.

134 'Art World Battles over *Numbers* Racket' *Sunday Democrat and Times* (28 March 1954).

135 O'Donoghue, 'Paint-by-Number', p. 172.

136 Walter Benjamin's definition of manual reproduction that he chiefly associates with forgery, is distinguished from processes of technical reproduction (photography and film). Walter Benjamin, 'The Work of Art in the Age of Mechanical Reproduction' in Walter Benjamin, *Illuminations*, trans. by Harry Zorn (London: Pimlico, 1999), p. 214.

137 Robbins describes the process as 'a painstakingly arduous task'. Robbins, *Whatever Happened*, pp. 48–50.

138 Robbins recalls Willie's 'Finger system' that involved 'smooshing' together different colours of wet paint to achieve comparable colours to Robbins's samples. For more on the production process of early paint-by-number see Dan Robbins, chapter five, 'Getting Ready', and chapter seven, 'First Test Run', in *Whatever Happened*, pp. 35–51 and 67–75.

139 Ibid., pp. 78–9.

140 David Pye, *The Nature and Art of Workmanship* in Glenn Adamson (ed.) *The Craft Reader* (Oxford: Berg, 2010), p. 342.

141 Bird, *Paint by Number*, p. 17.

142 Reatha Wilkins, 'Post-a-Reminiscence' (19 February 2002). For similar stories see Linda Beason (4 June 2001) and Kathryn L. Bergstrom (10 April 2001).

143 Lawrence Rinder, Introduction to 'Paint-by-Number' *Nest: a Quarterly of Interiors* (Spring 2001), p. 169.

144 Dario Gamboni, 'Ai Weiwei: Portrait of the Artist as Iconoclast' in Moore and Torchia (eds) *Dropping the Urn* (Glenside, PA: Arcadia University Art Gallery, 2010), p. 85.

145 For an account of paint-by-number after its boom in the 1950s and early 1960s, see Robbins, *Whatever Happened*, pp. 231–44.

146 John C. Welchman, *Art After Appropriation: Essays on Art in the 1990s* (Australia: G + B Arts International, 2003), p. 24.

147 Sue Taylor, 'Don Baum: Domus' (Madison, Wisconsin: Madison Art Center, 1988).

148 Thelma Adams, 'Context, Content and Intention: An Interview With Trey Speegle' in *Trey Speegle: What Are You Waiting For?* Cheryl Hazan Gallery (March–April 2008).

149 Trey Speegle, 'Artist Interview: Trey Speegle' *Artlog* (8 March 2011).

150 The show drew a crowd of 1,000 people on its first night. Mary Daniels, 'Count on It: Who Would Have Ever Thought Those Paint-by-numbers Compositions Would Reach Art Gallery Status?' *Chicago Tribune* (12 September 1993).

151 Selected newspaper coverage of this collecting boom includes V. E. Gehrt, 'By The Numbers: Dan Robbins Helped Generations of Americans Put a Piece of His and Their Creativity on the Living Room Wall' *Chicago Tribune* (1 January 1995). Lynn Van Matre, 'Another Brush with Fame: Fifty Years After Paint-by-numbers Kits Emerged, Nostalgia Over the Fad is Colouring Pop Culture' *Chicago Tribune* (18 January 1999).

152 Susan Sontag, 'Notes on "Camp" ' in Susan Sontag *Against Interpretation* (London: Eyre & Spottiswoode, 1967), p. 292.

153 Sophie Morris, 'Priceless! Art's Great Disasters' *The Independent* (31 July 2008), http://www.independent.co.uk/arts-entertainment/art/features/priceless-arts-great-disasters-881280.html (accessed 18 June 2014).

154 Matthew Higgs (ed.) *Thrift Store Paintings: A Primer* (London: Institute of Contemporary Arts, 2000).

155 Julian Stallabrass, 'Thrift Store Paintings' *New Statesman* (16 October 2000), pp. 42–3, http://www.courtauld.ac.uk/people/stallabrass_julian/PDF/Shaw.pdf (accessed 5 September 2011).

156 Neal Brown, 'A Noble Art/Jim Shaw' *Frieze* 57 (March 2001), http://www.frieze.com/issue/review/a_noble_art_jim_shaw/ (accessed 1 September 2011).

157 Brian O'Doherty, *Inside the White Cube: The Ideology of the Gallery Space* (Santa Monica, San Francisco: The Lapis Press), p. 15.

158 Colin Rhodes, *Outsider Art: Spontaneous Alternatives* (London: Thames and Hudson, 2000).

159 Andy Warhol is famous for saying 'If you want to know about Andy Warhol, just look at the surface of my paintings and films and me, there I am. There's nothing behind it'. Gretchen Berg, 'Andy Warhol: My True Story' *The East Village Other* (1 November 1966) in Kenneth Goldsmith (ed.) *I'll Be Your Mirror: the Selected Andy Warhol Interviews 1962–1987* (New York: Carroll & Graf, 2004), p. 90.

160 Auther, 'Wallpaper, the Decorative', pp. 115–30.

161 Alan R. Pratt (ed.) *The Critical Response to Andy Warhol* (Westport: Greenwood Press, 1997), xxii.

162 Meredith Schiff, 'I Think Everybody Should Be Like Everybody Else: The Hidden Significance of the Andy Warhol *Do It Yourself* Series of 1962' (unpublished master's thesis, University of Cincinnati, 2002), p. 2. Heiner Bastian (ed.) *Andy Warhol: Retrospective* (London: Tate Publishing, 2001), p. 24.

163 Schiff, 'I Think Everybody', p. 12.

164 Georg Frei and Neil Printz (eds) *The Andy Warhol Catalogue Raisonné* (London: Phaidon, 2002), p. 169.

165 Warhol manipulated the colour of these works. In *Do It Yourself (Seascape)*, the section numbered '18' should actually be '6' if the Venus Paradise kits colour instructions were adhered to; 'Navy Blue', not the smoky grey as seen in the final work. Frei and Printz, *The Andy Warhol Catalogue*, p. 169. A list of the original colour–number combinations of the Venus Paradise kits can be found at a WetCanvas forums thread entitled 'Venus Paradise Pencils' started by 'alleypond', http://www.wetcanvas.com/forums/showthread.php?t=228997 (accessed 12 October 2011).

166 Patrick Smith, *Warhol: Conversations About the Artist* (London: UMI Research Press, 1988), p. 60.

167 Arthur Danto, *Beyond the Brillo Box: The Visual Arts in Post-Historical Perspective* (Berkeley and London: University of California Press, 1992), p. 134.

168 Ibid., p. 66. See also Michael Lobel, *Image Duplicator: Roy Lichtenstein and the Emergence of Pop Art* (New Haven: Yale University Press, 2002).

169 Max Kozloff, 'Johns and Duchamp' *Art International* 8:2 (March 1964) in Carlos Basualdo and Erica F. Battle (eds) *Dancing Around the Bride: Cage, Cunningham, Johns and Duchamp* (New Haven and London: Yale University Press, 2013), p. 93.

170 Ibid., p. 95.

171 Nicolas Bourriaud, *Relational Aesthetics* trans. by Simon Pleasance and Fronza Wood (Dijon: les presses du réel, 2002).

172 Richard Noble, 'Painting By Other Means' Catalogue for *Jeff McMillan The Possibility of an Island* (London: PEER Gallery, 2009).

173 Ibid.

174 Gell, *Art and Agency*, p. 18.

175 Ralph Rugoff in Grace Kook-Anderson and Claire Fitzsimmons (eds) *Amateurs* (San Francisco: California College of the Arts, 2008), p. 11.

Chapter 2

1 Email conversation with James Rigler (21 May 2014).

2 Jackson Lears, *No Place of Grace* (Chicago and London: University of Chicago Press, 1981), p. 95.

3 Matthew Crawford, *The Case for Working With Your Hands: Or Why Office Work is Bad for Us and Fixing Things Feels Good* (London: Viking, 2009), p. 3. See also Hackney, 'Quiet Activism and the New Amateur', p. 174.

4 Antimodernism, according to Jackson Lears, describes the late nineteenth- and early twentieth-century reaction of American and European Arts and Crafts ideologues to 'overcivilization', exemplified by stringent labour organization, regularization and the cultural and moral degradation of cities and modern work. See Lears, *No Place of Grace*, pp. 4–5 and 60–3.

5 Henri Lefebvre, *The Production of Space* trans. by David Nicholson-Smith (Oxford: Blackwell, 2009), p. 6.

6 Ibid.

7 Ibid., p. 7.

8 Ben Highmore, *Everyday Life and Cultural Theory: An Introduction* (London: Routledge, 2002), p. 32.

9 Walter Benjamin, *The Arcades Project* trans. by Howard Eiland and Kevin McLaughlin (Cambridge, Massachusetts and London: The Belknap Press of Harvard University Press, 2002), pp. 517–21 and 568.

10 Joe Moran, *Reading the Everyday* (London: Routledge, 2005), pp. 12–13. See also Joe Moran, *Queuing For Beginners: The Story of Daily Life From Breakfast to Bedtime* (London: Profile, 2007).

11 Highmore, *Everyday Life and Cultural Theory*, p. 21.

12 Gaston Bachelard, *The Poetics of Space* (Oregon: Beacon Press, 1994), xxxvii.

13 Ibid., p. 67, and see p. 81 for a description of boxes as reflecting a need for secrecy.

14 Freud's approach in the *Psychopathology of Everyday Life* was to identify the common mundane slips, mistakes and forgetfulness of habitual human behaviour that unearth layers of meaning underneath civilization's veil. Sigmund Freud, *The Psychopathology of Everyday Life* trans. by Anthea Bell (London: Penguin, 2002).

15 Highmore, *Everyday Life and Cultural Theory*, p. 171.

16 Lefebvre, *Production of Space*, p. 14.

17 Ibid., p. 17.

18 Moran, *Reading the Everyday*, p. 23.

19 Michel de Certeau, *The Practice of Everyday Life* trans. by Steven Rendall (Berkeley and London: University of California Press, 1988), p. 25.

20 Ibid., p. 26.

21 Highmore, *Everyday Life and Cultural Theory*, pp. 153–4.

22 Lefebvre, *Production of Space*, p. 15.

23 Ibid., p. 71.

24 Ibid., p. 354.

25 Ibid., p. 385.

26 Highmore, *Everyday Life and Cultural Theory*, p. 122.

27 Karl Marx, *Capital: A Critical Analysis of Capitalist Production* trans. by Samuel Moore and Edward Aveling (London: Lawrence & Wishart, 1970), p. 209.

28 The division of labour is explained through the example of pin manufacture in Adam Smith, *The Wealth of Nations* (London: Penguin, 1970), pp. 109–10.

29 Marx, *Capital*, p. 181.

30 Karl Marx, 'Marx to Friedrich Bolte in New York' (23 November 1871) trans. by Donna Torr in *Marx and Engels Correspondence* (International Publishers, 1968), http://www.marxists.org/archive/marx/works/1871/letters/71_11_23.htm (accessed 9 September 2011).

31 Hannah Arendt, *The Human Condition* (Chicago and London: University of Chicago Press, 1958), p. 126.

32 Ibid., p. 133.

33 Karl Marx, 'The German Ideology' from *Karl Marx: Selected Writings* David McLellan (ed.) (Oxford: Oxford University Press, 2000), p. 185.

34 Arendt, *The Human Condition*, p. 88.

35 Ibid., pp. 117–18. See also Thorstein Veblen, *Conspicuous Consumption* (London: Penguin, 2005), p. 22.

36 John Ruskin, *The Nature of the Gothic* (London: George Allen, 1892), p. 15.

37 Martin Heidegger, 'The Thing', originally delivered as a lecture to the Bayerischen Akademie der Schonen Kunste [1950] in Glenn Adamson (ed.) *The Craft Reader* (Oxford and New York: Berg, 2010), p. 406.

38 Bernard Leach, *The Potter's Book* (London: Faber and Faber, 1976), chapter one, 'Towards a Standard', pp. 1–27.

39 Richard Sennett, *The Craftsman* (London: Allen Lane, 2008), p. 178.

40 George Obsourne, '2011 Budget: Britain is open for business', https://www.gov.uk/government/news/2011-budget-britain-open-for-business (accessed 31 May 2014).

41 Talia Schaffer, *Novel Craft: Victorian Domestic Handicraft and Nineteenth Century Fiction* (New York and Oxford: Oxford University Press), p. 5. Jennifer Harris, *William Morris Revisited: Questioning the Legacy* (London: Crafts Council, 1996), p. 54.

42 Henri Lefebvre, *Critique of Everyday Life* vol. 3 trans. by John Moore (London: Verso, 2008), p. 21.

43 Henry Heerup, 'All Art Ought to be Folkelig' *Helhesten* 2 (5–6) trans. by Kristina Rapacki in Primary Text feature of *The Journal of Modern Craft* 7:2 (July 2014), p. 209.

44 Arendt, *The Human Condition*, p. 7.

45 Gilles Deleuze and Félix Guattari's model mixture between 'smooth' and 'striated' space provides a conceptual precedent for the dialectical interaction amateur space and other spaces of everyday life. Gilles Deleuze and Félix Guattari, *A Thousand Plateaus: Capitalism and Schizophrenia* trans. by Brian Massumi (Minneapolis: University of Minnesota Press, 1987), pp. 474–5.

46 Charles Leadbeater and Paul Miller, *The Pro-Am Revolution: How Enthusiasts are Changing our Society* (Demos, 2004), p. 9, http://www.demos.co.uk/files/proamrevolutionfinal.pdf (accessed 13 June 2014).

47 Ibid., p. 12.

48 Francis Chilton-Young, *Every Man His Own Mechanic: A Complete and Comprehensive Guide to Every Description of Constructive and Decorative Work that May Be Done By the Amateur Artisan, At Home and in the Colonies* (London and New York: Ward, Lock & Co, 1886), p. 1.

49 Ibid., p. 4.

50 Most existing studies on 'do-it-yourself' locate the practice in the environment of post-war affluence rather than seeing its roots in late nineteenth-century, middle-class self-reliance, a feature of the historiography noted by Paul Atkinson in his special issue of the *Journal of Design History*. See

Paul Atkinson, 'Do It Yourself: Democracy and Design' special issue of *Journal of Design History* 19:1 (2006), pp. 1–8; Karal Ann Marling, *As Seen on TV: Visual Culture in Everyday Life in the 50s* (Cambridge, Massachusetts and London: Harvard University Press, 1994); Elizabeth Shove et al., *The Design of Everyday Life* (Oxford: Berg, 2007).

51 For an assessment of the dialogic apparatus of journals like *Amateur Work* see Stephen Knott, '*Amateur Work*: Reader Participation and Dialogism in Late Nineteenth Century Domestic Design Advice' *Interiors* 5:2 (July 2014).

52 *Amateur Work* 5 (1886), p. 134.

53 Tosh claims that in the Victorian era the house was 'by and large' not a productive unit and was constructed as a sentimental and emotional realm. John Tosh, *A Man's Place: Masculinity and the Middle Class Home in Victorian England* (New Haven and London: Yale University Press, 1999), p. 13. This hypothesis is challenged by Elizabeth Langland, *Nobody's Angels: Middle-Class Women and Domestic Ideology in Victorian Culture* (Ithaca and London: Cornell University Press, 1995).

54 Twenty thousand copies were sold in the first year (1859), increasing to 150,000 by 1889 and 250,000 by 1900. Asa Briggs, introduction to Samuel Smiles, *Self-Help: With Illustrations of Conduct and Perseverance* (London: John Murray), p. 7.

55 Samuel Smiles, *Self-Help: With Illustrations of Conduct and Perseverance* (London: IEA Health and Welfare Unit, 1996), p. 2.

56 Ralph Waldo Emerson, *Self-Reliance* (Massachusetts: Elizabeth Towne, 1916). Strong echoes of Emerson's ideas are seen in the work of Henry Thoreau, *Walden: Or, Life in the Woods* (London: Folio Society, 2001) and Lears, *No Place of Grace*.

57 Briggs, introduction to *Self-Help*, p. 30.

58 Ellis Davidson, *Amateur House Carpenter* (London: Chapman & Hall, 1875), ix.

59 'Amateurs' *Design and Work* 251 (19 February 1881), p. 142. Other works that stress avoidance of wastefulness and purposeless activity in line with this idea of the 'professional amateur' include John Black, *Saxon's Everyday Guide to Carpentry* (London: W R Russell & Co, 1898), preface.

60 'Amateur Inventors' *Design and Work* 264 (21 May 1881), p. 401.

61 Chilton-Young, 'Notes on Novelties', *Amateur Work* (1881), p. 428.

62 Davidson, *Amateur House Carpenter*, p. 4. Phillis Browne, *What Girls Can Do: A Book for Mothers and Daughters* (London: Cassell & Co, 1880), pp. 256–7.

63 Chilton-Young, *Every Man His Own Mechanic*, p. 4.

64 F.M., 'A Tradesman Opinion of *Amateur Work*' in 'Notes and Queries' *Amateur Work* 5 (London: Ward, Lock & Co, 1886), p. 94.

65 'In Our Time with Melvyn Bragg: Social Darwinism' (BBC Radio 4, first broadcast 20 February 2014).

66 Kyriaki Hadjiafxendi and Patricia Zakreski (eds) *Crafting the Woman Professional in the Long Nineteenth Century – Artistry and Industry in Britain* (Burlington: Ashgate, 2013), p. 12. See also the four essays under the chapter subheading 'Industrious Amateurs'.

67 Eric Hobsbawm, *Age of Revolution: 1789–1848* (London: Abacus, 1962), p. 228.

68 Frederick Winslow Taylor, *The Principles of Scientific Management* (London: Harper and Row, 1974), p. 25.

69 Ibid., p. 13.

70 Ibid., p. 43.

71 As with the paint-by-number case study, the mid-twentieth-century moment of amateur practice represents an intensification and exaggeration of features existing in the earlier moment of

modernity – the late nineteenth century. See footnote 50 concerning the expectation within the historiography that DIY had its origins in the context of post-Second World War affluence.

72 Ray Gill in David X. Manners, *Outdoor Living* (Greenwich, Connecticut: Fawcett Publications, 1960), p. 5.

73 Cheryl Buckley, 'On the Margins: Theorising the History and Significance of Making and Designing Clothes at Home' in Barbara Burman (ed.) *The Culture of Sewing: Gender, Consumption and Home Dressmaking* (Oxford: Berg, 1999), p. 57.

74 Saucré, *Le dessin à la peinture vitrifiables accessibles à tous pour la décoration des vitraux d'intérieur* (Paris: A Lacroix, 1894), pp. 9–10.

75 Roszika Parker, *The Subversive Stitch: Embroidery and the Making of the Feminine* (London: Woman's Press, 1984), p. 38.

76 Clive Edwards establishes a division between 'soft' do-it-yourself activities of women in the late nineteenth century, mainly confined to the realms of decoration, and the 'hard' equivalents undertaken by men, such as building furniture. Clive Edwards, 'Home is Where the Art is: Women, Handicrafts and Home Improvements 1750–1900' *Journal of Design History* 19:1 (2006), p. 19.

77 Chilton-Young, 'Notes on Novelties' *Amateur Work* (1881), p. 429.

78 Leo Parsey, 'Wood-Carving for Amateurs' *Amateur Work* (1881), p. 276.

79 David X. Manners, *How to Plan and Build Your Workshop* (New York: Arco Publishing Co, 1955), p. 8.

80 Sam Brown, *Planning Your Own Home Workshop* (Chicago: Popular Mechanics Press, 1949), pp. 48–9.

81 'Editorial', *Journal of Modern Craft* 6:3 (November 2013), p. 253. Parker, *The Subversive Stitch*, p. 16.

82 David X. Manners, *Home Improvements You Can Do* (Greenwich, Connecticut: Fawcett Publications, 1959), p. 64. Brown, *Planning*, pp. 91 and 47.

83 Chilton-Young, *Everyman His Own Mechanic*, pp. 403–6. Davidson, *Amateur House Carpenter*, pp. 38–41.

84 Black, *Saxon's Everyday Guide*, p. 31.

85 Davidson, *Amateur House Carpenter*, p. 26.

86 Ibid., p. 27.

87 Ibid. The editors of *Design and Work* positioned tool abuse as one sign of an unpractical 'bumptious amateur' who fails to take advice from others and vainly triumphs his own abilities. 'Amateurs' *Design and Work*, pp. 141–2.

88 For example, Manners, *Home Improvements*, p. 65; Manners, *How to Plan*, p. 45.

89 Manners, *How to Plan*, p. 46.

90 Martin Heidegger, *Basic Writings* trans. by David Farrell Krell (London: Routledge, 2008), p. 225.

91 Davidson, *Amateur House Carpenter*, p. 27.

92 Manners, *How to Plan*, p. 5.

93 Taylor, *The Principles of Scientific Management*, p. 77.

94 Harry Braverman, *Labour and Monopoly Capital: The Degradation of Work in the Twentieth Century* (New York and London: Monthly Review Press, 1974), p. 36.

95 Cecil Meadows, *The Victorian Ironmonger* (Princes Risborough: Shire, 2000), p. 16.

96 G. A. Hardy, *The Complete Ironmonger* (London: Offices of 'The Ironmonger', 1900), pp. 27–8. See also *The Ironmonger's Workshop* (London: Offices of 'The Ironmonger', 1904), pp. 161–4.

97 Rosalind Williams draws attention to the particular spatial logic of spectacle within the department store. Rosalind Williams, *Dream Worlds: Mass Consumption in Late Nineteenth Century France* (Berkeley and London: University of California Press, 1982), p. 72.

98 Hardy, *The Complete Ironmonger*, p. 38.

99 Manners, *How to Plan*, p. 6.

100 Ibid., p. 45.

101 Lewis Edwin Akers, *Particle Board and Hardboard* (Oxford: Pergamon, 1966), p. 162. Like all hardboard, perforated hardboard was made by exploding and compressing woodchip and is distinguished from particleboard due to the use of inherent adhesive properties of the wood pulp itself.

102 Manners, *Home Improvements*, pp. 64 and 84–5; Manners, *Outdoor Living*, pp. 132–3. Contemporary artist, Ryan Gander, also praises the adaptability of pegboard in Ryan Gander, *Ampersand: Notes on a Collection* (London: Dent-De-Leone, 2012), pp. 48–9.

103 Adverts for Masonite's pegboard stress its 'prefinished' nature. *Popular Mechanics* 118:4 (October 1962), p. 219 and *Popular Science* 181:4 (October 1962), p. 191. Manners, *Home Workshops*, pp. 78–80.

104 Akers, *Particle Board*, p. 136.

105 See adverts for Presto Pegboard in *Popular Science* 181:4 (October, 1962), p. 191; 181:5 (November 1962), p. 29; 183:3 (September 1963), p. 3; and *Popular Mechanics* 118:4 (October 1962), p. 219; 118:5 (November 1962), p. 219.

106 Siegfred Kracauer, 'The Mass Ornament' in *The Mass Ornament: Weimar Essays* trans. by Thomas Y. Levin (London and Cambridge, Massachusetts: Harvard University Press, 1995), p. 79.

107 Ibid., p. 83.

108 Rosalind Krauss, *Grids: Format and Image in the Twentieth Century* (New York: Pace Gallery, 1980), p. 3. Henri Lefebvre, in his critique of abstract space, also explains that the rationality of the grid is not 'above reproach' explaining how as a space it desires to eliminate contradictions 'to reduce the dialectical to the logical'. Lefebvre, *The Production of* Space, p. 367.

109 Ellen Lupton and J. Abbott Miller, *The Bathroom, The Kitchen, and the Aesthetics of Waste: A Process of Elimination* (Cambridge, Massachusetts and New York: Princeton Architectural Press, 1992), p. 2.

110 Ibid., p. 5.

111 Heidegger, *Basic Writings*, p. 225.

112 Brown, *Planning*, p. 90.

113 Ibid., p. 43.

114 Tag Gronberg critiques Penny Sparke's argument that women lose their agency in the modern space of streamlined kitchens, stating that individuals can find agency within this presumed 'deaestheticized' space. Tag Gronberg, 'The Gendered Object: As Long As It's Pink: The Sexual Politics of Taste' *Journal of Design History* 11:3 (1998), pp. 263–5.

115 Thomas Edward Brown, *Home Made Poultry Appliances* (London: A. Pearson, 1921), p. 13.

116 Harry Braverman, *Labour and Monopoly Capital*, p. 58.

117 Susan Stewart, *On Longing: Narratives on the Miniature, the Gigantic, the Souvenir, the Collection* (New York and London: Johns Hopkins University Press, 1984), p. 57.

118 Lewis Wright, *Illustrated Book of Poultry* (London: Cassell & Co, 1880); William Powell-Owen, *An Income From Backyard Fowls! The Working Man's Vade Mecum* (London: Poultry Press, 1911); Elizabeth Watts, *The Poultry Yard* (London: Routledge & Sons, 1893); Lewis Wright, *The Practical*

Poultry Keeper (London: Cassell & Co, 1899). This last book was in its 20th edition by 1899, demonstrating its popularity.

119 J. Roach, *Eggs at a Profit Everyday of the Year: Showing How It Has Been Done By a Backyarder* (London: J. Roach, 1918), p. 1. Introduction to Sidney Lewer, *The World's Poultry Congress. Handbook and Souvenir of the British Section* (London: The Feathered World, 1921), p. 11. Watts, *The Poultry Yard*, p. 29.

120 John Henry Walsh, *The Economical Housekeeper: Being Practical Advice for Brewing, Preserving and Pickling at Home, To Which are Added Directions for the Management of the Dairy, Poultry-yard, Laundry and Cellar* (London: Routledge & Co, 1857), p. 263. Wright, *The Practical Poultry Keeper*, p. 41.

121 Wright provides figures that prove the rise of French egg imports from £278,422 in 1856 to £1,265,484 in 1871. Wright, *Illustrated Book of Poultry*, 89. William Bernhard Tegetmeier, *Poultry for the table and Market Versus Fancy Fowls. With an Exposition of the Fallacies of Poultry Farming* (London: H. Cox, 1893), p. 59.

122 Susie Barson, 'Infinite Variety in Brick and Stucco, 1840–1914' in Andrew Saint (ed.) *London Suburbs* (London: Merrell Publishers, 1999), p. 93; David A. Reeder, *Suburbanity and the Victorian City* (Leicester: Victorian Studies Centre, 1980), pp. 3–4; H. J. Dyos, *Victorian Suburb: A Study of Camberwell* (Leicester: Leicester University Press, 1966), p. 22. For an account of growth of suburbia and its relationship to the emerging movement of studio craft see Lily Crowther, 'Et in Suburbia Ego: A Cultural Geography of Craft in the London Suburbs' *Journal of Modern Craft* 3:2 (2010), pp. 143–59.

123 The exceptions are the few works on 'hands-on' gentlemanly husbandry in the early modern period. See introduction to Michael Leslie and Timothy Raylor (eds) *Culture and Cultivation in Early Modern England: Writing and the Land* (Leicester: Leicester University Press, 1992), and Katrina Ramsey, 'Inside and Outside the Seventeenth Century Garden' (unpublished Master's thesis, Royal College of Art, 2008).

124 Wright, *The Practical Poultry Keeper*, p. 41.

125 An indication of the garden's spatial relationship to the home is indicated by streetmaps in Dyos' analysis of Camberwell. Dyos, *Victorian Suburb*, pp. 102 and 108.

126 Wright, *The Illustrated Book of Poultry*, p. 1; Davidson, *Amateur House Carpenter*, pp. 129 and 131; L. B. Collier, *Poultry Appliances and How to Make Them* (London: Poultry Press, 1921), p. 49; Fred Hobs, *Backyard Poultry Keeping* (London: Merrit and Hatcher, 1920), p. 7; H. Francklin, *Utility Fowl Houses and Appliances* (London: Dawbarn & Ward, 1903), pp. 3–4.

127 Chilton-Young, *Every Man His Own Mechanic*, p. 466.

128 Brown, *Home Made Poultry Appliances*, p. 15. Francklin, *Utility Fowl Houses*, p. 1.

129 Collier, *Poultry Appliances*, pp. 49–54; Brown, *Home Made Poultry Appliances*, p. 9. 'Amateur Woodworker', 'Combined Chicken and Pigeon House', in the 'Wrinkles for Amateurs' section *Amateur Work* 2 (1882), p. 1.

130 Powell-Owen, *An Income From Backyard Fowls*, p. 4; Watson (ed.) *Amateur Poultry Keeping* (London: Poultry Press, 1919), p. 5; Brown, *Home Made Poultry Appliances*, p. 39; Hobs, *Backyard Poultry Keeping* p. 7; Browne, *What Girls Can Do*, p. 276; Anne de Salis, *New Laid Eggs. Hints for Amateur Poultry-Rearers* (London and New York: Longman, Green & Co, 1892), pp. 2–3; 'Amateur Woodworker', 'Combined Chicken and Pigeon House', p. 10.

131 See for example Tegetmeier, *Poultry for the Table*, p. 101; Powell-Owen, *An Income From Backyard Fowls*, p. 7; Watson, *Amateur Poultry Keeping*, p. 7; Wright, *The Practical Poultry Keeper*, pp. 1–2; De Salis, *New Laid Eggs*, p. 6.

132 Authors who refer to their direct experience with working with backyard hens include Ellis Davidson, Anne de Salis and Lewis Wright. Davidson, *Amateur House Carpenter*, p. 135; De Salis, *New Laid* Eggs, v; Joseph Batty, *Lewis Wright and his Poultry* (Midhurst, West Sussex: Northbrook Publishing, 2001), p. 1.

133 Roach, *Eggs at a Profit*, pp. 2–3. Watson, *Amateur Poultry Keeping*, pp. 4–6, and Powell-Owen, *An Income From Backyard Fowls*, p. 4, both recommend using boxes from grocery stores. One amateur advised using broomsticks for perches. Hoc Signo, Comment in 'Notes and Queries' section of *Design and Work* 3 (29 September 1877), p. 398.

134 Wright refers to the determination of amateur poultry keepers who kept chickens on flat roofs in the high of the poultry keeping 'mania'. Wright, *Illustrated Book of Poultry*, p. 20. Tegetmeier refers to chicken being kept in attics. William Bernhard Tegetmeier, *The Poultry Book* (London: 1873), p. 1.

135 Wright, *Illustrated Book of Poultry*, p. 3; William Powell-Owen, *An Income From Backyard Fowls*, pp. 70–2; Davidson, *Amateur House Carpenter*, p. 132; Browne, *What Girls Can Do*, pp. 279–81.

136 Edwards, 'Home is Where the Art is', p. 19. Similarly, Steven Gelber argues that tool use was divided between the genders with men's 'heavy' tools and materials (wood and metal) distinguished from the female handicrafts (textiles), Steven Gelber, *Hobbies: Leisure and the Culture of Work in America* (New York: Columbia University Press, 1999), p. 180.

137 Davidson refers to his audience as 'gentlemen' or 'men of education' in his book *Amateur House Carpenter*, especially the introduction. See also Powell-Owen, *An Income From Backyard Fowls* and Francis Chilton-Young, *Every Man His Own Mechanic*.

138 Davidson, *Amateur House Carpenter*, p. 127.

139 Wright, *Illustrated Book of Poultry*, p. 1

140 Ibid., p. 9; Watson (ed.) *Poultry Press Annual* (London: Poultry Press, 1919), p. 111.

141 Mrs George O'Grady, *100,000 Chickens a Year on an Acre of Land. My System of Rearing Table Chickens by Mrs O'Grady* (London: Poultry Press, 1919). The *Poultry Press Annual* gives a list of the opportunities available to women in poultry keeping including the possibility of running a successful business. *Poultry Press Annual 1910–11*, p. 111.

142 Browne mentions that once the chicken coop had been built women could manage poultry keeping. Browne, *What Girls Can Do*, p. 274. See also Watts, *The Poultry Yard*, Barbara Elrington Fergusson Arbuthnott, *The Henwife* (Edinburgh: T. C. Jack, 1870) and Edith Park, *Farming for Ladies* (London: Vinton & Co, 1907). Flora Guest, *Every Woman's Book of Poultry* (London: Poultry World, 1916).

143 Elizabeth Langland, *Nobody's Angels: Middle-Class Women and Domestic Ideology in Victorian Culture* (Ithaca and London: Cornell University Press, 1995), p. 14. Further description of the middle-class woman's role as manager of domestic labour can be found on pp. 45–54.

144 De Salis, *New Laid Eggs*, vi.

145 Powell-Owen, *An Income From Backyard Fowls*, p. 13.

146 Lupton and Miller, *The Bathroom, the Kitchen, and the Aesthetics of Waste*, p. 15.

147 Arbuthnott, *The Henwife*, p. 272.

148 Prominent poultry manual author, Powell-Owen, stated that this shortage 'always' provided 'a good market'. Powell-Owen, *An Income From Backyard Fowls*, preface; Roach, *Eggs at a Profit*, pp. 15–16; See also, Edwards, *How the French Make Fowls Pay* (London, 1871), p. 11.

149 Edwards, *How the French*, p. 5.

150 Powell-Owen, *An Income From Backyard Fowls*, pp. 78–9. See also, Tegetmeier, *Poultry for the Table*, p. 102; Wright, *Illustrated Book of Poultry*, p. 20. De Salis gives instructions of how to kill a hen but admits her inability to kill fowls due to her own attachment to the 'poor things'; De Salis, *New Laid Eggs*, pp. 64–5.

151 Advertisements in supplement to Watson, *How to Feed Hens*.

152 Watts, *The Poultry Yard*, p. 6.

153 Edwards, *How the French*, p. 16. Powell-Owen, *Poultry Keeping*, p. 242.

154 Tegetmeier, *Poultry for Table*, p. 91. Powell-Owen, *Poultry Keeping*, p. 242.

155 Braverman, *Labour and Monopoly Capital*, pp. 77–8.

156 De Salis cites an example of a device that would release food at the sound of an alarm. De Salis, *New Laid Eggs*, p. 9. 'Will'o the wisp', 'Item 1446: Detector Battery' Notes & Queries section of *Design and Work* (3 February, 1877), p. 134. Wright noticed that 'otherwise honest people' were prone to stealing eggs and hens, suggesting that this petty crime was pervasive. Wright, *The Illustrated Book of Poultry*, p. 34; Arbuthnott, *The Henwife*, p. 29.

157 William Powell-Owen, *Poultry-Farming as a Career for Women* (London: George Newnes, 1918), pp. 9–10.

158 In a similar exposition of contradictions at the heart of the Victorian mentality, Deborah Cohen discusses the reconciliation of heightened Victorian morality with increased material wealth that came with the abundance of modern capitalism. See Deborah Cohen, *Household Gods: The British and their Possessions* (New Haven and London: Yale University Press, 2006).

159 Powell-Owen, *An Income From Backyard Fowls*, p. 12 and Powell-Owen, *Poultry Keeping*, p. 14.

160 Batty, *Lewis Wright*, pp. 5–9. For literature that disseminated 'standards' of examination for poultry see Wright, *Illustrated Book of Poultry* (1880) and William Bernhard Tegetmeier, *The Standards of Excellence in Exhibition Poultry, To Which is Added the American Standard* (London, 1874).

161 Arbuthnott, *The Henwife*, p. 57.

162 Veblen, *Conspicuous Consumption*, pp. 21–2.

163 Arbuthnott, *The Henwife*, xviii.

164 Sarah Davis, 'Darwin, Tegetmeier and the Bees' *Studies in the Philosophy of Biological and Biomedical Sciences* 35 (2004): 65–92.

165 David Barnaby, *Letters to Mr Tegetmeier* (Timperley: ZSGM Publications, 2004), viii.

166 Tegetmeier, *Poultry for the Table*, p. 3. Other authors shared Tegetmeier's strictly utilitarian viewpoint including Park, *Farming for Ladies*, p. 21.

167 Siegfried Kracauer, 'The Mass Ornament', p. 83.

168 Ibid., p. 84.

169 Thomas Y. Levin, 'Introduction' to Kracauer, *The Mass Ornament*, p. 18.

170 Powell-Owen, *An Income From Backyard Fowls*, p. 20; Ellet, *Modern Wyandottes: How to Breed, Manage and Exhibit* (London: Poultry Press, 1919), p. 19.

171 For information on poultry clubs see *Poultry Annual*, p. 188; Arbuthnott, *The Henwife*, xx; Powell-Owen, *Poultry Keeping*, pp. 199 and 120–1.

172 Watson, *How to Feed Hens*, p. 54.

173 R. W. Webster, *All About Black Minorcas: How to Manage, Breed and Exhibit Them* (London: Poultry Office, 1904), pp. 10–13; Powell-Owen, *An Income From Backyard Fowls*, pp. 15–17; Tegetmeier, *Poultry for the Table and Market* (London: Horace Cox, 1893).

174 Watts, *The Poultry Yard*, p. 40.

175 Natalie Haynes, 'Attilla the Hen' (BBC Radio 4, first broadcast 29 March 2011). An article in the trade magazine for poultry farmers claims that there were two to three million backyard chickens in the United Kingdom in 2011. 'Surge in Backyard Flocks' *Ranger* (September 2011), p. 23.

176 Susan Orlean, 'The It Bird: The Return of the Backyard Chicken' *New Yorker* (28 September 2000). Susan Merrill Squier, *Poultry Science, Chicken Culture: A Partial Alphabet* (New Brunswick: Rutgers University Press, 2011).

177 Lucy Siegle, 'Fresh way of life sweeps suburbia' *The Observer* (7 November 2004); Amy Iggulden, 'Chic Coops to House Urban Chickens' *The Guardian* (10 April 2004); Lewis Smith, 'Urban Hen Coop for the Designer Chic' *The Times* (10 April 2004). Tesco sales of hen houses have increased by 180 per cent in three years, prompting an expansion in their range, the company citing the attraction of self-sufficiency as a reason for the increase in sales. 'Surge in Backyard Flocks', p. 25.

178 FARM: Shop, Dalston, http://farmlondon.weebly.com/farmshop1.html (accessed 12 June 2014).

179 Sue Perkins, *Giles and Sue Live the Good Life* (BBC Two, first broadcast 8 November 2010).

180 See http://www.omlet.co.uk/products_services/products_services.php?view=Eglu%20Classic (accessed 5 July 2011).

181 Simon Starling, interview with Phillip Kaiser in *Cuttings* Phillip Kaiser (ed.) (Portchester: Art Books International, 2005), p. 2.

182 Simon Starling, *Back to Front* (London: Camden Arts Centre and John Hansard Gallery, 2000).

183 Juliana Engberg, 'Simon Starling: Apprentice of the Sun' in Starling, *Back to Front*, pp. 52–3; Francis McKee writes of a collapse of 'historical time through its reanimation of various events' in *Burn Time*, Francis McKee, 'Chicken or Egg?' *Frieze* 56 (Jan–Feb 2001).

184 Katrina Brown, 'Djungel Dwelling' in Simon Starling, *Djungel* (Dundee: Dundee Contemporary Arts, 2002), p. 57.

185 See Nigel Reynolds, 'Forget Painting, Turner Prize is Awarded to an Old Boatshed' *The Telegraph* (6 December 2005); Andrew Downie, 'Art for a Topsy-Turvey World' *The Sunday Times* (3 October 2004).

186 Laura Meyer, 'From Finish Fetish to Feminism: Judy Chicago's "Dinner Party" in California Art History' in Amelia Jones (ed.) *Sexual Politics* (Los Angeles: UCLA at the Armand Hammer Museum of Art and Cultural Center in association with University of California Press, Berkeley, 1996), p. 69. See also Glenn Adamson, *Thinking Through Craft* (Oxford: Berg, 2007), pp. 158–9.

187 John Roberts, 'The Amateur's Retort' in Grace Kook-Anderson and Claire Fitzsimmons (eds) *Amateurs* (San Francisco: California College of the Arts, 2008), p. 20.

188 McKee, 'Chicken or egg?'

189 Tanya Harrod notes Kieran Jones's use of the term 'professional amateurism' in 'Symbolic Crafting' Jerwood Makers Open (ex cat.) 2012. Published in the UK to accompany Jerwood Makers Open (Jerwood: London, 2012).

190 Brown, 'Djungel Dwelling', p. 23.

Chapter 3

1 John Stretton, *Thirty Years of Trainspotting* (Paddock Wood: Unicorn, 1990), p. 9.

2 Andrew Jackson, 'Constructing at Home: The Experience of the Amateur Maker' *Design and Culture* 2:1 (2010), pp. 19–20; Fiona Hackney, 'Quiet Activism and the New Amateur: The Power of Home and Hobby Crafts' *Design and Culture* 5:2 (July 2013), pp. 179–83; Betsy Greer, 'Craftivist History' in Maria Elena Buszek (ed.) *Extra/Ordinary: Craft and Contemporary Art* (Durham: Duke University Press, 2011), pp. 175–83.

3 Theodor Adorno, 'Free Time' in Theodor Adorno, *The Culture Industry: Selected Essays on Mass Culture* (London: Routledge, 1991), p. 168.

4 Karl Marx, *Economic and Philosophical Manuscripts* in Erich Fromm (ed.) *Marx's Concept of Man* trans. by T. B. Bottomore (New York: Ungar Pub. Co., 1961), p. 98.

5 Noted by Ian Carter, *British Railway Enthusiasm* (Manchester: Manchester University Press, 2008), p. 264.

6 Karl Marx, 'The German Ideology' from David McLellan (ed.) *Karl Marx: Selected Writings* (Oxford: Oxford University Press, 2000), p. 185.

7 Adorno, 'Free Time', p. 162.

8 Ibid.

9 Ibid., p. 165.

10 Ibid., p. 163.

11 Ibid., p. 164.

12 Ibid., p. 170.

13 Ibid., p. 167.

14 Harry Braverman, *Labour and Monopoly Capital: The Degradation of Work in the Twentieth Century* (New York and London: Monthly Review Press, 1974), p. 39.

15 Jean Baudrillard, *Mirror of Production* trans. by Mark Poster (St Louis: Telos Press), p. 104.

16 Johan Huizinga, *Homo Ludens* trans. by R. F. C. Hull (London: Routledge & Kegan Paul, 1949), pp. 7–10.

17 Ibid., p. 9.

18 Ibid.

19 Henri Lefebvre, *Rhythmanalysis: Space, Time, and Everyday Life* trans. by Stuart Eldon and Gerald Moore (London and New York: Continuum, 2004), pp. 19–23.

20 Thomas Henricks, *Play Reconsidered: Sociological Perspectives on Human Expression* (Urbana, Illinois: University of Illinois Press, 2006), p. 1.

21 Huizinga, *Homo Ludens*, p. 166.

22 Friedrich Schiller, *On the Aesthetics of Man* trans. by Elizabeth Wilkinson and L. A. Willoughby (Oxford: Clarendon, 1967), p. 101.

23 Henry Thoreau, *Walden: Or, Life in the Woods* (London, Folio Society, 2009), p. 262.

24 William Morris, *News from Nowhere* in Asa Briggs (ed.) *William Morris: Selected Writings and Designs* (Harmondsworth: Penguin, 1962). Glenn Adamson, 'A Global Concern' in Grant Gibson (ed.) *Collect: The International Art Fair for Collectors* (London: Crafts Council, 2014), pp. 8–13.

25 See Glenn Adamson, *The Craft Reader* (London: Berg, 2010), pp. 135–6. Tom Crook, 'Craft and the Dialogics of Modernity: the Arts and Crafts Movement in Late Victorian and Early Edwardian England' *Journal of Modern Craft* 2:1 (2009). Glenn Adamson, *Thinking Through Craft* (Oxford: Berg, 2007), pp. 103–37.

26 Fredric Jameson, *Archaeologies of the Future* (London: Verso, 2005), p. 3.

27 Mihaly Csikszentmihalyi, *Flow: The Psychology of Optimal Experience* (New York: Harper and Row, 1990), p. 6.

28 Ibid., pp. 3–4.

29 For example Steven Gelber, *Hobbies: Leisure and the Culture of Work in America* (New York: Columbia University Press, 1999), p. 9. Andrew Jackson, 'The Amateur Maker' *Design and Culture* 2:1 (March 2010), pp. 19–21; Hackney, 'Quiet Activism and the New Amateur', p. 171.

30 Csikszentmihalyi, *Flow*, p. 51.

31 Ibid., p. 39.

32 Ibid., pp. 40–2 and 48.

33 Henricks, *Play Reconsidered*, pp. 103 and 97. See also Adorno, 'Free Time', p. 168.

34 John Roberts, 'The Amateur's Retort' in Grace Kook-Anderson and Claire Fitzsimmons (eds) *Amateurs* (San Francisco: California College of the Arts, 2008), p. 21.

35 Roel Klassen and Bart Heerdink, 'The Fall and Rise of the Amateur', paper for the Second International Conference on Critical Digital. Harvard Graduate School, Cambridge, Massachusetts (17–19 April 2009), http://isites.harvard.edu/fs/docs/icb.topic559475.files/CDC2.Proceedings.pdf (accessed 11 August 2011), pp. 203–4.

36 Jameson, *Archeologies*, p. 5.

37 Klassen and Heerdink, 'The Fall and Rise', p. 206.

38 Lucy Lippard, 'Making Something From Nothing (Toward a Definition of Women's "Hobby Art")' *Heresies* 4 [1978] in Glenn Adamson (ed.) *The Craft Reader* (Oxford: Berg, 2010), p. 487.

39 Although the woman as a domestic embroiderer conformed to patriarchal expectations between the seventeenth and nineteenth centuries, Parker talks about the 'secondary gains [women] accrued from absolute conformity to the feminine ideal', namely the quiet subversion of home decoration, recycling and re-use. Roszika Parker, *The Subversive Stitch: Embroidery and the Making of the Feminine* (London: Woman's Press, 1984), p. 13. Rita Felski is another scholar who contributed to this historical revision: Rita Felski, *Doing Time: Feminist Theory and Postmodern Culture* (New York and London: New York University Press, 2000), p. 3.

40 Historical studies on women's role in late nineteenth-century design reform include Emma Ferry, ' "Decorators May Be Compared to Doctors": An Analysis of Rhoda and Agnes Garrett's Suggestion for House Decoration (1876)' in Grace Lees-Maffei and R. House (eds) *Design History Reader* (Oxford: Berg, 2010); Anne Anderson, 'Queen Victoria's Daughter and the Tide of Fashionable Female Philanthropy' *Women's History Magazine* 41 (June 2002), pp. 10–15; Anthea Callen, *Angel in the Studio: Women in the Arts and Crafts Movement, 1870–1914* (London: Astragal Books, 1979); Janice Helland and Bridget Elliott (eds) *Women Artists and the Decorative Arts, 1880–1935: The Gender of Ornament* (Aldershot: Ashgate, 2003).

41 Hackney, 'Quiet Activism and the New Amateur', p. 170. See also Betsy Greer, 'Craftivist History' and Kirsty Robertson 'Rebellious Doilies and Subversive Stitches: Writing a Craftivist History' in Buszek, *Extra/ordinary*, pp. 175–83 and 184–203.

42 Joost Smiers and Mareike Van Schijndel, *Imagine There Is No Copyright And No Cultural Conglomerations Too: An Essay* trans. by Rosalind Buck (Amsterdam: Institute of Network Cultures, 2009), p. 5. Amateurist Network 'About', http://amateuristnetwork.wordpress.com/about/ (accessed 6 June 2014).

43 See footnote 41 in Chapter 2. Victor Papanek, *Design for the Real World* (London: Thames & Hudson, 1972).

44 Anthea Black and Nicole Burisch, 'Craft Hard Die Free: Radical Curatorial Strategies for Craftivism' in Buszek, *Extra/Ordinary*, pp. 207–8.

45 The work of Mr X Stitch fuses embroidery and needlecraft with contemporary slang and swearing. Cited in Hackney, 'Quiet Activism and the New Amateur', pp. 183–5.

46 Jenni Sorkin, 'Pottery in Drag: Beatrice Wood and Camp' *Journal of Modern Craft* 7:1 (March 2014), p. 62.

47 Alice Walker, *In Search of Our Mothers' Gardens* (London: Women's Press, 1984), p. 241.

48 Glenn Adamson, 'The Spectacle of the Everyday' in Laurie Newell (ed.) *Out of the Ordinary: Spectacular Craft* (London: Victoria & Albert Museum), p. 15.

49 Georges Perec, *Life: A User's Manual* trans. by David Bellos (London: Harvill, 1988), xv.

50 Lefebvre, *Rhythmanalysis*, p. 7.

51 Felski, *Doing Time*, p. 84.

52 Hackney, 'Quiet Activism and the New Amateur', p. 172.

53 Jameson, *Archeologies of the Future*, p. 15.

54 Lesley Brown (editor-in-chief) *New Shorter Oxford English Dictionary* (Oxford: Oxford University Press, 1993), p. 312. McKibbin refers to this phenomenon in his comment on post-war British hobbies when he states that 'the hobby of many carpenters and painters was carpentry and painting'. Ross McKibbin, *Ideologies of Class* (Oxford: Oxford University Press, 1990), p. 160.

55 Nick Pisa, 'Tony Blair Begged Wife Cherie to Protect Him From Berlusconi's Bandanna' (24 May 2009), http://www.telegraph.co.uk/news/worldnews/europe/italy/5377843/Tony-Blair-begged-wife-Cherie-to-protect-him-from-Berlusconis-bandanna.html (accessed 26 June 2014).

56 Jameson, *Archeologies of the Future*, p. 16.

57 Thoreau, *Walden*, p. 92.

58 Albert Roland 'Do-It-Yourself: A Walden for the Million?' *American Quarterly* 10:2 (1958), p. 163.

59 John Pocock, *Model Engine-Making* (London: Swan Sonnenschein and Co, 1888), p. 1. For an echo of this defence of making models of trains see Carter, *British Railway Enthusiasm*, pp. 192–3.

60 The notion of 'instructive amusement' was used in one of the earliest retailers of model trains called Stevens's Model Dockyard. See the introduction of *A Catalogue of Model Ships, Engines, Boilers, Fittings, Instructive and Scientific Amusements* (London: Stevens's Model Dockyard, 1914). William Tennant, 'Introductory note' in Henry Greenly, *The Model Locomotive: Its Design and Construction* (London: Percival Marshall & Co, 1904), iv and p. 8.

61 'Answers to Notes and Queries' section of *Amateur Work* 4 (London and New York: Ward, Lock & Co, 1885) pp. 205–6, 307, 358, 401, 453. These same firms are also recommended in the earlier publication *Design and Work: A Home and Shop Companion* 1 (London: George Purkess, September 16, 1876), p. 298. Paul Hasluck states that there were kits on the market that only required a screwdriver to assemble them. Paul Hasluck, *The Model Engineers' Handybook* (London: Crossby Lockwood and Co, 1889), p. 21.

62 Allen Levy, *A Century of Model Trains* (London: New Cavendish, 1986), p. 7.

63 A Hide, 'Model Yachts: How to Design and Build Them' *Amateur Work* 4 (1885), pp. 4–6, 52–5, 97–9, 166–70.

64 John Humphreys, 'Peter Snow shows John Humphreys his Model Railway' *Today* (BBC Radio 4, first broadcast 3 December 2010), http://news.bbc.co.uk/today/hi/today/newsid_9251000/9251362.stm (accessed 17 August 2011).

65 Pocock, *Model-engine Making*, p. 30.

66 'Stadt Dresden', *Amateur Work* 5 (1886), p. 526.

67 See Percival Marshall, *The Beginner's Guide to the Lathe* (London: The Model Engineer Series, 1904). Percival Marshall, *Induction Coils for Amateurs: How to Make and Use Them* (London: The Model Engineer Series, 1902) and other work for the Model Engineer Series. For more on the early history of the Society of Model Engineers see Eric Ball, *100 Years of Model Engineering: A History of the Society of Model and Experimental Engineers* (London: Society of Model & Experimental Engineers, 1997), pp. 1–23.

68 Editorial, 'Scale and Gauge Standards' *The Model Engineer and Electrician* 9:116 (London: Dawbarn & Ward Ltd, 16 July 1903), p. 71. For a history of the gauge standards of international railways as they development, including an explanation for Britain's smaller loading gauges see Douglas Puffert, *Tracks Across Continents, Paths Through History: The Economic Dynamics of Standardization in Railway Gauge* (Chicago: Chicago University Press, 2009).

69 Harold Soper, *The Model Engineer* 9:121 (20 August 1903).

70 Henry Greenly, 'Scale and Gauge Standards' *The Model Engineer* 9:140 (31 December 1903), p. 641.

71 Henry Greenly, *The Model Locomotive: Its Design and Construction* (London: Percival Marshall & Co, 1904), p. 18. Other contributors to *The Model Engineer* scale-gauge debate who were happy with this degree of looseness include E. L. Pearce, H. A. Bennett, 9:121 (20 August 1903), pp. 188–9; F. K. Cobb, 9:122 (27 August 1903), p. 210; Geo Loudon, 9:126 (23 September 1903), p. 369.

72 Chris Graebe, *The Hornby Gauge O System* (London: New Cavandish, 1985), pp. 64–5.

73 Levy, *A Century of Model Trains*, p. 79.

74 Clive White, 'The Model Railway Club "First 100" ', *The Model Railway Club Bulletin* 454 (May–June 2010), p. 4.

75 The railway layout can still be seen on specific days throughout the year at Pendon Museum, http://www.pendonmuseum.com/about/madder.php (accessed 17 August 2011). For a sample of articles by John Ahern on scenic modelling see *Model Railway News* 16 (London: Percival Marshall & Co, 1940), pp. 115–18, 210–12; *Model Railway News* 17 (1941), pp. 2–4, 28–30, 86–8, 172–5.

76 Henry Greenly, *TTR Permanent Way Manual . . . Layout and Operation of the Trix Twin* OO *Gauge Model Railway* (London: Trix, 1937).

77 Ball, *100 Years of Model Engineering*, p. 5.

78 Clive White and members of the Model Railway Club, 'MRC Layouts' in *100 Years of the MRC: The 100 Year History of the Oldest Model Railway Club in the World. British Railway Modelling* supplement (2010), pp. 9–16.

79 Tim Watson, *Model Railway Club Bulletin* 458 (January–February 2011), p. 4.

80 Ibid., p. 7. The 'glacial' pace of railway modelling is also remarked upon by critic Michael Ned Holte upon seeing Jean-Pierre Gorin's 1986 film *Routine Pleasures*, which charts the activities of a railway modelling group in San Diego. Michael Ned Holte, 'Termite Tracks: Routine Pleasures and the Paradoxes of Collectivity' *Afterall* 22 (Autumn 2009), p. 99.

81 Tim Watson, 'Copenhagen Fields: Frequently Asked Questions' *Model Railway Club* website, http://themodelrailwayclub.org/CopenhagenFields.aspx (accessed 17 August 2011).

82 Interview with Mike Chrisp, Chairman of the Society of Model and Experimental Engineers (Sandown Park, 11 December 2010).

83 Norman Simmons, *How to Go Railway Modelling* (Cambridge: Stephens, 1980), p. 10.

84 Copenhagen Fields is made from several pieces of baseboard that are carried to exhibitions in a 35cwt Luton van. Tim Watson, 'Copenhagen Fields' *Model Railway Club Bulletin* 458 (2011), p. 6.

85 Helen Carnac, 'The Concept' described on the website *Making a Slow Revolution*, http://makingaslowrevolution.wordpress.com/about/opportunities/ (accessed 18 August 2011).

86 John Ahern, *Miniature Building Construction: An Architectural Guide for Modellers* (London: Percival Marshall & Co., 1947), v.

87 Peter Snow, 'Peter Snow shows John Humphreys his model railway'.

88 Adnan Morshed, 'The Aesthetics of Ascension in Norman Bel Geddes's Futurama' *Journal of the Society of Architectural Historians* 63:1 (March 2004), p. 91. See also Rem Koolhaas, *Delirious New York: A Retroactive Manifesto for Manhattan* (London: Thames and Hudson, 1978).

89 Umberto Eco, 'The Myth of the Superman' in Umberto Eco, *The Role of the Reader: Exploration in the Semiotics of Texts* (Bloomington and London: Indiana University Press, 1979), p. 107.

90 See Kimberley Chandler, 'The Eiffel Tower and the Ferris Wheel: Transfixed Immobility and the Performance of the Modern in the Late Nineteenth Century' (unpublished Master's thesis, Royal College of Art, 2009).

91 Koolhaus, *Delerious New York*, p. 155.

92 For more on the idea of models as useful prototypes see Louise Valentine (ed.) *Prototype: Design and Craft in the 21st Century* (London: Bloomsbury, 2013). Glenn Adamson provided an eloquent précis of the importance of models when planning the Postmodernism show at the Victoria and Albert Museum. Glenn Adamson, 'Designing Postmodernism, Part 2: The Model' *From Sketch to Product* blog (Victoria and Albert Museum, January 2011), http://www.vam.ac.uk/things-to-do/blogs/sketch-product/designing-postmodernism-part-2-model (accessed 18 August 2011).

93 Friedrich Nietzsche, *Thus Spoke Zarathustra* trans. by R. J. Hollingdale (London: Penguin Books, 2003), p. 136.

94 Interview with Mike Chrisp. Hornby has proved particularly adept at marketing its trains to evoke this nostalgic sentiment. Peter Randall, *The Story of Gauge O Hornby Trains* (London: Cranbourn Press Ltd, 1975), pp. 21–2 and see Richard Lines, *The Art of Hornby: Sixty Years of Model Railway Literature* (Kingswood: Kay & Ward, 1983).

95 Great Western Railway, London Midland and Scottish, London and North East Railway, Southern Railway were the companies formed from this act.

96 Interview with David Crossley, Exhibition Manager of the Chiltern Model Railway Association (St Albans, 15 January 2011).

97 Susan Stewart, *On Longing: Narratives on the Miniature, the Gigantic, the Souvenir, the Collection* (London: Johns Hopkins University Press, 1984), p. 23.

98 Interview with Leslie Bevis Smith, Chairman of the Model Railway Club (9 December 2010).

99 Mickelover Model Railway Group, 'Farkham' *St Albans Model Railway Exhibition 2011 Programme* (Chiltern Model Railways Association, 2011), p. 39.

100 Peter Bossom, 'Whatlington' *St Albans Model Railway Exhibition*, p. 54.

101 'Places of Interest: Gypsum Mine' *The Parish of Mountfield* website, http://www.mountfield.org.uk/page30.htm (accessed 5 September 2011).

102 For details of these layouts see *St Albans Model Railway Exhibition*, pp. 20–1 and 46–7, respectively.

103 See Roger Boyes, 'Sex and Violence as Life with Model Trains Goes off the Rails' *The Times* (8 February 2007). http://www.timesonline.co.uk/tol/news/world/europe/article1350239.ece (accessed 5 September 2011).

104 John Ahern, letter in response to Longridge's article 'Railway Modelling as an Art' in 'Our Mailbag' section of *Model Railway News* 17:201 (September 1941), p. 144.

105 Greenly, *TTR Permanent Way*, p. 54.

106 Information about Norman Eagles gathered from a lecture by Leslie Bevis-Smith, 'Sherwood Section of the LMS' (13 January 2011).

107 Mike Hughes, 'Norman Eagles' thread on ModelGeeks.com forum (25 June 2004), http://www.modelgeeks.com/Uwe/Forum.aspx/uk-rail/1485/Norman-Eagles (accessed 5 September 2011).

108 Visitor of Eagles's layout, quoted by Bevis-Smith, 'Sherwood Section of the LMS'.

109 Jon Humphreys, 'Peter Snow shows John Humphreys his model railway'.

110 The 'OO' gauge standard creates a width between the rails of 16.5 mm that is 2.33 mm off the scale standard of 18.83. The EM gauge gains greater scale accuracy by widening the gauge to 18.2 but P4 is the most accurate, achieving the 18.83 standard gauge track at the 4 mm to the foot scale standard.

111 Interview with David Crossley.

112 Conversation overheard during visit to the Model Railway Club (9 December 2010).

113 Davis Lennard, *Obsession: A History* (Chicago and London: Chicago University Press, 2008), p. 38.

114 Ibid., p. 14.

115 Gelber, *Hobbies*, p. 234.

116 Émile Zola, *The Masterpiece* trans. by Thomas Walton (Oxford: Oxford University Press, 2008).

117 Davis, *Obsession*, p. 195. See also Jane Green and Leah Levy (eds) *Jay Defeo and the Rose* (Berkeley and London: University of California Press, 2003).

118 Richard Sennett, *The Craftsman* (London: Allen Lane, 2008), p. 262.

119 Interview with Leslie Bevis Smith.

120 Ned Holte, 'Termite Tracks', p. 104.

121 John Ahern, *Miniature Landscape Modelling* (London: Percival Marshall, 1951), vii.

122 Michael Longridge, 'Editorial' *Model Railway Club Bulletin* 36 (October 1957). Longridge also argues that railway modelling should be seen as an art in much the same way as photography. See Michael Longridge, 'Railway Modelling as an Art' *Model Railway News* 17:1999 (July 1941), p. 210.

123 Watson, 'MRC Layouts', p. 7.

124 Mickelover Model Railway Group, 'Farkham', p. 39.

125 Jameson, *Archeologies of the Future*, p. 47.

126 Ibid., p. 44.

127 Georges Friedmann, *The Anatomy of Work: The Implications of Specialisation* trans. by Wyatt Rawson (New York: Free Press of Glencoe, 1964), pp. 110–11.

128 'Many model railway club members spend weekends as volunteer workers on preserved lines. Many professional railwaymen also devote much time to running preserved railways working alongside these amateurs'. Carter, *British Railway Enthusiasm*, p. 6. This point is also made by Steven Gelber. Gelber, *Hobbies*, p. 48.

129 Friedmann, *The Anatomy of Work*, p. 158.

130 Ed Smith, 'Are We Too Professional?' *Intelligent Life* (Winter 2009), p. 126. See also Ed Smith, 'Amateur Hour' *Spectator* (26 March 2011), p. 24; and Ed Smith 'Is Professionalism Killing Sport?' for *Inside Sport* (BBC Two, first broadcast 21 September 2010).

131 Michel Foucault, 'Of Other Spaces' in Roland Ritter and Bernd Knaller-Vlay (eds) *Other Spaces: The Affair of the Heterotopia* (Graz: Haus der Architektur, 1998), p. 28.

132 The designers involved were: Amos Merchant, Carl Clerkin, William Warren, Gareth Neal, Gitta Gschwendtner, Chris Eckersley, Rory Dodd, Suzanne Barnes and Dave Green.

133 'Green Woodwork Courses with Gudrun Leitz'. Homepage for Gudrum Leitz's Green woodwork courses, http://www.greenwoodwork.co.uk/index.html (accessed 18 July 2011).

134 Mary Greensted, *Gimson and the Barnsleys: 'Wonderful Furniture of a Commonplace Kind'* (Stroud, Gloucestershire: Alan Sutton, 1991), p. 43.

135 Grant Gibson, 'The Bodgers' Parade' *Crafts* 224 (May/June 2010), p. 41.

136 David Pye, *The Nature and Art of Workmanship* (London: The Herbert Press, 1995), p. 20.

137 Gibson, 'The Bodgers' Parade', p. 41.

138 This development of the project was known as the 'Cov Bodge', named as such because Dave Green's factory is situated near to Coventry. *Bodging Milano* website, http://www.bodgingmilano. co.uk/section482362.html (accessed 18 July 2011). Since the project, Gareth Neal's chair has been bought by the Shipley Art Gallery – my thanks to Chris Eckersley for this information.

139 'V&A Broomstick Bodge' *Bodging Milano* website, http://www.bodgingmilano.co.uk/ section483925.html (accessed 18 July 2011).

140 For more information on these projects see David Sokol, 'We Work In A Fragile Material' *American Crafts* (Apr–May 2009), pp. 34–5; and the collective's website, http://www. weworkinafragilematerial.com (accessed 18 July 2011).

141 Glenn Adamson, 'We Work In A Fragile Material: We built this city' on collective's website, http://www.weworkinafragilematerial.com (accessed 18 July 2011).

142 Glenn Adamson, 'Fragile's State of Mind' *Crafts* 219 (Jul–Aug 2009), p. 61.

143 'Happy Campers' (New York, 20–23 May 2006) on the collective's website, http://www. weworkinafragilematerial.com (accessed 18 July 2011).

144 In an interview with Christina Zetterlund, We Work In A Fragile Material explicitly claim their aversion to providing a specific education. Christina Zetterlund, 'We Work In A Fragile Material: Interview' in *Tumult* (ex cat.) (Gustavsbergs: Gustavsbergs Konsthall), p. 139.

145 Peter Dormer, 'Chapter Three: Learning a Craft' in *The Art of the Maker* (London: Thames and Hudson, 1994), pp. 41–9.

146 Charles Fourier, *Passions of the Human Soul: Volume II*, trans. by Rev J. R. Morell (London: 1851), p. 31.

147 Ibid., p. 34.

148 Jameson, *Archeologies of the Future*, p. 249.

149 Aram Sinnreich, 'Re-mix Speaker Interviews' *Re-mix Symposium* part of the 2010–11 *Masters of Amateurism* series, http://www.premsela.org/en/peoples-republic_1/re-mix_1/ (accessed 6 September 2011).

150 *Les Misérables* and *The Hunchback of Notre-Dame* are among Victor Hugo's well-known novels. For Focillon's critique see Henri Focillon, *Technique et sentiment: études sur l'art moderne* (Paris, 1952), p. 43.

151 Marie-Laure Prévost, 'The techniques of a Poet-Draftsman' in Florian Rodari (ed.) *Shadows of a Hand: The Drawings of Victor Hugo* (New York and London: The Drawing Center in association with Merrell Holberton Publishers, 1998), p. 31.

152 David Pye, *The Nature and Art of Workmanship*, p. 134. Julia Bryant-Wilson, *Art Workers: Radical Practice in the Vietnam War Era* (Berkeley: University of California Press, 2009), p. 127.

153 Winston Churchill, *Painting as a Pastime* (London: Odhams Press, 1948), p. 17. 'Churchill voted greatest Briton' BBC News (24 November 2002), http://news.bbc.co.uk/1/hi/entertainment/2509465.stm (accessed 6 June 2014).

INDEX

Page numbers in *italics* indicate images